An inspiring and instructive journey to the wide ... pioneering a sustainable global future.

Jakob von Uexküll, founder of the Right Livelihood Award and former member of the European Parliament

One of the most powerful questions asked of us by our world crisis is: "How can we live together in ways that allow us to 'be the change' together?" Karen Litfin's book gives us answers. These ecovillage experiments – idealistic, imperfect, courageous, creative, and honestly described – will help us transform our consciousness and find our way forward.

Terry Patten, co-author (with Ken Wilber, Adam Leonard, and Marco Morelli) of *Integral Life Practice*

In these times of political gridlock and myopia, Karen Litfin's tremendously engaging and informative exploration of ecovillages around the world points the way to a viable and attractive future very different from the bleak place to which we are now headed. You will enjoy this book!

James Gustave Speth, author of *America the Possible: Manifesto for a New Economy*, former Dean, Yale School of Forestry and Environmental Studies, Yale University

Nature teaches us that nothing disappears when it dies; it merely becomes something new. Karen Litfin's lucid and heartfelt book reveals the new life emerging in the cracks of failing systems. Through her eyes, we meet people everywhere who are building high-joy, low-impact communities. Litfin is the perfect guide: intellectually rigorous, spiritually awake, and deeply caring. If you want to create a richer, gentler life for yourself and your community, read this book!

Vicki Robin, bestselling author of *Your Money or Your Life* and *Blessing the Hands That Feed Us*

Karen Litfin is a perceptive, thoughtful, and gifted observer of the human predicament. In writing *Ecovillages*, Litfin combines her intellectual prowess with her sensitivity and compassion to tell a hugely important and inspiring story.

Chris Uhl, author of *Developing Ecological Consciousness*, Professor of Biology at Pennsylvania State University

The world is in for a major transition, a huge downshift, ready or not. For those inclined to roll up their sleeves and get ready, ecovillages can offer insight and hope. As Litfin shows in this compelling book, they exemplify an "affirmative politics," a politics at once ecological, economic, community-oriented, and spiritual. Ecovillages aren't for everyone but, in these uncertain times, their lessons may be.

Thomas Princen, author of *The Logic of Sufficiency*, Professor, School of Natural Resources and Environment, University of Michigan

Karen Litfin has not only written a book of great importance to all of us at this pivotal moment in history, she has also done it in a way that is lively, moving, informative, and compelling. This first-rate book deserves to reach the widest possible audience; we must pay attention to the issues Litfin addresses if we are going to thrive as a species on this fragile planet.

Nina Wise, performance artist and author of *A Big New Free Happy Unusual Life*

Karen Litfin understands that today we need inspiration as much as information to forge the vibrant communities that will carry us into an enduring future. The success stories she brings to life are just what we need to revivify our existing communities on a planet perched at the precipice.

Kurt Hoelting, author of *The Circumference of Home: One Man's Yearlong Quest for a Radically Local Life*

# ECOVILLAGES

For my teachers

# ECOVILLAGES

## LESSONS FOR SUSTAINABLE COMMUNITY

### KAREN T. LITFIN

polity

First published in 2014 by Polity Press
Reprinted in 2014

Polity Press
65 Bridge Street
Cambridge CB2 1UR, UK

Polity Press
350 Main Street
Malden, MA 02148, USA

ISBN-13: 978-0-7456-7949-5
ISBN-13: 978-0-7456-7950-1(pb)

A catalogue record for this book is available from the British Library.

Typeset in 10.5 on 12 pt Sabon
by Servis Filmsetting Ltd, Stockport, Cheshire
Printed and bound in the United States of America by Edwards Brothers Malloy

For further information on Polity, visit our website: www.politybooks.com

# CONTENTS

# LIST OF FIGURES

# ACKNOWLEDGMENTS

It has literally taken a planetary village to write this book. First and foremost are the fourteen communities who invited a curious academic to live in their midst and the 140 ecovillagers who gave lengthy interviews. My research was greatly facilitated by the following people who served as community liaisons: Aly Mansare and Mariama Guldagger (Colufifa); Alan Corbett and Max Lindegger (Crystal Waters); Macaco Tamerice (Damanhur); Diana Leafe-Christian (Earthaven): Liz Walker (EcoVillage at Ithaca); Michiyo Furuhashi (Konohana); Lois Arkin (Los Angeles Ecovillage); Bandula Senadeera (Sarvodaya); Kosha Anja Joubert (Sieben Linden); Sigrid Niemer (UfaFabrik); Ina Meyer-Stoll (ZEGG). I also thank Bagnaia, the charming Italian ecovillage where I convalesced while too sick to travel. For consulting with me about the journey, I owe a special debt of gratitude to Jonathan Dawson, Ross and Hildur Jackson, Kosha Anja Joubert, and Diana Leafe-Christian.

Each of the fourteen micro-societies I visited is like a world unto itself, with its own ethos and ambiance. As much as I endeavored to dive deeply into each one, what I could glean in a matter of weeks was necessarily shallow – particularly because most interviews required English translation – and only a small portion of that has found its way into the book. Moreover, my field is global environmental politics, not community development. Consequently, I have inevitably made mistakes and glossed over important aspects of each community. While a cast of thousands stands behind this book, I alone am responsible for the shortcomings. For these, I apologize with the hope that the overriding transformative message nonetheless shines through.

There were those who facilitated the journey and those who supported the writing. To the extent that you are now holding a lively and accessible book rather than an academic tome, Margaret Bendet is largely responsible. Not only is Margaret, with her keen sense of nuance and authenticity, my favorite writing teacher, but she also became a treasured friend. For our serendipitous Easter meeting at the Whidbey Institute, I thank my friend and colleague Johnny Palka.

To all those who read the manuscript, entirely or in parts, I owe a debt of gratitude: Sarah Ellison, Wendy Visconty, Anya Woestwin, Chris Uhl, Lauran Zmira, Leanne Do, Vicki Robin, Tim Richards, and David Marshak. For research assistance, I thank Mark Visconty, Julie Johnson, and David Wilkerson. For help with the index, I thank Catherine Quinn and Angela Gaffney. My thanks also to Stephen Dunne for computer assistance. I am especially grateful to my dear friend Donna Gregory for enlivening the early chapters and offering wise counsel throughout. For bringing this book to fruition, I thank my editorial team at Polity, especially Louise Knight, Pascal Porcheron, Clare Ansell, and Gail Ferguson. They have shepherded the project with good humor and the greatest of care.

To have the freedom to write this book – a highly personal seven-year project – is a great privilege. I acknowledge the Department of Political Science at the University of Washington for enabling this unconventional international relations scholar to fully engage her academic freedom. In particular, my sincere thanks go out to my chair Peter May and my colleagues Jamie Mayerfeld and Christine DiStefano for their encouragement, and to Aseem Prakash for challenging me to scale it up.

For helping me to begin thinking of myself as a writer, I thank the Mesa Refuge for a residency in a lovely cottage overlooking Tomales Bay. I will never forget the day the agricultural levees came down and the Pacific Ocean trickled up the tributaries, bringing new life to an old wetland. It was the perfect metaphor for this book. My thanks, as well, to Carroll Smith and Janice Giteck for their Whidbey Island guest cottage, where I organized more than two thousand pages of research notes.

This book would not have been possible without the loving support of my friends and family. I am especially grateful to Rand Hicks for grasping and emboldening my larger vision; to my dearest friend, Anya Woestwin, who sees my higher self and always finds a larger framework for the rest; to my daughter, Maya Jacobs, who inspires me every day and loves me no matter what; and to my mother, Kathleen Wilkinson, who believed in me even when she couldn't understand me. And there's no question that my journey was inspired by Laura, who lived the possibility and sent me on my way.

ACKNOWLEDGMENTS

It is an odd thing to buy a farm and start a community in the midst of writing a book and teaching full time, but that is what I did. Thanks to Dan Neumeyer and Bill Copperthwaite for coordinating the building workshop for the tapered-wall wooden yurt where this book was written. The beauty of the wood inspires me every day. Thanks, too, to my former students and Maya's friends who, in pulling thistle and whacking blackberry, helped me keep the faith. Of all those who have endured the innumerable hours I've spent incommunicado these past four years, the members of SkyRoot Community top the list. For their patience and generosity of spirit, I offer my heartfelt gratitude to Sarah Gillette, Beth Wheat, Anne Wheat, TraceyJoy Miller, Joanne Pontrello, and Byron and Raven Odion. I promise to be more present.

This book is not only *about* the pioneers who are writing the story of planetary interdependence with their lives; it is a *consequence* of an invisible web of personal and global community. I am the beneficiary of that web in more ways than I can possibly acknowledge.

## Ecovillages at a Glance

| Community | Country | Approximate Population (2012) | Landscape | Founding Date | Primary Worldview |
|---|---|---|---|---|---|
| Auroville | India | 2,000 | Rural | 1968 | Spiritually focused |
| Colufifa | Senegal, the Gambia | 350 traditional villages | Rural | 1964 | Interreligious |
| Crystal Waters | Australia | 200+ | Rural | 1984 | Secular |
| Damanhur | Italy | 1,000 | Rural | 1975 | Spiritual |
| Earthaven | USA | 55 | Rural | 1995 | Spiritually eclectic |
| EcoVillage at Ithaca | USA | 160 | Suburban | 1991 | Secular |
| Findhorn | UK | 600 | Rural | 1962 | Spiritually focused |
| Konohana | Japan | 80 | Rural | 1994 | Spiritually focused |
| Los Angeles Ecovillage | USA | 45 | Urban | 1994 | Secular |
| Sarvodaya | Sri Lanka | 15,000 traditional villages | Rural | 1957 | Interreligious |
| Sieben Linden | Germany | 140 | Rural | 1997 | Spiritually eclectic |
| Svanholm | Denmark | 140 | Rural | 1979 | Secular |
| UfaFabrik | Germany | 35 onsite | Urban | 1979 | Secular |
| ZEGG | Germany | 80 | Suburban | 1991 | Spiritually eclectic |

# — 1 —

# LIVING A NEW STORY

For years, I've had the perfect job: a tenured professorship in a field I love at a major research university. The perks include a stable income with good benefits, a downhill bicycle ride to my office each morning, and a podium from which to encourage thousands of bright young people to ponder the most momentous issues of our time. Soon after the beginning of the new century, my once-obscure field of global environmental politics began climbing to the top of the public agenda. Suddenly students were hungry to learn what I was teaching – maybe not all of them but enough to make my work exciting. At last I could lecture about climate change, the mass extinction of species, and resource depletion without sounding like Chicken Little. I've been giving these lectures for two decades now, and the big picture hasn't changed much in that time. What *has* changed is that a lot more people are beginning to see that perhaps the sky (along with the rest of the biosphere) might well be falling, or at least changing in some palpable ways. Ways we can see, hear, and feel – warmer winters, fiercer storms, holes in the ozone layer. Nature has been giving us a wake-up call for quite some time now, and people are finally beginning to wake up. For one who thinks about this stuff nonstop, this is very good news.

As a professor, my job is to acquire and communicate a lot of knowledge. On these issues, though, I'm fascinated by what I *don't* know – indeed, what it seems nobody today *can* know. We don't know, for instance, how many species there are or which of them are critical to our survival; we only know that because of human behavior other species are disappearing a thousand times faster than before the industrial era. We don't know what it will be like to live on Planet Earth when it's 3–10°F warmer; we only know that the

1

Figure 1.1. Humor helps to lighten the mood in my classes

scientific consensus is that's where we're headed. We don't know when oil production will peak or whether it already has; we only know that we're utterly dependent on the stuff and we've already picked the low-hanging fruit. I find this combination of knowledge and ignorance utterly compelling. We can't be completely certain, but the evidence points to a profoundly disturbing conclusion: our way of life is driving us into the perfect storm. For the young adults in my classes, this comes as a rude awakening.

Over the years, I've learned to temper all this gloom and doom with a healthy dose of humor. I start each lecture with a political cartoon. Soon after I've pointed out what nobody knows about what's coming toward us as a species, I usually show one of my favorites: "Goldilocks Goes Global."

A dark sense of humor may help in the moment, but relief is temporary. One upshot of my perfect job is that I was making thousands of students fearful, angry, depressed, and guilt-ridden. Having steeped myself in the available information, I also inflicted these states upon myself. Until, finally, I said "stop!"

If in the face of the end of civilization as we know it, the best I can do is cite statistics and a few woefully ineffective treaties, what kind of teacher am I? I want to empower my students, not paralyze them, which means that I have to be empowered. Passion grounded in fact is what ignites personal power and transforms responsibility from a moral burden to a genuine ability to respond.

The response, as with the issue, is inevitably multifaceted and must come from a variety of sources. All told, the bottom line is that we need to find viable ways of living with one another and our home planet, changing some systems from within and restructuring others entirely. Some responses – corporate social responsibility, government subsidies for renewable energy, municipal recycling programs – offer tangible ways to work within the system. Personally, I'm inspired by responses that reinvent life from the ground up, and of these I'm most intrigued by the ecovillage. This is a gathering of individuals into a cohesive unit large enough to be self-contained – that's why it's a village – and dedicated to living by ecologically sound precepts. I find ecovillages compelling because they weave together the various strands of sustainability into integrated wholes at the level of everyday life and because they've sprung up spontaneously all over the world.

This is, of course, a book on ecovillages, but, before focusing on the subject at hand, I want to present a bit more of the big picture, the framework within which ecovillages have emerged, so that it's clear what "reinventing life" truly means.

## A new story

For some time now, I've been looking for a way to make sense of this unfolding environmental mega-crisis. It's one thing to see and feel that we're in a pickle. It's another to put our recognition into an intellectual framework. How did we, who view ourselves as the pinnacle of evolution, become the most destructive force on the planet? If every culture lives out its core story, what cultural stories have engendered humanity's current morass? And since our survival as a species requires harmonizing ourselves with our home planet, what new stories might foster our capacity for doing that? For decades, I hunted for answers to these questions in disciplines ranging from economics to philosophy, from geology to theology.

In a nutshell, I concluded that *homo sapiens* is a splendid oddity in the natural world: the species with the capacity of separating itself from the whole – at least in our own minds. The very term "environment" assumes that separation. One of our culture's most compelling stories has been our conquest of nature through technology. We've told ourselves that our comforts and conveniences would protect us from the vagaries of nature – and to a great extent they have. But now the tattered ozone layer and collapsing ice shelves are evoking a new story: *we are not separate*. If we take this story to heart and follow its radical implications, it offers some very good news – for the biosphere and for ourselves.

Humanity has become a force of nature, a geophysical force operating on a planetary scale. We didn't get here overnight. The story of separation, which crops up in one way or another across many cultures, has deep roots; only recently did it produce epic consequences. With the scientific and industrial revolutions, knowledge engendered power in new ways. Starting with seventeenth-century Europe, Earth was carved up into a patchwork of sovereign states. The economic and psychological counterpart of the sovereign state was the rational self-interested individual who, alongside nations and firms, found himself (*sic*) in fierce competition for resources, power, and wealth. The collisions and conglomerations of these "particles" were like Newtonian particles in a mechanical universe. Nature was reduced to territory and property, a vast storehouse of resources for human consumption, and an unlimited repository for our waste.

Three centuries ago, when most Europeans never reached their thirtieth birthday, that story made sense. With only a billion people on Earth and a vast frontier in the New World, nature seemed unshakably robust and inexhaustibly abundant. Today, with 6.8 billion people inhabiting an increasingly vulnerable planet, that same story is, to put it mildly, evolutionarily maladaptive. The impulse toward self-protection has mutated into a fearsome capacity for self-destruction, particularly in the wealthy countries. Yet, as the story of separation and conquest reaches the end of its tether, the unfolding crisis carries within itself the seeds of a new story.

If "independence" was the by-word of the old story, "interdependence" is the by-word of the new. If the old metaphors were drawn from Newtonian physics, the new metaphors are rooted in ecology, where symbiosis is the rule. Whatever its political utility in the past, independence was always a biological fiction; current trends are driving that point home. The so-called individual is inextricably reliant on a vast web of external ecosystems and internal microbial networks.

At the level of international politics, sovereignty is being eroded by global networks of communications, finance, crime, terrorism, disease transmission, ecology, and transnational activism. Europe, the birthplace of the sovereign state and the epicenter of two world wars, is now home to a particularly intriguing post-sovereign entity, the European Union. The 2008 economic meltdown highlights the same lesson that the even thornier issues of climate change and peak oil challenge us to learn: we now live in an era of planetary interdependence (for an explanation of peak oil, see Box 3.5).

No longer relegated to a collection of objects to be consumed, nature (albeit a profoundly altered nature) emerges as teacher and we her students. When we grasp the meaning of "nonrenewable," we learn to favor bicycles over cars. When we learn that living systems, being cyclical, generate no waste, we see that there is no "away" in which to throw our garbage and pollution. And we discover the value of compost. As our knowledge grows, so too does our sense of homecoming to our place on Earth.

When we come home, we do so in a specifically human way. Like other animals, we are eating, drinking, breathing creatures. *And* we are equipped, perhaps uniquely so, to come into conscious harmony with the rest of creation. In doing so, we find our individuality not in our ability to *acquire*, but in our capacity to *inquire* – and then to express ourselves as unique parts of the whole. Like cells in the larger body of the living Earth, we become that aspect of Gaia that is growing into awareness of herself. From this large perspective, "sustainability" is just a dry word for our new story's central plotline: coming home to our place within the larger community of life that sustains us. The upshot of this story is that there are no environmental problems. There is only the age-old *human* problem, now writ large: how, then, shall we live? Benjamin Franklin's purported words to his compatriots at the signing of the US Declaration of Independence now have a global ring: "We must hang together, gentlemen . . . else, we shall most assuredly hang separately."

## The challenge of "hanging together"

So how *do* we "hang together?" How do we forge enduring symbiotic relationships that acknowledge our interconnectedness? How do we live *with* one another? It's not easy, as many of us have found, to live in groups. We face challenges even in pairs, as I saw in my brief attempt at cohabitation with my daughter's father. To forge a stable matrix of relationships among individualistic modern people, within tribal- or village-size groups ... Group living of any kind requires a commitment to something higher than the fixtures and plumbing of life.

I had my first experience of conscious group living in my early twenties in California when a friend and I started the Orange County Peace Conversion Project – right in the belly of the beast, as we liked to put it. Those were the years when political leaders talked seriously about winning an all-out nuclear war. So we set out to inspire people, especially workers in the local military industries, to consider how the money and expertise being poured into war preparations might be used to enhance life. Within three years, we had five thousand supporters. We were against nuclear weapons, but our focus was mostly on what we were *for*: a life in harmony with one another and with the Earth. We didn't know it at the time, but we were muddling our way toward a politics of "yes," despite being surrounded by so much that seemed negative. Living by example was an essential ingredient in our homespun recipe. When a generous woman donated her house to our project, several of us, all in our twenties, moved in and lived hand to mouth. We grew our vegetables, ate low on the food chain, bicycled whenever possible, converted our driveway into a neighborhood recycling center, and made our decisions by consensus. That was 1979, long before the term *ecovillage* was coined.

Like many adventures in community living, our idealistic experiment dissolved for mundane reasons: couples broke up, people left, and eventually our generous donor wanted her house back.

Over time, life's disappointments and a certain dry pragmatism buried my ideals under a heap of obligations and responsibilities. After those quixotic years in Orange County, I entered a fourteen-year period of intellectual intensity on my way to academic freedom, first as a PhD student and then as a single mother and a professor on the tenure track. During those years, I learned to hone my mind, weave complex webs of thought, dress them up in suitable jargon, and get them published. I wrote about what mattered most to me, the human face of global ecology, but always in the stilted academic language that remains impenetrable to ordinary people. I was in a protracted rite of passage. Some day, I imagined, I would make a difference. Some day.

When I first came to the University of Washington in 1991, I considered group living once again. Alone in a new city, I didn't want to raise Maya, my daughter, in isolation. Besides, I knew we could live more sustainably in community than in a single-family home. The most promising possibility was Songaia, a new group that owned

11 acres in a semirural area north of Seattle. I attended meetings for several months as we developed a site plan and got to know each other. Every meeting ended with boisterous songs and a shared meal.

In the end, as much as I cherished the prospect of raising Maya in such a wholesome environment, I was deterred by yet another of the classic issues associated with group living: location. I was daunted by the commute. For me, the ecological and social benefits of community life were not worth long hours on the freeway. So I bought a house near the university and, bowing before the academic dictum "publish or perish," I put my nose to the grindstone.

As I've said, it was the perfect job, but something was missing, something big. I cared about my subject, thought about it constantly, saw it as vital – and yet I was not *living* as if it were true. My lectures, painstakingly researched, all pointed to one extremely inconvenient truth: our everyday actions are unraveling our home planet's life-support systems. And *our* actions included *my* actions. For me, this was even more inconvenient. No matter how inspiring my lectures might be for others, what did it matter if I didn't change my own life! Sure, I bicycled to work, ate organic, recycled, and shopped at thrift stores. Without any huge effort and even including my international flights, I was able to reduce my ecological footprint to just over half the American average. Still, if everybody on the planet lived as I did, we would need two and a half Earths. Who was I to talk about coming into conscious harmony with the living Earth? There was a yawning gap between my lofty notions of planetary sustainability and my own economic consumption. At the end of the day, as I bicycled homeward up the long hill, I felt like a fraud. But what more could I do?

## Enter Wonder Woman

Then one evening, a ruddy-faced woman came knocking on my front door. With her close-cropped hair, at first glance I took her for a man. "Is this where the meditation group meets?" she asked. It was. As she took her seat in our weekly meditation circle, I was curious about this new arrival: she seemed different.

At the next meeting of the meditation group, Laura confirmed that she was, indeed, different. My toilet stopped flushing, and, while the rest of us sat in the living room bemoaning the high price of plumbers, Laura asked for my toolbox and did the repair. In time, I found out that she could fix just about anything. She could build, plumb, and wire a house. She could grow anything rooted in the earth. Whereas

I, and virtually everybody I knew, used money to navigate through the material aspects of life, Laura relied upon her skills, her personal relationships, and her ability to barter.

Inspired in her youth by St Francis, Laura had decided to live simply. Her inner life and a handful of deep friendships came first for her. She lived on her earnings, less than US$6,000 a year. By the time she knocked on my door, she had been living with outer simplicity and inner wealth for twenty-five years. I could see that, with all my degrees, I had a lot to learn from this high-school dropout – who is, by the way, at least as well read as my overeducated friends and I.

Laura was master of the spontaneous project. In the time she lived in my vicinity, my home and garden got a substantial upgrade. When I complained about the ugly shrub blocking my living room window, she was back in a flash with her chainsaw and shovels. After one look at my chaotic garage, so many years of detritus from a middle-class life, Laura masterminded the dreaded clean up. A conversation about the evils of concrete led to half my driveway being transformed into a terraced strawberry bed. With every project, I navigated new equipment (a hammer, a chisel, a drill, a handsaw, an electric saw) and learned new skills (how to dig without hurting my back, how to make yogurt, how to build soil, how to compost my own shit). Laura's guiding question seemed to be: How can we maximize our effectiveness and minimize our harm to the Earth? And how can we do it having the most fun?

One huge consequence of Laura's material simplicity is her spacious approach to time. People say time is money, but perhaps it's more accurate to say time is wealth. Although Laura had virtually no money, she seemed to have all the time in the world, while I had money but so little time. If a conversation was important to her, Laura would give an entire day to it. If she felt like making art with rocks, she would give an entire day to that. If I needed help around the house, Laura was right there. I, on the other hand, was constantly rushing from one appointment to the next. I could buy time from other people – the plumber, the massage therapist, my daughter's music teachers – but I had no time myself, while Laura couldn't buy other people's time but her time was her own. When I told her how I often felt squeezed by the lack of time, she teased me. "Litfin," she said, "you're the victim of your own choices!"

I started to make different choices. I bought a pedal-activated electric bicycle, made it my primary mode of transportation, and within three years put more than four thousand miles on it. Growing food takes more time than buying it, but it's a lot more fun. So I took a comprehensive organic gardening course, built several large vegetable beds, and, along with my daughter, began growing vegetables. Maya pitched in with enthusiasm, taking pride in her strawberries. We found a recycled wooden box and enlisted worms to compost our food waste. We shrank our weekly garbage to half a grocery bag. Little by little, I was learning to walk my talk. And I found it fun.

I had many more dreams – fantasies of building an earthen home, harvesting rainwater, installing solar panels .... These didn't feel ungrounded as long as I had a friend who could actually *do* all these things. Perhaps I couldn't do them, but in Laura's company I knew they were doable. The doors of my life were opening up to a whole new world of possibilities.

Those doors closed abruptly when my personal Wonder Woman moved on to a warmer, sunnier place. Long-distance conversations were small consolation for the loss of my mentor for a life of integrity. On every level, it was a long, soggy Northwest winter.

Come spring, I was at a crossroads. With my comfortable salary and "perfect job," it would have been easy to continue giving my ideas free rein to gallop beyond my material existence. Maybe I would never live in conscious harmony with the rest of creation, but at least I could inspire my students in that direction. After all, they were young, and there were hundreds of them. I was just one middle-aged egghead.

As the clouds lifted, my sense of what was possible once again expanded. The sustainability crisis is global, and I knew beyond certainty that people all over the world are addressing it collectively at the level of their everyday lives. Surely there must be Wonder People all over the place, and surely some of them would have joined together to share their knowledge. I began asking myself how I could find those who were not just theorizing about planetary interdependence but were living those lessons and forging a viable future. They had to be out there, and I wanted to find them, to see them "hanging together" in a real and viable way.

## Seedlings for a viable future

My quest led me to visit communities all over the world, to study ecovillages where people were hanging together so closely they looked like the facets of a single gem. The word "ecovillage" may conjure up images of shabby rural outposts populated by long-haired iconoclasts, but I found that these communities and their residents cannot be so easily pigeonholed.

9

Ecovillages are diverse in every way you can imagine – cultural, architectural, economic, climatic. The smallest I visited was like a big family – 40 people – and the largest, Auroville, has a population of 2,000, bigger than some small towns. These sustainable communities are appearing in tropical, temperate, and desert regions; among the rich and the very poor; in cities and in all parts of the countryside. People living in ecovillages espouse beliefs rooted in all the major world religions, paganism, and atheism, as well as by a spectrum of moral codes.

Though you won't find the term "ecovillage" in most dictionaries, the Global Ecovillage Network (GEN) with its regional divisions was established in 1995, and with that, the movement went from local to global. The GEN website (http://gen.ecovillage.org/) lists about 400 ecovillages worldwide, and this doesn't include the traditional rural villages in the Third World that belong to participatory development networks within GEN. Put these ecovillages into the mix and the number leaps to 15,000. Yet if "sustainable" means "continuable into the indefinite future," then most ecovillages are really *aspiring* ecovillages. For that reason, GEN has published a Community Sustainability Assessment, available on its website in four languages, which enables ecovillages to gauge their sustainability.

That spring I read everything I could find about ecovillages, online and in print. I found that they describe themselves in glowing prose, packed with organic imagery. Consider this passage from GEN's online ecovillage design curriculum, Gaia Education:

> In preparation for the emergence of a new worldview, "seed" people will begin to appear, inoculating the collective consciousness with new ideas and concepts – evolved interpretations about the nature of reality. Initially, these seed people will be perceived as a cultural "fringe," an idiosyncratic minority whose new interpretations can be easily discounted and disregarded because of their incongruity with established, officially sanctioned, interpretations of reality. Eventually, however, as the precepts of the old paradigm are revealed to be increasingly inept at managing and providing a meaningful context for the evolving, emerging situation, the seed people will gain credibility. . . . Ecovillages are the "seed" communities of the not-too-distant future.

Seed people from the cultural fringe inoculating the larger culture? This verbal feast left me with an immense hunger for the meat of experience. I had lots of questions.

- Is it true that ordinary people on every continent are coming to similar conclusions about the global predicament and how to address it? If so, I wanted to know about them.

10

- Are ecovillagers consciously supplanting the old story of separation with a new story of wholeness? Is it just so much verbiage, or is it a narrative grounded in everyday life?
- Do these seeds of sustainability live up to their glowing accounts? How do they deal with conflict? Child rearing? Questions of ownership? Income disparities? Power imbalances? Aging and death? I wanted to know.
- Are they populated from the mainstream or by hippies and fractious malcontents?
- And if some, or even all, of the ecovillages are failing to live up to their image, I wanted to know that as well. There is much to learn from ambitious experiments.

My daughter had just graduated from high school and had saved money for her own dream trip, working on organic farms around the world – WWOOFing, as it's called. That left me free to explore ecovillages. Wanting to write a personal book, I tapped my savings and financed the journey myself. I got the time by taking a sabbatical from my teaching job and shepherded my research proposal through my university's human subjects review. In this regard, I signed an agreement not to interview minors and not to quote anyone without their express permission.

## Box 1.1 Ecovillages: Intellectual and Social Roots

For centuries, people have come together in small groups to find ways of living in harmony with each other and with life itself. Now, in the face of social alienation and a creeping global ecological crisis, this communitarian impulse has coalesced globally in the form of ecovillages. Individually, these ecovillages trace their roots to diverse lineages:[1]

- the ideals of self-sufficiency and spiritual inquiry that have historically characterized monasteries and ashrams and, more recently, Gandhian movements;
- the social movements of the 1960s and 1970s, including the environmental, peace, feminist, and alternative education movements;
- in affluent countries, the "back-to-the-land" movement and, beginning in the 1990s, the co-housing movement;

[1] Jonathan Dawson, *Ecovillages: New Frontiers for Sustainability*, Devon, UK: Green Books, 2006.

11

- in developing countries, the participatory development and appropriate technology movements.

Unlike many alternative communities, ecovillages are not isolated enclaves; rather, they have a strong educational mission. Since 1995 with the formation of the Global Ecovillage Network (GEN), they have joined forces in order to share and disseminate sustainable living practices among themselves and with the larger world.

GEN has its roots in a 1991 conference organized by two couples, Ross and Hildur Jackson from Denmark, and Robert and Diane Gilman from the United States. As a pioneering software designer and successful international currency trader, Ross Jackson had become convinced that the global economy was unsustainable. In 1987, he and Hildur founded Gaia Trust, a philanthropic organization dedicated to fostering a transition to a sustainable society.[2] Meanwhile, the Gilmans were publishing *In Context: A Quarterly Journal of Humane Sustainable Culture*. Robert had left his earlier career as an astrophysicist because "the stars could wait, but the planet couldn't."[3] At the 1991 conference in Denmark, the Gilmans presented a survey of the world's ecovillages, which they defined as "human-scale, full-featured settlements in which human activities are harmlessly integrated into the natural world in a way that supports healthy human development and can be successfully continued into the indefinite future."[4] In 1995, the first international ecovillage conference was held at Findhorn. The 400 participants established GEN and its three regional centers: GEN-Europe and Africa, the Ecovillage Network of the Americas, and GEN-Oceania and Asia.

Yaacov Oved, a scholar and member of Israel's kibbutz movement, traces GEN to a larger process of "globalization from below," which includes a growing interest in international relations among intentional communities since the 1970s.[5] Since the 1990s, this process has been greatly facilitated by the internet revolution. The original vision of GEN – that new ecovillages would sprout like mushrooms – has not taken place. Instead, the primary impact of ecovillages has been to make existing communities look more like ecovillages through educational programs offered all over the world. My own sense is that this is exactly as it should be.

---

[2] Ross tells the story of GEN's inception, including how a spiritual experience he had with Swami Muktananda inspired him to create Gaia Trust, in J. T. Ross Jackson, *We ARE Doing It: Building and Ecovillage Future*, San Francisco: Robert D. Reed Publishers, 2000.

[3] www.context.org/about/who-we-are/robert-gilman.

[4] www.context.org/iclib/ic29/gilman1.

[5] Yaacov Oved, *Globalization of Communes, 1950–2010*, New Brunswick, NJ: Transaction Publishers, 2012.

## Mapping the journey

Beginning in September 2007, I visited fourteen ecovillages on five continents. Starting in North Carolina, I worked my way eastward from Europe to Africa to Australia to Asia until I ended up in Los Angeles. The sampling of communities I chose reflects their diversity worldwide: rural and urban, rich and poor, spiritual and secular. I also chose some ecovillages that seemed like places where middle-class Americans like me could imagine living.

So, why fourteen ecovillages? Why not ten? Or forty? Writing has been described as the art of winnowing, and a topic as vast as this global movement requires a great deal of winnowing. That said, there are some important gaps in this material. I did not visit Brazil's vibrant ecovillage culture nor any other Latin American communities at all. Nor did I visit any of the 200-plus Anastasia communities in Russia nor any of Israel's 200-plus kibbutzim. Had I visited them all, I might still be on my journey now, and the final book might be too heavy to lift.

Because I wanted inspiration and practical guidance, I chose these fourteen ecovillages with an eye to their success. Given that these living laboratories are works in progress, how would I know success when I saw it? Several objective criteria came to mind.

- *Longevity*: Communities with staying power have been able at least to sustain themselves across time. Findhorn, founded in 1962, is the oldest ecovillage I visited, and Sarvodaya, a Sri Lankan village network, was established in 1957.
- *Size*: All things being equal (which of course they never are), 100 people pioneering a viable way of living is a greater accomplishment than 10 people doing the same thing – especially if we want to apply their lessons to the larger society.
- *Resource consumption and waste*: This is a book about green living, so the ability to grow food, build homes, move about, and process waste without harming the Earth are obvious signs of accomplishment.
- *Economic prosperity*: If the price of a green lifestyle is a sense of impoverishment, then this would be a one-sided success. Yet, as I had learned, there are many avenues to wealth besides having more money.
- *Ripple effect*: Some ecovillages have a strong emphasis on public education and have become internationally recognized models of sustainability. All fourteen of the ecovillages on my itinerary have attained that status.

Of the hundreds of ecovillages I might have visited, the ones in this book were especially strong on some combination of these criteria. Before setting out on my journey, I ran my list of fourteen ecovillages by Jonathan Dawson, then president of the Global Ecovillage Network. He agreed: these were the ones to visit.

Yet, there were other, more subjective criteria that I could only gauge through firsthand experience and getting to know the ecovillagers themselves. Being a social scientist and also the person I am, these were the human factors I found most compelling:

- *Cohesiveness*: A felt sense of belonging, of trust, honesty, and reciprocity – these are intangible yet crucial elements of community.
- *Embodied vision*: While many ecovillages have posted impressive mission statements on the web, I was looking for a sense of shared purpose among the community members and whether they were able to *live* their vision.
- *Happiness and satisfaction*: Even if an ecovillage were wildly successful with respect to every objective criterion, it would only be truly successful if its members *enjoyed* living there. They need not be perpetually happy; to enjoy the challenges of collective problem solving can also be a source of great satisfaction.

I set out on my journey hoping to find success stories, but my quest was tempered by an awareness that we can also learn from apparent failures. My goal was not to be a cheerleader for ecovillages but to truly study them, to transform my own life in light of what I might learn, and to share my gleanings with ordinary people who want the *information* about how to transform their lives and the *inspiration* to actually do so.

# — 2 —

# AROUND THE WORLD IN FOURTEEN ECOVILLAGES

Ultimately, sustainability will not be a choice. It is the nonnegotiable precondition for our earthly existence. Only because of the superabundance of nonrenewable resources and Earth's seemingly infinite capacity to absorb our waste were we able to persuade ourselves otherwise. Like teenagers with our parents' credit cards, many of us have been operating under the illusion that living within our means was optional. We've acted as if we had the resources of five Earths at our disposal. And it wasn't just that we *could* behave like this; our culture told us (in so many ways, ranging from advertising to perverse government subsidies) that this is how we *should* behave.

As the tectonic pressures on our global socio-ecological system mount, we are fast approaching the day of reckoning. For some, that day has arrived, and they have transformed their lives accordingly. Having reached the day of reckoning in my own life, I set out to learn from those who have gone before me. As demonstration sites for every aspect of sustainable living, ecovillages were the natural place to go. Having taken the road less traveled by opting out of consumer society, ecovillagers have left tracks in the sand. I was determined to follow those tracks, to apply the lessons to my own life, and to share them with people who might never set foot inside an ecovillage.

Starting on the East Coast of the United States in the fall of 2007, I worked my way around the world via Europe, Africa, Asia, and Australia, concluding my journey in Los Angeles nine months later. I lived in each community for at least two weeks. This was long enough to see more than solar panels and composting toilets, long enough to get to know a few people. I interviewed ten members of each community, listening to their personal stories about their choice to leave the beaten path, along with the trials and triumphs entailed in that

15

choice. I wanted to learn how contemporary people worldwide were answering that age-old question: how, then, shall we live?

The answers I found were diverse. Urban ecovillages focus on having fewer cars and higher-density dwellings, while rural communities focus on growing more food. Low-tech communities emphasize manual labor and locally available materials, while high-tech communities use expensive state-of-the-art environmental technologies. Ecovillages in affluent countries seek to overcome social alienation and reduce material consumption, while those in the less affluent countries aim to make existing villages economically and ecologically sustainable. Many ecovillagers are politically active on issues ranging from district school boards to climate change and genetically modified food, while others express their political views only through their lifestyles.

With these differences, I found some striking commonalities among ecovillagers in their basic perceptions about the world and themselves:

- The web of life is sacred, and humanity is an integral part of that web.
- Global environmental trends are approaching a crisis point.
- Positive change will come primarily from the bottom up.
- Saying yes is a greater source of power than saying no.

As a consequence of these beliefs, ecovillagers are unusually sensitive to their actions' consequences, both near and far, and unusually open to sharing. Indeed, if I had to choose one word to express the taproot of ecovillage life, it would be "sharing."

Because ecovillages share resources like land, food, living space, cars, and tools, the per capita consumption for every community is substantially lower than the average for its home country. I'll speak about this in some detail in chapter 3. Many ecovillages have found creative ways of limiting their participation in the global economy, and so their average income is generally quite low. Yet the experience of community members seems to be one not of deprivation but of abundance. In the words of Capra, a member of the Italian ecovillage of Damanhur, "Even though I have less money, I feel richer here. There's so much support."

The sense of wealth seems to rest upon the intangible kinds of sharing that are the essence of community – the sharing of knowledge and skills, joys and sorrows, births and deaths. These are the signs of community I looked for in my nine months of ecovillage living. I experienced a principle I'd been theorizing about for years: the foundation for ecological sustainability is social sustainability, person to person.

16

In many of the ecovillages I visited, I saw concrete demonstrations that a self-replenishing social order is based on relationships of trust and reciprocity. This isn't easy to quantify, but I heard it expressed in many interviews and felt it, palpably, in the tenor of conversations during meals and community meetings.

For example, I attended a Sunday afternoon meeting at EcoVillage at Ithaca, where the future of their community farm was in question. Its profits were in negative figures. I braced myself for a tedious exercise in interminable decision-making, but I actually had fun. Like so many meetings at ecovillages, this one began with a ten-minute check-in, with each person saying a few words about how they were doing. A woman, whose husband had been ill, thanked people for bringing them meals. Several parents spoke about how their children were doing in the new school term. And there was a lot of excitement about a three-way birthday party that would be happening in the common house that evening. Those ten minutes seemed to clear the air and set the stage for tackling a tough agenda with a team spirit. People were succinct in their comments and friendly, even in their disagreements; they obviously took pleasure in being together.

Later, I asked a member of the ecovillage's governing board, a university scientist, whether he would want to live in the community. He ducked the question but implied that, no, he would not want to spend alternate Sunday afternoons in meetings like this one. "Who would want to live with a bunch of idealists who discuss every issue!" he said with a laugh. But he added, "I've been pleasantly surprised, however, by the high quality of discussion. Frankly, it's better than the university. The quality of the ideas is just as good, but it feels better because there's not the arrogance." From what I saw, he was right. For some at least, ecovillages offer fertile soil for the shift from individualism to synergistic interdependence.

This is not to say that ecovillagers are without ire or self-interest or tunnel-vision idealism. Those who decide to join a community can themselves endanger the success of that noble experiment because of personality quirks, destructive habits, and the glaring inconsistencies between their words and their actions. Arguments in ecovillages have become feuds, and feuds have led to pitched battles of will, as ecovillagers search for the right balance between forestland and fields, animal husbandry and animal protection, green values and creature comforts. At Earthaven, a rural ecovillage in North Carolina, debates over felling trees and drilling wells erupted into what one member called "a civil war." I speak about this in greater detail in chapters 3 and 5; for now, it's enough to say that disagreements over land

17

use sparked a crisis of solidified stances all around. Ultimately, a few members left and the rest of the community entered into a two-year review of its mission and governance process.

In other words, ecovillages are not utopias; they are living laboratories. Some experiments may be successful and others not, but they are all opportunities for learning, and the people I met in these living laboratories seemed infinitely more interested in learning than in comfort, convenience, and security. It's not that ecovillagers sacrifice all comfort and convenience; it's that these are not their highest priority. Their commitment to learning – from one another, from other communities, from the larger world – is a big part of what sharing means to them. Ecovillages share information about conflict resolution, consensus training, straw-bale construction, wastewater treatment, and so much more. In this sense, ecovillagers are like applied scientists, running collective experiments in every realm of life: building, farming, waste management, decision-making, communication, child rearing, finance, ownership, aging and death.

Hearing the stories of ecovillagers from all over the world, I came to appreciate that choosing to live in a hotbed of learning is not necessarily an easy path. It is a path of adventure.

## Step by step

As I traveled from ecovillage to ecovillage, people were inevitably curious to learn about other communities and to hear my take on what I was seeing. While most ecovillagers had heard of the other communities I was visiting, few of them had ever seen a community other than their own. About midway through my journey, at Damanhur in Italy, a group asked me to do a slide presentation. A few dozen people came to see that embryonic version of the slideshow, which continued to evolve and grow in my travels. Each time I shared my photographs and experiences, I was grateful to have something from this project to offer the people who were giving so generously of their time to support it. Since returning from my journey, I've presented the ecovillage slideshow in churches, lecture halls, retirement homes, and family living rooms, enabling people in search of sustainability to circumambulate the globe with me from the comfort of their chairs.

The slideshow remains the simplest way of encapsulating my journey, and now, thanks to the wonders of technology, I can share it with a wider audience. To view these photographs, see the companion website for this book at www.ecovillagebook.com. The title, "Fourteen Seed Communities Take Root," expresses both the diminutive scale of these ecovillages and also their extraordinary resilience and growth.

I like to think of ecovillages as a pioneer species. In botany, it's known that whenever land has been devastated, whether through natural causes like fires and floods or through human activities like plowing and clear-cutting, there are certain tenacious plants that are the first species to grow. The pioneer species have deep roots that are strong enough to fracture rocks and release their minerals into the soil. These plants also serve as nitrogen fixers, fertilizing the soil by pulling nitrogen out of the air. And when the pioneer species die, their decomposition produces soil for later species. Typically, the pioneer species are not the most glamorous of plants – think thistle – but their restorative work is absolutely essential.

This is why, when criticism is leveled at ecovillages, I tend to defend them. Like pioneer species, ecovillages are preparing the ground for a viable future, and we can all learn from their experiments. These communities are attempting so much that I feel they must be forgiven if at times their greatest strength turns out to be, as well, their greatest challenge.

Consider Auroville, an international township in South India that sees itself as an experiment in human unity. Participating in this experiment are some 2,000 individuals from 40 countries. Aurovilians are, however, primarily from Europe and tend to be quite well educated. This means that Auroville is, actually, a bunch of highly educated white folks plunked down amid 40,000 Tamil villagers living at subsistence level. So, Auroville's experiment in human unity can be seen as a dressed-up version of neo-colonialism, with all the subjugation and exploitation that the term implies. Almost all the physical work in Auroville is done by Tamils. At the same time, this employment, along with the educational and health benefits that come to neighboring Tamil villagers, means that Auroville's presence substantially improves the lot of those who live around it.

This is not a simple issue, and, in fact, there is enormous complexity involved in each of the ecovillages I visited. Every ideal has its shadow. Yet, to my mind, even casting a shadow should be seen as an act of service; there's a lot to be learned from investigating shadows. What follows in this chapter is not so much an investigation as a glimpse of each of the fourteen communities I visited. In-depth discussions of the issues will come in later chapters.

## Earthhaven, USA

My first stop was Earthaven, a picturesque ecovillage with earthen-plastered homes in the Blue Ridge Mountains about an hour's drive from Asheville, North Carolina. Established in 1994, Earthaven is an off-grid community and educational center with about 50 members who share an affinity for permaculture. I explore permaculture in greater depth in the next chapter. For now, suffice it to say that it is a radical ecological approach to designing settlements and agricultural systems that is thought to be permanent because it attempts to follow the functioning of nature. I was impressed by what the people at Earthaven had managed to create in less than fifteen years: an expertise in forestry, a range of natural building styles, 100 percent energy and water self-sufficiency, and several thriving farms – all in what was once 320 acres of raw forest.

Yet, as I learned on my visit, a shared affinity for permaculture is not enough to hold a community together. For one thing, people can have very different ideas about what it means to design from nature. With Earthaven's spring-fed water system, the North Carolina State Health Department had concerns about water sanitation and closed the community down to overnight guests. This one action simultaneously undercut Earthaven's educational mission and a big chunk of its income. The solution seemed to be to drill wells; but for a small, vocal minority, this would be a violation of the planet. Because this ecovillage is also committed to governance by consensus, meaning that everyone has to accept all decisions, the ensuing debates over water were painful for everyone.

Earthaven's difficulties underscore something that applies wherever we live: social sustainability is a foundation of ecological sustainability. Healthy ecosystems may provide the material support for all human activities, but we will be able to sustain those ecosystems only if we find a way to work together. So far as I know, no community has ever collapsed because it lacked composting toilets, but many have failed when human relationships fractured.

Earthaven is a community I was able to visit twice. When I returned two years later, I found among residents a sense of cautious optimism. The wells were dug, broken relationships were mending, and the community was completing its review of the governance process.

## EcoVillage at Ithaca, USA

EcoVillage at Ithaca (EVI), with its architectural designs and angular wooden construction, sees itself as a model for Middle America. A suburban co-housing community with roughly 100 adults and 60 children living on 175 acres in upstate New York, EVI has succeeded in reducing its average per capita ecological footprint to 14 acres, just over half the US average, while enjoying most of the comforts and conveniences of the proverbial American Dream. Still, if everyone in the world were to follow the lifestyle of EVI, we would need two or three Earths to sustain ourselves.

During my visit, construction was about to begin on the community's third neighborhood, bringing EVI one step closer to its projected population of 500. This is definitely a boom town, especially for young families.

One of the missions of EVI is to heal the schism between urban dwellers and the rural farms from which they get their food. To this end, EVI has a 10-acre organic farm, which feeds both EVI and hundreds of Ithaca residents.

## Findhorn, Scotland

Findhorn began in 1962 when three spiritual seekers with no previous gardening experience transformed a barren, windy bluff on the North Sea into a cornucopia. They attributed their success to their contact with nature spirits. Their astonishing results, inexplicable by normal scientific criteria, were broadcast globally; by the 1970s, Findhorn had become a Mecca for New Age seekers. Now, Findhorn's members are working as consultants with the United Nations and multinational corporations. The community has grown to 600, with hundreds more supporters living nearby, and is widely perceived as "the mother of all ecovillages."

Findhorn long ago shifted its focus from growing vegetables to what its literature terms "growing people." This happens through a popular smorgasbord of conferences and workshops on spiritual and ecological themes.

I enjoyed Findhorn's spiritual eclecticism and the atmosphere of openness and tolerance, but I also wondered about the glue of this community, with its dozens of businesses and nonprofits, its revolving door of world-class teachers, and its steady stream of visitors. A few people have told me the emphasis on ecological living has made Findhorn lose touch with its spiritual roots.

21

Hoping to gain some insight into the essence of this world-acclaimed ecovillage, I enrolled in Findhorn's most popular course: Experience Week. Designed as an intense immersion into both the community and one's own inner life, the course has attracted over 30,000 participants over the years. My favorite part of the week was the service work, where I got to partake in the rhythms of Findhorn. To my delight, I got my first choice: Cullerne Gardens, the direct descendant of the garden where the founders grew forty-pound cabbages and strawberries the size of beefsteak tomatoes. Each morning, about ten of us began by gathering in an "attunement circle." The facilitator, called the "focalizer," would tell us what needed to be done and then we each "attuned" to our specific task – listening within not for what we *wanted* to do but for what we felt *called* to do. We worked together for three hours each day, and as I worked, I had the sense of being a cell within a larger body. Whether harvesting beans or thinning lettuce seedlings, I gave myself fully to the task at hand. My senses were alive, picking up sights and sounds I would normally miss, and I was continually amazed by how much fun it was to work like this – and how much we were able to accomplish, even with a mid-morning tea break. Working in these bountiful gardens, I found one core teaching from Findhorn's early years alive and well: "Work is love in action."

## Svanholm, Denmark

Svanholm is a rural Danish community of 80 adults and 45 children. With nearly half of its 988 acres devoted to organic farming, the scale of Svanholm's farms (and its meat production) dwarfs that of most ecovillages. What most interested me, however, was this commune's thirty-year commitment to income sharing. If sharing is the essence of ecovillage life, then surely full-on financial sharing deserves some attention – especially when the community is as prosperous as Svanholm.

While the vast majority of the back-to-the-land communes of the 1960s and 1970s failed, this one has flourished. The key to Svanholm's economic success seems twofold: discernment and trust. Svanholm's lengthy membership process ensures that new members are able to support themselves, both economically and emotionally. The community rarely admits recent divorcees or single-parent families, and the norm of financial transparency is so strong that the community's bookkeeper didn't hesitate to show me a list with everyone's income. Yet I sensed another, more subtle reason for

Svanholm's ability to stay the course: its child-centered culture makes it a wonderful place to raise a family. Family values and communal living might seem like an odd mix, but at Svanholm they are perfectly compatible.

## UfaFabrik, Germany

UfaFabrik is an urban ecovillage that began in 1979 when about 100 squatters occupied the former Universal Film Studios in the heart of West Berlin. Their Cold War message was "Peace through culture and ecology." Their main mission was educational, but always with a splash of humor. Eventually, they gained title to the land and trans- formed the old film studio into a 160,000-sq.-ft., state-of-the-art ecological demonstration site. Today, UfaFabrik is a bustling hub of activity. While only 35 adults live on site, another 150 are employed in its organic café and bakery, social services, performance hall, children's programs, martial arts studios, and more. An estimated 200,000 visitors come through UfaFabrik every year. As I sat in the cozy café doing interviews, I got the sense that UfaFabrik's motto was, "If it's not fun, don't do it."

My visit happened to coincide with a performance by a South Korean drumming and dance troupe with close ties to UfaFabrik. Koreans and Germans, my host told me, know how it feels to live in a divided country, and they know that the universal language of music and dance can help span the chasm. I sat spellbound for two hours as brilliantly festooned dancers executed amazing feats in a perfor- mance that was pure extravagance – and seemingly well outside the bounds of my ecovillage research. Yet in their cross-cultural celebra- tion of the human spirit, these Korean dancers were displaying their own answer to the question "How, then, shall we live?" In joyful self-giving.

## ZEGG, Germany

Ninety minutes by train from Berlin, outside the town of Belzig, is ZEGG, the Center for Experimental Cultural Design (*Zentrum für esperimentelle Gesellschaftsgestaltung*), which was founded in 1991 on a former Nazi sports camp. ZEGG's eighty members believe that the life force of humanity, including our capacity for building a sustainable society, will only be liberated when we learn to take a nonpossessive approach to sexuality. I had strong reservations about visiting ZEGG, but many people with no interest in polyamorous lifestyles said it was a must. Having survived all manner of emotional upheaval among its members, ZEGG has developed a cluster of techniques called the Forum, which draws highly charged feelings into the open in group settings. The Forum has proved to be both successful and portable. For the last fifteen years, ZEGG has presented the Forum in other communities as a tool for fostering greater self-awareness and social bonding.

Had I followed my fears, I would not have experienced ZEGG's rare atmosphere of emotional transparency. By the time of my visit, the founder who established this community on a foundation of sexual exploration had moved on. What I imagine was, in the past, not an optimal environment for raising children is now beginning to attract young families. Monogamy and even celibacy have become viable options, and many residents seem to be less focused on sexuality than on spirituality.

## Sieben Linden, Germany

Sieben Linden, which is named for seven linden trees on the land, is another ecovillage that sprouted in the fertile soil of East Germany after reunification. Founded in 1997, this off-grid community of about 150 now occupies roughly 200 acres of farmland and pine plantation. The community's tiny ecological footprint, just over 25 percent of the German average, rests in part on its labor-intensive commitment to vegan agriculture and its "Peace Contract with Animals," which I discuss in chapter 3. During my visit, Sieben Linden experienced the first death of one of its members. I found myself moved by the community's response to the death: how they treated the body, shared their grief, performed the funeral, integrated the children into the process, and how at this tender time in their community they included even me – a foreigner and English speaker who was in every way an outsider.

Witnessing the community members' organic handling of this unexpected death and, as well, their ongoing conversations about whether or not to kill animals for food gave me an inkling of how secure one might feel living in a culture where every aspect of life is approached with reflection. At the end of my visit as I walked to the bus stop, I found that I was looking at the silent winter landscape of rural Germany in a new light. When I arrived, I'd seen it as foreboding; now it seemed like a vast, brooding potential. I was pleased to observe that, in the intervening weeks, what had changed was my own perspective.

24

## Damanhur, Italy

A spiritual community in the foothills of the Italian Alps, Damanhur has its own molecular biology lab for testing for genetically modified food and a smartphone for every member. It may be the world's most fast-paced, high-tech ecovillage. It may also be the world's most fanciful, beautiful, and prosperous ecovillage. About 600 Damanhur residents live in 30 communities, called "nucleos," spread across a spectacular subalpine valley, each devoted to a specific field: solar energy, seed saving, organic meat production, education, healing, and so on. Appropriately, I stayed in a new nucleo dedicated to international exchange.

I was perpetually mystified by what I encountered in Damanhur, oscillating between admiration and skepticism throughout my visit. Who would not be awestruck by Damanhur's elaborate underground Temples of Humankind? I did not, however, so readily take in the esoteric philosophy behind these temples. I attended weekly talks by Damanhur's spiritual teacher, Falco, with simultaneous translation into several languages. But even with English translation, I had difficulty grasping his meaning. Falco spoke about time travel and cosmic guides, galactic laws and intergalactic communication. In addressing the effect of humankind on our own planet, he had this to say: "What is natural in a world where humans have altered everything? We should set aside any prejudgments, telling ourselves that this is natural and this is not. We need to overcome that distinction through magic. Magic is the only act where those who act and those who don't are in balance."

On my final day, I visited a tree-based nucleo with the assigned task of communicating with plants. The residents hooked up a machine of their invention to various plants to track their connection with those plants. I was initially doubtful, but with several tries and a session of meditation, I could actually hear that communication had been established between myself and a white cyclamen. I'll speak more about this in chapter 6.

## Colufifa, Senegal

Colufifa is a French acronym for the Committee to End Hunger (*Comité de lutte pour la Fin de la Faim*). This is not an ecovillage per se; it is a network of 350 West African villages seeking to become self-sufficient through organic farming, microfinance, adult literacy, and malaria prevention. In Africa, as in the rest of the developing world, the work is not to build new villages but to make the existing ones sustainable. Founded in 1964, Colufifa predates the ecovillage movement by decades and joined the Global Ecovillage Network because the network's leadership shared GEN's commitment to village self-sufficiency. Yet while Colufifa's impoverished villagers have minuscule ecological footprints – by far the smallest I encountered – the term *ecovillage* meant nothing to most of them: their austerity is involuntary.

I visited Colufifa's headquarters in Faoune, a village in southern Senegal, and I also went to several nearby member villages. In all of these villages, the vast majority of young men have left, hoping to find employment in African cities or in Europe. Their departure may have contributed to a sense of despair, and it has certainly created a peculiar de facto women's empowerment in this traditionally patriarchal Muslim culture. Each village greeted me as if I were royalty, even though I had nothing to offer them, save my ability to listen and to relay their stories. In one village where every young man had left, a group of women who called themselves the Fools welcomed me with local dances, which they performed for over an hour with ground-shaking force. The dancing, common in these villages, and ubiquitous prayer were the images I took with me as I left Colufifa.

## Crystal Waters, Australia

In 1984, when Crystal Waters Permaculture Village was founded in northeastern Australia, it was the world's first permaculture village. Some 200 residents now live on its 85 private one-acre lots, with another roughly 500 acres held in common as a wildlife sanctuary. In a region plagued by drought, Crystal Waters is a sparkling oasis whose intricate system of dams has transformed rainwater into streams and lakes. Even under severe drought conditions such as these, however, hydrology is a far simpler matter than human relationships. On my visit, the community – and a number of residents informed me that this is *not* a community – was in crisis. Most owners of internal businesses, including all of the farmers, were in the process of leaving. I asked Max Lindegger, one of Crystal Waters' founders and a world-renowned permaculture designer, what he made of this. He said, "We're not hungry enough yet." Personally, I'm hoping that hunger is not a prerequisite to sharing.

Crystal Waters is a fascinating case study of how social environment can be influenced by structure, both physical and financial.

Crystal Waters' homes are sold on the open market, the only requirement for joining the community being that new owners receive a copy of the by-laws. There is neither a common house nor a dedicated community meeting space. Even though one-acre lots are considered high density in rural Australia, the distances and the steep terrain reinforce the existing car culture. Since I had no car, my host loaned me his 24-speed bicycle. As I pedaled along the rollercoaster of a road that spans the length of Crystal Waters, I only needed two gears: first and twenty-fourth. Not once did I see another adult on a bicycle, but I did see hundreds of kangaroos and wallabies.

## Auroville, India

Auroville, established in 1968 as an international township and "a living laboratory," is first and foremost a spiritual community, not an ecovillage. For Auroville's founders, however, the first order of business was transforming a severely eroded plateau into a habitable ecosystem. Having planted and tended more than three million trees, Auroville is now one of the few places on Earth where biodiversity is actually increasing. The community is also a world leader in compressed-earth building techniques, rainwater harvesting, plant-based sewage treatment, and solar and wind energy. I experienced Auroville as a beehive of activity overlaid with an atmosphere of ease and fluidity, truly one of the most hopeful places I've ever encountered.

Yet behind this hopefulness, as I mentioned earlier, I perceived a shadow. Auroville's dynamism is partly due to its proximity to 40,000 traditional Tamil villagers, many of whom work in Auroville's guesthouses and its construction and cottage industries. In this rural setting, there were morning and evening "rush hours" with hundreds upon hundreds of Tamil villagers streaming past on bicycles and motorbikes. While by American standards most Auroville residents live very simply, their lifestyle is opulent compared to that of the surrounding Tamil villages. The inevitable tensions that arise from this economic disparity suffuse every aspect of Auroville's existence – from housing policies, to the division of labor, to race and gender relations.

What can human unity possibly mean, I found myself wondering, under conditions of extreme economic inequality? As I considered the dawning era of planetary interdependence and the new story it heralds, that question hit me with a sense of urgency.

## Sarvodaya, Sri Lanka

When people ask how many ecovillages there are in the world, I tell them it depends upon whether you count the 15,000 Sri Lankan villages working with Sarvodaya. Sarvodaya, which literally means "the awakening of all," began in 1957 when its founder, Dr A. T. Ariyaratne, decided to bring Gandhi's vision of village self-sufficiency to his country. The basic premise is that, by working together to meet their needs, villagers can enhance their material wellbeing, their social relationships, and their spiritual consciousness. As they say, "We build the road, and the road builds us."

Of Sarvodaya's thousands of villages, only one, Lagoswatte, was designed and built as an ecovillage from the ground up. Constructed in the aftermath of the 2004 tsunami under the guidance of Crystal Waters co-founder Max Lindegger, this village is now a world-class environmental learning center. Its cheerful yellow compressed-earth homes are each equipped with a single solar panel, a rainwater cistern, and a home garden. Lagoswatte's green living and its self-governance are new for the residents, who are all displaced tsunami victims. While the village is impressive, the residents' transformation is even more so. Harit, the village president, told me that, once a drunkard, he became an international environmental educator under Sarvodaya's influence.

Yet in Sri Lanka – and in the world itself – Lagoswatte is a tiny drop amid an ocean of unsustainable development. I voiced my concern during a two-day road trip I took with Dr Ariyaratne, and this octo-genarian Buddhist stalwart reassured me with a bit of the philosophy that has kept him working these five decades. "The tiny drops living in harmony with the cosmic laws of interdependence," he said, "are more important than the whole ocean of harmful practices." I want to believe him.

## Konohana Family, Japan

Konohana Family, an ecovillage that sits under the towering presence of Japan's Mount Fuji, takes its name from the goddess once thought to inhabit this venerable mountain. On my first night, I received the warmest welcome I've ever received as a stranger: a personal perfor-mance by Konohana's singers. With passionate honesty, they sang songs they had themselves written about such personal matters as giving up selfishness and coming to love one another and the Earth. As other guests arrived during my visit, I realized that they do this for everyone who comes.

Each day I was at Konohana, I marveled at the community's prodigious rice, soy, and vegetable fields – the basis of its collective economy as well as its efforts to come into harmony with nature. One of the farmers showed me how to make Konohana Kin (pronounced *keen*), a potent mixture of "effective micro-organisms" that boosts the productivity of the fields. Community members also drink this concoction daily, and apparently they rarely get sick. The farmer explained that "going to war with bacteria" is the Japanese way. "Here at Konohana," he said, "instead, we make friends with the beneficial bacteria." I don't know whether it was just the idea that this wine-like beverage was good for me, but I found myself wanting to drink it at every meal.

Like a family, Konohana's fifty-some members share close quarters (even by Japanese standards) and homegrown food three times a day around one long table. The community glue is the intense after-dinner conversation that ensues every evening and lasts sometimes until the early morning hours. Under the guidance of Isadon, the village patriarch, Konohana's members use this time to reflect on how well they were able to implement God's will that day. This is not just an individual process, and the residents have no compunction about poking and prodding into one another's psyches as well. This style of group self-inquiry didn't appeal to me, but apparently it works for this community. Anyway, Konohana seems to function better than most families I've seen.

## Los Angeles Eco-Village, USA

After nearly nine months on the road and in the air, I came full circle, returning to my home country by way of the graffiti-strewn East Hollywood neighborhood that is home to Los Angeles Eco-Village (LAEV). Having lived for fourteen years in Southern California, the epicenter of American hyper-individualism, I was curious to see what fifty adults committed to green living in a gritty neighborhood could accomplish. At first glance, their two renovated tenement buildings had little to catch my eye: a few more trees out front, a whimsical cob bench in the shape of a dragon, and permeable sidewalks that prevent rainwater runoff. Around back in the wide courtyard between the buildings, however, I found something extraordinary: a lush garden, somewhere between wild and tame, with picturesque sitting nooks and twenty-seven varieties of fruits and vegetables. Compared to the tacky strip-mall jungle outside, this was Eden!

I also found another way of looking inside LAEV: through the

29

hearts and minds of its members. The founder, Lois Arkin, had a social justice vision for LA Eco-Village right from the start. Troubled by the 1992 Los Angeles riots, she abandoned a plan to build on an 11-acre lot on the city's outskirts and, instead, created this ecovillage in the inner city. As a consequence, Los Angeles Eco-Village is the most ethnically diverse community I visited. In addition, because most of the community members work as full-time environmental and social justice advocates, LA Eco-Village has a huge ripple effect. This inner-city ecovillage is the only community I visited with no children. At night, as sirens blared outside and police helicopters circled overhead, I understood why.

## E2C2: four windows into sustainability

I returned to my home in Seattle with a sense of excitement about ecovillages, with a renewed commitment to align my life with my core values – and, most importantly for me, with some essential knowledge about how to do that. My next task was to share this journey that now lives inside me.

During my travels, I leapt from rural outposts to inner-city ghettos, from opulent temples to abject poverty. How could I bring a sense of coherence to such disparate experiences? How could I tell such a complex story? What are the common threads that run through this diverse tapestry? Certainly there is a common commitment to sustainable living. But what is this elusive thing known as "sustainability"?

One popular approach to sustainability is sometimes called the three-legged stool: ecology, economy, and society. This is a good start because it acknowledges that we don't want only to sustain natural ecosystems; we also want to sustain our livelihoods and our human relationships. But the metaphor is problematic because it reduces sustainability to a balancing act between three separate poles when, in fact, ecology, economics, and social relationships are all unavoidably interconnected. Saving energy, for instance, might look like an ecological practice, but when I read my utility bill, saving energy becomes a matter of economics, and when I offend people by telling them to turn off the lights, it's definitely a social issue.

Another problem with the three-legged stool is that it ignores the inner dimension of sustainability, the deeper questions of meaning and cosmological belonging that have informed human existence for ages. While some ecovillages eschew the term "spirituality," others – like Findhorn, Damanhur and Auroville – are first and foremost spiritual communities. In the online Gaia Education curriculum associated with the Global Ecovillage Network, the image of the stool is replaced with a fourfold mandala that includes "worldview." I prefer to call this elusive yet all-important subjective dimension of sustainability "consciousness." Ultimately, how I live outwardly will express who I am inwardly.

My own metaphor of choice for sustainability is a house with four windows. We live in houses, after all, and sustainability is, ultimately, a question about our planetary household. Imagine four windows looking into a house, each representing a different vantage point. From each perspective, the house looks different and yet it is still the same house. And if the house is small enough – as my house of sustainability would be – then each window would offer a view of every other window. So, we can look into ecovillages, and any human endeavor you might think of, through any or all of these windows: ecology, economics, community, and consciousness – or E2C2 for short.

Like individuals and cultures everywhere, each ecovillage tends to highlight certain elements of E2C2. Yet the house of sustainability always has four windows, and each of them is a valid, even essential, perspective. Crystal Waters Permaculture Village, for instance, is famous for its hydrological tour de force in rainwater catchment, but the fact that its homes are sold on the open market makes for some challenging social and economic dynamics. In its economic work to overcome hunger, Colufifa has simultaneously helped to empower women and spread organic farming in West Africa. And while only half of the ecovillages I visited have an overt spiritual focus, questions of deeper meaning and cosmological belonging are very much alive in even the most secular communities. One Svanholm member who claimed to be "allergic to spirituality" waxed eloquent when he explained his sense of himself as one cell in the living body of Gaia.

Over and over again, I came to see that the four dimensions of sustainability are interconnected, each reflecting and refracting the light from the others. Because ecovillages take a strongly integrative approach, E2C2 takes on a dynamic, self-reinforcing character. The ecological focus of Sieben Linden, for instance, is the basis of its social life. As they work to eradicate poverty, Third World networks like Colufifa and Sarvodaya strengthen the health of both communities and ecosystems. And the spiritual perspectives of Findhorn and Auroville are the very soil from which their ecological, social, and economic practices grow.

E2C2 constitutes the fourfold structure for the next four chapters:

ecology, economy, community, and consciousness. Each chapter is an essay on that topic, assembling illustrations from the stories I gleaned, encounters I had, and observations I made in these fourteen ecovillages. My purpose is to sketch a global portrait of the leading edge of sustainable living in the early twenty-first century. This portrait, of course, has been filtered through my eyes and my own idiosyncratic approach to the art of winnowing. I returned from my journey with more than a thousand pages of interview notes, my mind and heart brimming with information and inspiration. I have attempted to cull the best of the material – the most useful, the most inspiring, the most fascinating, the most puzzling, and the most paradoxical – interweaving it with my own story of learning and adventure.

Of course, I hope that you will read this book cover to cover. In case you don't, the fourfold structure will enable you to easily focus on the areas of your own life you are most interested in transforming.

This book assembles the story of my global journey and stories from fourteen ecovillages against the backdrop of perhaps the most compelling story of our time: that of our species groping its way toward a viable future. As I've said, sustainability is not an option; it is the ground rule for inhabiting our home planet. Ecovillages have a big head start in figuring out how to make sustainability work. Ecovillages may not be *the* answer to humanity's problems, but they are one of the answers, and we need all the answers we can get. I see ecovillages as seeds of hope sparsely sown across the global landscape. These seeds are small and time is short. It seems clear that we can't all go out and build new ecovillages. We can, however, apply the lessons of the ecovillage in our homes, neighborhoods, cities, countries, and even internationally. The basic principle is simple: sharing – sharing material resources, ideas, dreams, skills, stories, joys, and sorrows. We don't need to be in ecovillages to share. And if we did share, then our communities would begin to look like ecovillages.

# — 3 —

# ECOLOGY: LIVING IN THE CIRCLE OF LIFE

One cold November morning, I went walking in the pine forest that Sieben Linden inherited from the former East German owners. Initially, I felt buoyed by the discovery of the huge pines, but after a short while I became aware of a strange silence. Beyond the occasional bird, I saw no wildlife. Finally, it dawned on me that this was not a forest at all; it was a plantation. Row upon row of virtually identical pines stood arrayed in all directions like mass-produced monoliths. For years I had been telling my students about the ecological devastation wrought by monoculture plantations, and still I was unprepared for the lifeless feeling of this forest. After some time, I encountered a young woman from Sieben Linden. She explained that in the late nineteenth century, the native forests had been cleared to produce charcoal for the iron smelters that fueled Germany's industrialization. The deciduous trees were replaced with fast-growing pine. Now, the combination of sandy soil and acidic pine needles made it impossible for this desolate forest to regenerate itself.

The young woman showed me how Sieben Linden has begun to restore the forest. She led me to an area where, after harvesting some pines for construction and firewood, the community had planted native oak and beech saplings and fertilized them with composted human manure from the community's toilets. With 150 members, there is plenty of compost! Once the trees are established, their fallen leaves will eventually regenerate the soil, which will in turn restore the forest – a process requiring several decades.

Consider how the thinking behind this ingenious system differs from the thinking behind the monoculture plantation. In the industrial model, systems are segregated into linear paths that run from resource to production to consumption to waste. The forest is one thing (an energy source for industry) and the flush toilet is another (a convenient way of getting rid of human waste). In a whole-systems approach, forest and toilet are integrated into mutually beneficial cycles. If Sieben Linden manages its forests well, its members will have a self-regenerating source of firewood for its high-efficiency wood-gasification furnace and an on-site source of quality timber for building. With a thriving native forest, birdsong will enliven their days. Of course, most of us live in cities where health codes prohibit fertilizing forests with composted human excrement, but the basic principle – integrate, don't segregate – can be applied anywhere. Sieben Linden offers just one example of the synergistic effects that ensue when systems for "waste" treatment, construction, energy, water, and wildlife are interwoven into a well-integrated whole. In this context, economics, community, and consciousness itself begin to serve the circle of life.

In the simplest terms, ecology is the study of how living organisms – including us – relate to each other and their geophysical surroundings. There's quite a bit to this because, as John Muir so aptly put it, "everything is hitched to everything else." Yet we live in a world of distinctions; a healthy body, like a healthy ecosystem, requires both healthy parts and harmonious relationships between them. When we discover and nourish the mutually enhancing interconnections across these distinctions – and this entails thinking outside the linear industrial model – life becomes very exciting.

In the rest of this chapter, I address various ecological aspects of ecovillage life, devoting one section apiece to permaculture, building, energy, water, food, transportation, collaborative consumption, and wildlife conservation. And, because of the integrative character of ecovillage life, we frequently catch glimpses of the other dimensions of E2C2.

## Box 3.1 The Ecological Footprint

A simple tool for measuring our environmental impact is the ecological footprint, an estimate of the amount of land needed to generate the resources and absorb the waste associated with a particular lifestyle.[1]

---

[1] A related concept, the carbon footprint, measures the impact of an activity or lifestyle on global warming. While the ecological footprint is more comprehensive, the two are correlated because fossil fuels, the primary cause of global warming, also drive the global economy.

These footprints can be expressed both in acres (or hectares) and as the number of Earths a lifestyle would require if every person on Earth lived this way, assuming today's world population. Thus, the average US footprint is 26 acres, or about five Earths, whereas the average footprint in the Gambia is about half an acre. In other words, one American has the ecological impact of fifty Gambians. Of all the footprint calculators available online, my favorite is http://myfootprint.org. No calculator is fully accurate but this one is based upon an enormous body of research and offers a good starting point for assessing our impact on the planet – as well as for understanding global inequality.

Shortly after the footprint exercise was developed by Mathis Wackernagel in 1992, I began using it with my students, and I've found it never fails to spark a lively discussion. I first ask students to calculate their footprint as a US resident and then, using the exact same numbers, to recalculate it as if they lived in a developing country. Initially, they're baffled by the results: why should identical numbers register as 20 acres in the United States and nine acres in India? They tend to blame it on a programming error, but I press them to make sense of the numbers. Their faces light up and then cloud over as the answer dawns upon them: their American footprints reflect the global web of technology that underpins their lifestyles – the roads, mines, oil rigs, factories, shipping lanes, military bases, feedlots, data storage centers, etc. Even using the lowest feasible numbers, they find that they cannot live in the USA on a one-Earth footprint. Sustainable living turns out to be more than a personal lifestyle choice; it is also about infrastructure – and is therefore a social and political matter. The footprint exercise helps my students to grasp that they are not merely consumers; they are citizens.

Why, then, would I, as a political scientist, take an interest in ecovillages? First, their average footprints are 10–50 percent less than their home country averages. Second, ecovillages demonstrate what is possible when communities come together to transform not only their physical infrastructure but every dimension of E2C2. Third, as we see in chapter 5, ecovillages are not isolated enclaves; they are deeply engaged in the larger social and political sphere. And finally, when people all over the world start transforming their lives through holistic thinking and action, it is inherently worth our attention.

# Permaculture: a holistic approach to technology and consumption

At the outset of my courses, I find that most students are hoping for a technological fix: more hybrids and solar panels. But their hopes are at odds with reality. The average American consumes as much as twenty people living in the developing world – many of whom would like to live as we do – and today's population of seven billion is expected to increase to nine billion by 2050. So our behavior is at least as problematic as our technologies. Yet, in a culture where personal and social wellbeing have been tied to ever-increasing consumption, there is a strong taboo against questioning that consumption.

It turns out that there are several reasons why it is counterproductive to focus on technological solutions without addressing levels of consumption. First, most efficiency gains from new technologies are offset by increased consumption. Our cars might get better mileage, but there are more cars than ever before – especially if you're taking a global count and considering China and India. Second, when we compute the environmental savings of green technologies like solar panels and electric cars, most of us don't consider their *embodied energy*, the accumulated energy required to assemble the necessary raw materials, manufacture a product, and transport it. This is typically much greater for high-tech goods. Third, because technological solutions to the sustainability crisis usually involve obtaining something new, they run the risk of reinforcing the "let's-buy-it" mania that's at the heart of the problem.

When we attend to *both* technology and consumption, as ecovillages are doing, we can dramatically reduce our environmental impact. With the exception of photovoltaic solar panels, double- and triple-glazed windows, and internet access, which were almost universal, the ecovillages I visited have diverse approaches to technology. Some plow their fields with horses while others zip around in electric vehicles. Low-tech ecovillages like Earthaven and Sieben Linden build with straw, timber, and clay – inexpensive natural materials that can be found locally, obviously an environmental benefit. High-tech communities like EcoVillage at Ithaca and Damanhur build with state-of-the-art manufactured materials like SIPS (Structural Insulated Panels) and computerized household climate-control systems. Damanhur has a molecular biology lab that tests its food to make sure none has been genetically modified, a high-energy endeavor that would be unthinkable at Earthaven. And everyone at Damanhur had their own smartphones, while Sieben Linden relied primarily on landlines.

36

Figure 3.1 An Aurovilian web designer works with clients from his home, a thatch-hut in the forest

Figure 3.2 A Damanhurian software engineer lives in a tree house

Table 3.1   Permaculture Design Principles

| | |
|---|---|
| Observe and interact | Use small and slow solutions |
| Catch and store energy | Produce no waste |
| Obtain a yield | Use edges and value the marginal |
| Design from pattern to details | Integrate rather than segregate |
| Apply self-regulation and accept feedback | Use and value diversity |
| Use and value renewable resources | Respond creatively to change |

Source: Based on David Holmgrem (http://permacultureprinciples.com).

Some of my favorite finds were what I like to call "high-lo tech": a computer programmer who lives in a tree house at Damanhur and a French website designer who lives in a mud hut in Auroville. Most of the designer's clients are in Paris, he told me, and they assume he is as well.

As I went from one to the next, I found myself hunting for the underlying ideas that unite these diverse ecovillages. If I had to name the single most popular source of ecological insight among the ecovillages I visited, it would be permaculture.[2] Permaculture, which speaks to both technology and consumption, is not so much a formula for sustainability as a set of guiding principles built upon the premise that human systems are a subset of nature and so should be – ultimately, *must* be – harmonized with nature. Most important, permaculture promotes bottom-up social change rooted in design principles observable in nature, starting with the individual and the household.

Gaia Education, an offshoot of the Global Ecovillage Network (GEN), offers a free downloadable curriculum that borrows heavily from permaculture. Tellingly, GEN's original Ecovillage Design Education is now entitled Education Design for Sustainability. This shift reflects an awareness that GEN's primary task is not to persuade people to build more ecovillages but to bring ecovillage principles into the world.

While not every ecovillage I visited traces its roots to permaculture, most speak in the language of permaculture and all embrace the core idea of harmonizing human systems with nature. Some ecovillages, like Earthaven and Crystal Waters, were founded by permaculture design teachers who pioneered those communities' focus on renewable energy and wildlife preservation. There were other ecovillages where I never encountered the permaculture terminology and yet the

---

[2]  See http://gaiaeducation.org. The curriculum is taught at ecovillages around the world as well as through the Open University of Catalonia in Spain.

residents seemed to be living in accordance with its principles. These twelve design principles don't delineate how to build your home or produce your electricity, but they do offer some general guidelines for greening your life. Unlike the mechanical way of parsing the world into separate systems, permaculture is a holistic approach to living that integrates human systems of building, energy, water, food, and transportation into existing ecosystems to form a well-functioning whole. In other words, it is a way of thinking in circles.

## Building

I expected to find lots of tiny energy-efficient buildings in the ecovillages I visited – and so I did. But I also often found many beautiful, comfortable homes, and that I had not expected. Along the way, I learned that simplicity can be entirely compatible with comfort and beauty. Compared to what I was used to, ecovillage homes felt less intrusive; often they enhanced the landscape. Their angles were more rounded, they had plenty of natural light, and they felt somehow healthier. Harmonizing the built environment with nature can be as good for people as it is for the Earth. If I had to find one word to describe how ecovillages look and feel – especially the ones that have built themselves from the ground up – it would be "organic."

And, yes, I did see a few funky structures built entirely from natural or recycled materials – including some I would never want to live in. I saw one house that had started as a canvas yurt, a circular one-room dwelling. Over the years, the owner had affixed several wooden alcoves so that, by the time I visited, it was a marginally functional jumble of spaces reeking of mold. Not my cup of tea.

I saw, as well, any number of homes that had never, probably *could* never, pass a building inspection in their own country and yet were attractive models of efficiency. I visited one woman who had lived for years in a two-story timber-framed earthen triplex that was approved as a garden shed. "When the building inspector came," she recalled, "he just said, 'I don't know what these people do at night time.' I'm always glad for those officials who quietly support us by turning a blind eye to what we're doing." This off-grid triplex cost US$90,000 to build, including electrical, water, and heating systems, and the three women who live there will never have to pay a utility bill. Their "garden shed" home, with its rounded earthen walls, warm wooden beams, and large south-facing windows, was the picture of rustic beauty. If success means reducing resource consumption and

39

waste while enhancing people's sense of wellbeing, I would count the vast majority of ecovillage building experiments as whopping successes – including most of those "illegal" structures where people have been living for years. It makes me wonder whether building codes shouldn't be updated.

## Green building and natural building

The ecovillage homes I saw ran the gamut from high tech to low tech, with most in between. The low-tech ecovillage building strategy uses locally available materials, including wood, clay, sand, stone, and straw from the land, as well as salvaged windows and doors. The high-tech strategy uses state-of-the-art materials, like large arrays of solar panels or cogeneration plants that produce both heat and electricity. While these may require an enormous initial outlay, they can be ecologically and economically efficient over the long haul.

The most impressive high-tech building I encountered was Damanhur's award-winning Aval, a 6,000-sq.-ft. house (plus basement) for twenty-one permanent residents and twenty-one guests. For some time, I stood in the basement bewildered by the assemblage of climate-control machines and computers that looked like something out of a sci-fi movie. No matter how cold or hot it is outside, these machines keep the indoor temperature constant. Everything I could see, plus the geothermal heat pump, radiant-floor heating system, and triple-paned windows and doors, came from Germany. Damanhur also happens to be home to one of my favorite low-tech experiments: Arboricoli, where people live in tree houses held together without nails, only rope.

Some low-tech experiments are pure genius, like Findhorn's Barrel Cluster. One resident's search for local, renewable building materials led him to the leftover oak barrels from one of Scotland's most famous industries: Scotch whiskey. He trucked in a few, dried them out, turned them upside down, insulated and painted them, and then assembled them into attractive modular homes. "We changed them from one kind of receptacle for spirits to another kind," he said.

If I wanted a small, inexpensive, Earth-friendly home and didn't have access to whiskey barrels, I would probably choose one of Earthaven's micro-huts. I stayed in one of these 12 ft-by-12 ft homes, complete with kitchen, office, living area, and a bedroom in the loft, and enjoyed its ultra-efficient use of space. Ditto for its energy efficiency, with its passive solar design, photovoltaic panels, solar hot water, and a tiny wood stove. The only inconvenience was that the shower and composting toilet were outside. The cost of this tiny home? Between US$20,000 and US$30,000, depending upon amenities, and the owner will never pay a utility bill.

When I reflect upon my journey, one of my most pleasant memories is of sitting inside on cool days – even frigid days – and basking in the sun's warmth without turning on the heat. I had this experience at half the ecovillages I visited. My stay at Sieben Linden coincided with a deep freeze, yet I found myself peeling off layers as I interviewed residents in their sunlit living rooms. At EcoVillage at Ithaca, I sat in several homes that were never warmer than 75°C, even when the outdoor temperatures topped 95°C. What did these homes have in common? Passive solar design. In the northern hemisphere, that means big windows on the south side, large overhangs to block summer sun, and a thermal mass (usually an earthen structure like cob or masonry) to absorb and store the sun's radiant heat. Having experienced this level of comfort and efficiency, my only explanation for why builders continue to orient homes toward the street rather than the sun is that cars dominate not only our landscapes but also our minds.

There's something else that these passive solar ecovillages have in common: they were built from the ground up. As a consequence, their designers were able to *choose* their materials and the orientation of their buildings. Given the choice, who wouldn't opt for free heat and light from the sun? And yet most of us live in cities and suburbs where there are plenty of buildings, many of them far larger than we need. Ultimately, therefore, most of us must work with what we have – and that means retrofitting.

Some ecovillages, especially in cities, have retrofit with intelligence, creativity, and flare. Having inherited a campus full of ugly, inefficient buildings built by Nazis and the former East German secret police, ZEGG embraced the challenge of transforming this dark legacy. Since the original walls were too thin for insulation, they gutted the buildings, built the walls out several inches, and installed high-efficiency insulation. They removed toxic paints, installed double-pane windows, and converted the old coal-burning furnace into a high-efficiency wood chip furnace that heats the entire community with net-zero carbon emissions. And they beautified each room with their own vibrant artwork. Even though I could still feel the institutional character of ZEGG's buildings, I often stopped to admire the paintings, contrasting their warmth with the place's bleak history.

As impressive as these transformations were, I still felt most drawn to the ecological and aesthetic benefits of building from the ground up – particularly when low-impact natural building strategies were employed. In weighing my assessment, I had to consider the question of embodied energy. *Green building* uses high-efficiency manufactured materials whereas *natural building* uses only materials that come directly from the Earth, like clay, sand, wood, and straw that can often be found on site. The embodied energy of green building materials is much higher. Because fossil fuels have been plentiful and cheap, it has been possible (at least in the affluent countries) to sidestep the problem of embodied energy. Of the ecovillagers I encountered, most – though not all – were hyper-conscious about embodied energy.

When I asked one of the builders of Aval, Damanhur's award-winning mega-house, about the embodied energy of that building's components, he said he had never considered the issue. His blank response reminded me of a friend who was quite pleased with herself for buying a Prius. She was oblivious to the fact that half the energy her beloved Prius will ever consume was already expended before the car hit the sales lot. So far as Earth is concerned, she would have been better off buying a used Honda Civic. By succumbing to the illusion that we can buy our way to sustainability, she was unwittingly reinforcing another pernicious delusion: that ecology is a luxury for the affluent.

Some people assume that, since the technologies associated with green building are . . . well, green, then we need not exercise restraint in using them. I encountered an example of this faulty logic at Findhorn. Back in the 1990s, they allowed private developers to build model green homes on a plot of land that came to be known as the Field of Dreams. When people at Findhorn spoke to me about "the ecovillage," they didn't necessarily mean their community as a whole; they were often referring to this colorful array of homes, ranging from the practical to the extravagant. For two weeks, I lived in a compact ultra-efficient eco-home on the Field of Dreams and enjoyed it immensely, never turning on the heat even when nighttime temperatures dipped into the low forties. But each day as I gazed up at the overbearing three-story homes around me, I wondered whether this was the best use of resources. At least one resident, a former member of Findhorn's planning committee, shared my doubts. "We made some mistakes," she admitted. "We had size limitations, but we granted too many exceptions." One disgruntled member went further; he called the Field of Dreams "the ego-village."

It was as if my Prius-driving friend now felt entitled to drive twice as much as she had before. Indeed, psychological research suggests that when people take one action to benefit Earth, they often feel entitled to act harmfully elsewhere. We tell ourselves things like, "I bicycle so I can fly to Hawaii in the winter."

Green building materials might require more energy to produce than clay, sand, and straw, but we've not found a way of procuring things like double-paned windows or blown cellulose (an insulation material made from recycled newspaper) directly from the planet. Virtually every natural builder uses some high-end materials. It's always a question of balance, and there's no question that green building can shrink our footprint. Homes at EVI, for instance, use less than half the energy of standard American homes – even with no lifestyle changes among the residents. Cutting our energy footprint in half is a good start but, as I said earlier, if everyone in the world lived like EVI, we would still need two or three Earths to sustain us all.

Personally, I felt more drawn to the natural building experiments of ecovillages like Earthaven and Sieben Linden. A University of Kassel study of Sieben Linden put their ecological footprint at 28% of the German average – and the German footprint is already half the American! But what really caught my eye was Club 99, a Sieben Linden neighborhood where the residents (according to the same study) have managed to reduce their footprints to 10% of the German average – or 5% of the American average. And these were not rural villagers in Africa!

Club 99's commitment to natural building was most evident in its 900-sq.-ft. common house. Over the course of its lifetime, that structure will use about 2% as much energy as a typical German house the same size. Martin Stengel, an engineer and builder at Sieben Linden, recounted the construction process. Except for some floorboards, everything in the house was either recycled or procured from Sieben Linden's land, and the entire structure was built without machinery. The cost? "Less than €8,000 (US$12,000)," Martin said. "But you must realize that we put 16,000 hours of work into this house, a lot of it from unskilled but very willing friends."

So, time is a cost that keeps us from seeing more of this kind of inexpensive, Earth-friendly and communitarian building.[3] Another

---

[3] Because natural building is so labor-intensive, it can be a great way to establish skills and, at the same time, a sense of community. The 15 members of Emerald Earth, a small ecovillage in the California redwoods, spend most of their waking hours building together. Because each hand-sculpted earthen home takes a year to complete, they can only expand their membership slowly – a conscious choice. I did not want to include such a small community in this book, but photos are available on the companion website at www.ecovillagebook.com.

Figure 3.3 Sieben Linden's Strohpolis incorporates
straw-bale construction, passive solar design, and
rainwater catchment

deterrent is that natural materials and the techniques that employ
them are only gradually finding acceptance in building codes. This is
why there's more natural building in rural areas, where such codes are
either nonexistent or rarely enforced. Violating codes creates problems: the danger of getting caught and the unlikelihood that others
will follow your example. This is why Sieben Linden has worked hard
to get natural building legalized in Germany. When its three-story
townhouse complex (known as Strohpolis) was completed in 2006, it
was the largest straw-bale building in Europe. After compiling extensive research on the fire safety of straw-bale construction, the builders
succeeded in getting this material written into the German codes. And
because German standards are among the most stringent, builders
around the world took note.

Of all the benefits of natural building, the one most compelling to
me is how it feels. One pitch made by natural builders is "the homes
that love you back," and, after living in some of these homes, I tend
to agree with them. I'd always accepted the hard angles of conventional building as the norm. Only after I discovered the warmth and
softness of natural building's colors and textures did I come to recognize my body's apparently inborn aversion to rectilinear building.

Figure 3.4 EVI's SONG neighborhood demonstrates passive solar and shared-wall design

## Natural building in the Third World

Of course, until recently *all* building was natural building. That's no longer the case in the affluent countries, and it's changing fast in the developing world. In some ways, those changes make sense. Screens and corrugated metal roofs are an asset in an area plagued by mosquitoes and torrential rains. What concerns me, though, is the knee-jerk preference for modern technologies I saw in Africa and Asia. Take cement buildings: they're ugly and uncomfortable, and their embodied energy is very high. Worldwide, cement is the largest material source of greenhouse gas emissions, adding as much carbon dioxide to the atmosphere as aviation. Yet many rural villagers would happily trade their well-insulated mud-brick homes for a modern cement box that's cold in the winter and hot in the summer.

Auroville, being a juncture of East and West, is home to some of the most intriguing building experiments I encountered. The traditional Tamil home, a latticework of branches and jute rope covered with thatch, is dark and poorly ventilated. Aurovilians modified the basic idea to bring in more space and light, but the structures, being composed of plant matter, attract rodents and snakes. During the week

I slept in one, I heard plenty of critters overhead and one morning woke up with a scorpion in my bed. Suddenly, I understood the popularity of the ugly concrete box with a corrugated metal roof.

The Auroville Earth Institute has pioneered an attractive and sustainable alternative to both thatch huts and concrete boxes: compressed-earth bricks made with a hand-operated machine, the Aurum. The bricks are made from the red soil found on site, usually from digging the building's foundation or its future wastewater treatment system. Auroville is dotted with hundreds of compressed-earth homes, schools, apartment buildings, and community buildings. Their graceful domes and arches, often painted white on top to reflect the sun's rays, allow for ventilation, making them a brilliant way to live outside of the box.

## Assessing needs

During my travels, I grew more sensitive to how my own physical and psychological wellbeing is affected by my living space. I also saw that some ways of building foster a greater sense of community than others. Bicycling along the five-mile rollercoaster of a road that links Crystal Waters' neighborhoods, I noticed that the widely dispersed single-acre lots reinforced the prevailing Australian car culture. Like Crystal Waters, EcoVillage at Ithaca (EVI) is predominantly middle class, and yet, because the American ecovillage used a co-housing model, I felt a far greater sense of community there. The common house (which included a guest room where I stayed and which any resident could book) served as a social hub, with a constant flow of people using the laundry, meeting spaces, and children's playrooms. Since parking at EVI was relegated to the periphery, I could go all day without seeing a car. Every day and well into each evening children – even toddlers – played safely in the courtyard without supervision. Crystal Waters' sprawling neighborhoods had none of these features, yet by rural Australian standards, eighty-five households living on less than 100 acres is high density. Building, like every aspect of ecovillage life, is context dependent.

If we are living between stories – between the old story of hyper-individualism and the new story of planetary interdependence – then we need models that can serve as bridges. As much as I might have an intellectual understanding about the drawbacks of hyper-individualism, I am a product of that culture. Simply put, I was uncomfortable in the high-density living spaces I encountered in Africa's traditional villages. Even Damanhur, where each person in a 20-member nucleo has their own room in a large house, would be too dense for me. Co-housing, with its integration of private and shared living spaces, felt like the right balance. Strohpolis, Sieben Linden's beautiful three-story straw-bale townhouses, also felt comfortable – especially when I experienced how well straw insulates against sound and considered the ecological benefits of shared wall space.

As I observed my responses to the built environment in fourteen different ecovillages, I found myself tucking little tips and images into my mental storehouse of ideas for my own home. My mind continually returned to questions about balance: how to find the right balance between my needs for privacy and community, between the trade-offs that come with low-tech and high-tech, between my personal preferences and planetary wellbeing. If the essence of sustainable living is sharing, then how much – and what – am I willing to share? Gardens? Laundry? Energy and water systems? Kitchen? Bathroom?

An even more basic question is this: what do I truly *need* to be comfortable? Of all the discoveries I gleaned on this journey, one of the most satisfying was that my physical and psychological needs with respect to living space are entirely compatible with what Earth can actually offer. At this critical juncture in history, every culture has assembled a body of knowledge about how to build; now that knowledge is available to more people than ever. Just as ecovillages are tapping into this vast human database, so can the rest of us.

## Box 3.2 The End of Straw-bale Idealism at Earthaven

I asked Chris Farmer (aka Farmer) what he had learned from working for ten years as one of Earthaven's principal builders. His answer surprised me. "I'm against natural building," he said. But he was smiling. "I say that tongue-in-cheek," he added, "because I'm *doing* natural building – with wood. But when people talk about natural building, they don't usually include wood. It's all straw-bale, adobe, rammed earth, cordwood ... *hurdy, gurdy, gurdy*! So much labor, just for exterior wall systems! They don't address foundations, roofs, floors, mechanical systems. What's the cheapest, easiest part of conventional building? Exterior wall systems, hands down. Here, we've learned how to use low-grade poplar studs – and the last time I checked, wood is natural. Why were we importing straw bales from the Midwest when we live in 300 acres of forest? I did timber framing and straw bale for awhile. If I could sit anyone down who wants to build sustainably, I would beg them, 'Please, use stud framing for your exterior walls!'"

"Maybe environmentalists have a taboo against killing trees," I mused.

Farmer gestured to the lush green pastures outside – land that was once heavily forested and is now home to his integrated farming experiment – and said, "I've gotten over that one!" He laughed and added, "The important thing is to engage the reality on which we depend."

Arjuna da Silva, an Earthaven resident who had been building her 900-sq.-ft. earthen home (christened Leela) for six years when I met her, had a different perspective. Leela incorporates just about every conceivable way to build with earth and straw. Leela was the focus of natural building at Earthaven for a number of years (http://naturalbuildingschool.com). As many as 200 people have helped to build Leela, primarily through workshops and internships. Even with so much unpaid labor, Arjuna put the final price tag at about US$170,000 – not a lot by mainstream standards but extravagant at Earthaven. Arjuna felt certain that Leela would be worth both the price and the wait.

Down the road stands a relic of Earthaven's early days of natural building. This lovely circular straw-bale structure, with mud walls and colored bottle inserts that give the impression of stained glass, was originally the community's temple. When mold made the temple a health risk, it became a five-star barn – and an enduring symbol for what the farmer who inherited it called "the end of straw-bale idealism at Earthaven." The straw-bale construction that works so well in Germany (annual rainfall: 20 inches) seems to be more problematic in North Carolina (annual rainfall: 60 inches).

## Energy

Buildings account for much of the world's energy consumption and greenhouse gas emissions – in the United States, some say as much as 40 percent. A structure's long-term energy use can be reduced by features like passive solar design and shared-wall construction. Equally important are the surrounding infrastructure and the occupants' habits. Ecovillages excel at saving energy on all fronts. While most of the world's heat and electricity are generated by coal, oil, and natural gas, ecovillagers primarily use renewable solar, wind, wood, and micro-hydro energy. Besides technological changes, they also decrease their consumption by making changes in their behavior.

Decades ago, the badge of honor for green living was "off-grid": fully self-sufficient for energy and water. So I was surprised to find that among the ecovillages I visited, only Earthaven, with solar panels on most of its buildings and two hyper-efficient turbines in its creeks, wore that badge. The dearth of off-grid ecovillages is not a sign they've been co-opted, however; rather, it means the mainstream is catching up. Most of the ecovillages I visited are *grid-tied* because they generate more energy than they use and are selling it back to the grid. Sieben Linden, for example, was able to take advantage of Germany's commitment to purchase renewable energy from private citizens at a premium.[4] As one Sieben Linden resident put it, "We're about self-reliance, more so than self-sufficiency. The goal isn't autonomy anymore; it's interdependence." For those of us who are grid-tied, which in the US is virtually everyone, this is good news. The downside of this interdependence, though, is that when the grid goes down, so does the power of everyone who doesn't have backup batteries or a generator.

I found solar power in nearly every ecovillage I visited, and at Findhorn and Svanholm I also found wind turbines, the world's fastest growing source of electricity. At a cost of about US$1 million per megawatt, these three-armed giants are out of reach for all but the largest and most prosperous ecovillages. On a smaller scale, cogeneration, the simultaneous production of heat and electricity, is gaining popularity. As I traveled south from Denmark to Italy, I found Stirling engines, or heard them mentioned, in every European ecovillage I visited. Stirling engines run on waste wood from local pulp and timber industries, making them carbon neutral.[5]

The ecovillagers I spoke with consistently cited two specific global problems that drive their energy decisions: climate change and declining reserves of oil and natural gas. In some cases, the renewable path also saved them money, but often it was more costly. Still, given the choice between cheap fossil fuels and expensive renewables, ecovillagers often opt for the latter – despite the fact that, as we see in the next chapter, many subsist on tiny incomes. "You have to consider the long-term cost of energy not just for yourself but also for the world," one resident of ZEGG said. I heard this sentiment echoed repeatedly during my travels.

Fossil fuels are nonrenewable on a human timescale, and their use is destabilizing Earth's climate, but they have been an amazing gift. Coal, oil, and natural gas have given us far-flung transport systems, an industrialized global food system, and

---

[4] Despite its suboptimal weather conditions, Germany leads the world in solar energy production, in large part because of policies like this one.

[5] Being dependent on "waste" as a fuel, of course, means that Stirling engines are tied to the system that generates that waste.

flick-of-the-switch heat, light, and water. Just a few spoonfuls of petroleum are equivalent to eight hours of manual labor. Consider how far your car would go if you had to push it! Yet, given the twin peril of peak oil and climate change, the prudent response would be to follow the ecovillage model and say, as my fellow political scientist Thomas Homer-Dixon says in *The Upside of Down*, "So long, cheap slaves!"[6]

## Box 3.3 Doing the Laundry

One way ecovillages reduce energy is by having people join forces on laundry. Each of the thirty-household neighborhoods at EcoVillage at Ithaca (EVI) shares three washing machines and three dryers – just one of each for ten households, or 90 percent fewer than the American norm. To my surprise, all three dryers in the EVI common house were running day and night, despite the unseasonably warm weather and the empty clotheslines just outside the door.

Perhaps busy people don't want to take the time to hang their clothes, or perhaps it's a habit: throw the wet wash into the machine, push a button and return in an hour to that luxurious feeling of warm fluffy clothes. Or, as I began to wonder as I traveled through Europe, maybe it's an American ritual. Electric clothes dryers are uncommon even in conventional European homes and virtually nonexistent in ecovillages. As I traveled through Europe, rarely seeing a clothes dryer, the question percolated in the back of my mind.

One cold morning as I was hanging my clothes in the basement of a German ecovillage, I asked a resident who had lived in the USA what he made of this phenomenon. He too had been struck by the prevalence of these energy-sucking machines. His interpretation took me by surprise. He said, "I think Americans are uncomfortable showing their underwear in public."

It was an explanation I hadn't considered! Whatever the economic, psychological, and cultural reasons for Americans' affection for the clothes dryer, finding three dryers running around the clock at EVI on a hot, sunny day suggests that the attachment runs deep.

[6] Thomas Homer-Dixon *The Upside of Down: Catastrophe, Creativity, and the Renewal of Civilization*, Washington, DC: Island Press, 2008, p. 77.

## Water

The energy extravaganza of the twentieth century shapes every aspect of our lives in the twenty-first century, including our use of water. The machinery for drilling into aquifers, pumping and transporting water across long distances, and building massive sewage systems is mostly manufactured with and powered by fossil fuels. If we had to carry our water, we couldn't possibly use the roughly 100 gallons required by the average American household each day – to say nothing of the far greater quantities required to feed us. While we *could* live without fossil fuels, we *can't* go for long without water – three days at the most. It's amazing to me that, even as freshwater systems all over the world are threatened, little is being done to reduce water consumption. We might turn off the water when we're soaping up or brushing our teeth, but this frugality has a minimal impact because the main problem is systemic. From our toilets and washing machines to our lawn sprinklers and industrialized food system, we are enmeshed in a water-intensive infrastructure. Because ecovillages are self-contained collective endeavors, they can address water consumption both behaviorally and systemically. While mainstream buildings are tied to municipal sewers and septic systems that degrade freshwater into wastewater, ecovillages are closing the circle in three ways: by filtering their so-called "wastewater," harvesting their rainwater, and using less water.

The most elaborate water treatment facility I saw was Findhorn's Living Machine, a gravity-fed system of holding tanks in a large greenhouse that uses plant roots and bacteria to clean all the wastewater for 350 residents. Karen Collins, the young woman running the facility, walked me through the various anaerobic and aerobic tanks that transform wastewater into clean water in just four days. At the far end of the Living Machine was an impeccable garden with a lovely fountain with sparkling clean water flowing from it.

I was curious to learn about Karen's technical background. Was she a biologist? "No," she said. "I'm a grade school teacher and a mom. Here, it's been on-the-job training. You don't need to know the science of bacteria; you just need to know how the system works. I work here alone 16 hours a week, with outside help for heavy work now and then."

The electricity from Findhorn's windmills pumps 10,000 gallons of clean water uphill to the community every day. By filtering its wastewater and replenishing its well through wind power, Findhorn is closing the circle for both energy and water. Later, I did the math: A

Figure 3.5 Findhorn's Living Machine recycles the community's
water supply –10,000 gallons – on a daily basis

Findhorn resident uses about 30 gallons of water per day – less than
the UK average of 40 gallons and about one third the US average.
Findhorn's residents are clearly changing their behavior, not just their
technology.

Built in 1996, Findhorn's Living Machine relies on older technology. Today, an apparatus this size could service an entire town. Still,
Findhorn's global reputation draws municipal officials from around
the world to see its experiments in green living, including the Living
Machine. On any scale, the principle is the same: purify water in the
way a wetland does but with greater intensity. Most of the ecovillages
I visited had some form of plant-based wastewater system.

The second part of water conservation is harvesting rainwater.
Rain barrels beneath gutters are an increasingly common sight in
American neighborhoods, but most of these hold only 50 or 60
gallons. Many of the ecovillage homes I visited had cisterns capable
of storing 1,000 gallons. Just one inch of rain falling on 1,000 hori-
zontal square feet generates more than 600 gallons of water, so the
potential is enormous. Collecting that water, however, requires a

nontoxic metal roof, which itself requires forethought. For anyone building a new house, harvesting rainwater is a relatively simple matter. In fact, some building codes, especially in arid countries like Australia, now require it.

The third means of water conservation is minimizing consumption. Behavioral changes can be significant, but, again, changes in infrastructure – like drought-resistant and perennial plantings and permeable pavements – have a far greater impact. Take the flush toilet. One person using the lowest-flow toilet currently available sends thousands of gallons of water down the drain each year. So when an ecovillage with a hundred people uses composting toilets, the impact is exponential. Plus, as Sieben Linden and Earthaven have learned, the rich organic matter contained in human urine and feces can be used to enrich the soil.

The toilet is, in many ways, a metaphor for modern society's relationship with nature. Decades ago, I read a description of the "Toilet Assumption" by social theorist Philip Slater, and it has stuck in my mind to this day. According to Slater, "unwanted matter, unwanted difficulties, unwanted complexities, and obstacles will disappear if they are removed from our immediate field of vision."[7] Out of sight, out of mind. It's not just our toilets; it's the vast unseen waste stream associated with our everyday actions. Slater went on to observe that the result has been "to remove the underlying problems of our society farther and farther from daily experience and daily consciousness, and hence to decrease, in the mass of the population, the knowledge, skill, resources, and motivation necessary to deal with them." Rather than treating energy and water as infinitely abundant, ecovillagers are supplanting the Toilet Assumption, whose linear logic moves from production to consumption to waste, with the cyclical logic of living systems. In so doing, they at once empower themselves and model a viable alternative for the rest of us.

## Food

Food is a perhaps the most intimate point of intersection between ourselves and the biosphere. Food is prepared in the home, it requires the taking of life, and it is the part of the environment that we ingest. Food is simultaneously a biological necessity and a profound source

---

[7] Philip Slater, *Pursuit of Loneliness: American Culture at the Breaking Point*, Boston: Beacon Press, 1976, p. 19.

of cultural meaning and social bonding. Little wonder, then, that people everywhere are preoccupied with food. The sustainability movement, with the dilemmas of its omnivores, herbivores, and loca-vores, is no different in this regard. Nor are ecovillages.

I was not surprised to find some shared perceptions about food in the ecovillages I visited, commonalities that are captured well by the twelve permaculture principles. Organic and local food, edible land-scapes, compost bins, beekeeping, and activism against genetically modified food: these are ubiquitous. Most of the rural ecovillages I visited were growing more vegetables than they ate, and all of the urban ecovillages made it a point to source their food from nearby organic farms. What did surprise me were the points of divergence, the impact of certain ecovillages on the larger society's relation-ship to food, and the creative possibilities that emerge when people start thinking outside the box. Located on the edge of a small city, EcoVillage at Ithaca illuminates these possibilities nicely.

## Community-supported agriculture

For Joan Bokaer, the woman whose ideas gave birth to EVI, food was at the core from the beginning. A white-haired woman with angular features, Joan describes her vision in practical terms: "A livable city needs a symbiotic relationship with its source of food." Joan believes that EVI's primary work is to support urban agriculture.

Joan's daughter, Jen, is helping to make that vision a reality. Jen returned to EVI from college with her future husband, John – both of them having a passion for organic farming and an interest in estab-lishing a community-supported agriculture (CSA) system. The essence of the CSA model is both economic and social: to spread the financial risk of small-scale farming while strengthening the bonds between producers and consumers. Consumers purchase advance shares in the harvest, thereby sharing the risks and benefits of farming and remov-ing the sense of anonymity that pervades the dominant agribusiness model. At Jen and John's ten-acre West Haven Farm, leased from EVI, member households pay US$360 a season and purchase most of the harvest. The rest is sold at the local farmers' market. All told, Jen and John supply high-quality produce to about a thousand people for six months of the year. Without EVI, it is doubtful that a flourishing farm would exist on this prime real estate at the city's edge.

West Haven Farm gives new meaning to community-supported agriculture: it exists within the community that supports it. Unlike most CSA farmers, Jen and John live side by side with their most committed members. This proximity, both geographic and emotional, bodes well for the farm's future. But in a world where organic food is mass-produced by industrial farms, the success of West Haven Farm is far from assured.

## The question of meat

Svanholm's sprawling farm has expanded community agriculture to another level. One of my favorite pastimes at this Danish ecovillage was a brisk late-afternoon walk up a rutted path in the community forest to a sunset vista. Some thoughtful person had built a bench at the clearing, a quiet spot where I could survey the undulating patchwork of fields. No doubt, the boundary of Svanholm's thousand acres was somewhere in view, but gazing out over the vast countryside, I couldn't say where. One thing was certain: Svanholm's influence on Danish farming practices – and therefore the European Union – stretched far beyond its property line.

Svanholm's chief crop farmer, a sturdy man in his mid-forties named Jørgen Kloster, gave me an overview of the ecovillage's food production: about 300 tons of grain and 200 tons of root vegetables – all organic and all for human consumption. Add 100 cows for beef and milk, 200 lambs, several acres of sun-loving vegetables in plastic tunnels, plus the fruit orchards and one thing became crystal clear: Svanholm grows a *lot* more food than most ecovillages.

With this scale of production, I envisioned the farm as Svanholm's largest business, but Jørgen corrected me. The forestry business and the two building companies are much larger; the farm employs only a handful of members and often loses money because it must compete with still larger farms. This scale of production, while 100 percent organic, requires heavy machinery – a controversial practice among ecovillages. Still, the farm reflects Svanholm's commitment to food self-sufficiency and organic agriculture.

Ecovillages have a wide range of answers to the question of meat, and Svanholm comes down solidly on the side of *yes*. Jørgen told me the basics of integrated farming. Cow manure is the linchpin in soil fertility; waste from pigs and poultry is secondary. Beef production puts the grasslands to good use. Clover, which builds the soil and feeds the cows, is planted on a rotation. "Without animals, we could not be profitable," Jørgen said. "And, yes, we like to eat meat!"

To learn about Svanholm's leadership in the European organic farming movement, I spoke with Bø Læssø, Svanholm's first farmer. Bø met me for lunch in the sunny south-facing dining room, still dressed in his bright orange coveralls. At 63, Bø's weathered skin and wiry body gave the impression of one who has worked outside most of his life.

As the only community member with a farming certificate, Bø turned out to be a key person at Svanholm. In the early days, most back-to-the-land communities wanted to withdraw from society, but Bø hoped to change the larger society from the bottom up. In order to educate aspiring organic farmers, he started the Farm Study Group. That group grew into a union of growers, processors, stores, and consumers who, together, created Danish standards for organic food – which were eventually used to help set European Union standards. Bø chaired this group until 2000, when he had a massive heart attack.

"I never imagined this adventure would take off in such a big way," he said. "It now looks possible that the whole country could go organic. It's being seriously studied, and we've had a big impact on that!"

I was curious to know if Bø's heart attack had changed his views on eating meat. While he agreed with Jørgen about the role of meat in integrated farming, Bø said he'd begun eating less meat for health reasons. "A conscientious person will eat a lot less meat," he said. "At Svanholm, we might have it two or three days a week, compared to the average Dane who eats meat maybe six days a week."

On the question of animals, Germany's Sieben Linden takes another approach. Since a vegetarian diet is one way to shrink one's ecological footprint, most Sieben Linden residents eat little or no meat. After several years of intense back-and-forth, the residents adopted what they call a Peace Contract with Animals: no animals living at Sieben Linden will be slaughtered there or anywhere else. This contract effectively precludes the possibility of mainstream organic farming, which uses animal manure as its primary fertilizer. Sieben Linden plows its fields with horses; when they are too old to work, they will be euthanized or allowed to die naturally.

And Club 99, Sieben Linden's most radical neighborhood, goes a step further. First, as vegans, they abstain from *all* animal products, including eggs and dairy. But even a typical organic vegan diet relies upon animal fertilizers. So Club 99 practices vegan farming, a labor-intensive practice that employs "green manure." These soil-enhancing cover crops are planted each year and then dug into the soil. This requires enormous time and labor, which means that vegan agriculture is not economically viable in today's markets. Nonetheless, vegan farming, combined with the use of draft animals rather than tractors, has helped Club 99 residents to cut their ecological footprints to one-twentieth of the US average.

Yet the debate at Sieben Linden continues. Shortly before my arrival, the diet debate was rekindled by the discovery that a toddler's mental retardation was linked to the vegan mother's vitamin B12 deficiency. While some vegans were reconsidering their diets, one woman claimed that modern hygienic processes might be part of the problem for today's vegans. Traditional vegan communities in India apparently have no problems with vitamin B12 because they unwittingly consume countless insects. As I listened to the divergent perspectives, I felt a deepening appreciation for the social and ethical complexity of food.

Leaving the Spartan atmosphere of Sieben Linden, I dove directly into the esoteric playfulness of Damanhur – and found it something of a cultural and culinary shock. I arrived at Dendera, Damanhur's nucleo devoted to international work, just in time for a splendid dinner. Twenty of us sat at a long table, passing bottles of wine and plates of pasta, sauce, meat, vegetables, olives, cheese, and bread. I asked Goura, the quiet young woman sitting next to me, about Damanhur's approach to food.

"In Damanhur, we eat first what we produce, then local food. We're not food self-sufficient, but we aim to be. I've been a vegetarian for most of my life, so eating meat was a change for me. We don't eat lots of meat, only some. We tend to eat only the meat we produce, and we grow all of the grain for our animals. Our molecular biology lab tests all the food we eat, including meat, for GMOs." She explained that Damanhurians believe that genetically modified food has not been proven safe.

"For us, Planet Earth is a sentient being. We tap into Earth's intelligence through plants and animals. That's why we take plant and animal names – to come into closer contact with these realms." Goura herself was named for a bird. "We believe humans are omnivores, that our bodies are alchemical laboratories that absorb the intelligence of what we eat," she said. "So we eat a little of many diverse things." And it seems they do: of twenty different foods before us on the table, there were just two platters of meat.

## Stacking functions

Of all the ecovillage farms I encountered, I was most inspired by Earthaven's tiny Gateway Farm. Located at the entrance to the community, just beyond the standard green street sign that reads

"Another Way," Gateway Farm is the brainchild of Chris Farmer and Brian Love. As Farmer explained the farm's interlocking pieces to me, the phrase that came to mind was "exponential permaculture." On the lowest area, he and Brian had dug a pond at the confluence of two creeks and stocked it with sunfish and bass. A 25-ft embankment, a riparian zone, shades the pond, providing a habitat for the fish. The surrounding forest was being logged sustainably to produce lumber for building and furniture. Berry bushes and fruit trees lined the creek, and sheep, turkeys, and chickens grazed in the fields. The Voisin method of rotational grazing – "Bah, gobble, cluk," Farmer calls it – builds the soil and prevents overgrazing. The chickens produce eggs and meat throughout the year, and most of the turkeys would be slaughtered for Thanksgiving. The female sheep give milk, the males give meat, and both give wool. These Icelandic sheep, with their unique dual-coated, multicolored fleece, can be sheared twice a year. Earthaven uses some wool for value-added fiber arts and sells the surplus to local artisans. Behind the pastures lie vegetable beds.

Most organic farmers integrate animal husbandry into their vegetable production, but the plan for Gateway Farm adds an unusual innovation: fuel production. Already, Farmer and Brian have begun bringing spent grain from a local organic beer brewery and feeding it to their animals and worms. Within a couple years, they hope to be transforming this spent grain into ethanol to power Earthaven's cars and biodiesel for the community's trucks, tractors, and other heavy equipment. If their vision becomes reality, the 5-acre Gateway Farm will be the Mighty Mouse of agriculture, a shining example of intensive, petroleum-free food production.

Together, agriculture and transportation consume most of the world's fossil fuels and produce most of the world's waste. In the United States, conventional agriculture requires ten calories of energy for every one calorie of food produced. As Farmer explained the technical details of making 180-proof ethanol, which uses only half the energy required to produce the 200-proof ethanol sold at the pump, and converting Earthaven's vehicles to operate on this lower-grade fuel, my mind traveled to the sign just down the hill: Another Way indeed.

### Farming to end hunger

Ecovillages in developing countries are also focused on food, but for very different reasons. Hunger was rarely a topic at American and European ecovillages, but it was top of the agenda in Colufifa's villages in Africa. Indeed, Colufifa is a French acronym for the Committee Fighting for the End of Hunger, a coalition that formed in 1985 in response to widespread drought and famine in West Africa. The food crisis was partly a consequence of international development projects that promoted water- and fertilizer-intensive crops like peanuts. The challenge for Colufifa was to find economically and ecologically sustainable alternatives.

At the time, it seemed sesame was the answer. I met with Djibril Balde, Colufifa's assistant director, on the veranda of his simple concrete home. "Sesame does not need much water, and it helps the soil," he explained. "Our parents grew it – it was an ancient tradition and an important medicine, but it disappeared with peanuts. Only the Gambia was growing sesame because they were less developed, so they taught us. In two years, we had ten tons of sesame."

The downside of sesame for Colufifa was being a tiny player in a global market where prices are controlled by Indian and Chinese middlemen who export sesame oil to the Middle East. "After a few years, we saw that we needed to find a way for villagers to be more self-sufficient – especially women because most of the men are gone. It is women who take care of poultry and vegetable gardens, so we started a microfinance project to help women raise chickens and grow vegetables. The chicken manure helps to make compost for the garden." Given the volatility of the global food economy and its utter dependence on cheap oil, village self-sufficiency is probably a safer bet for Colufifa's villages.

As I traveled to some of Colufifa's villages along the Gambia River, I felt overwhelmed by the stark reality of the global condition from this vantage point. The jeep bounced along the rough roads for hour after hour, and my mouth hung open at the sight of thousands – maybe millions – of mango and cashew trees. How could people go hungry here? One pound of these crops, all grown organically even if not certifiably so, could fetch the equivalent of US$10 in Europe. (To put this price in context, my Gambian translator, Djibril Ba – known as Jiby – told me that he supports his family of five on the equivalent of about US$100 a year.) What happens to the unfathomable harvest of mangoes and cashews?

"Most of it rots on the ground," said one of the farmers traveling with us. "We have no way to bring our mangoes and cashews to market. Last year, an Indian businessman came with a truck and bought several tons of our cashews for 75 *sefa* per kilo." That's less than a nickel a pound.

Virtually all of Senegal's cashews perish on the ground while India, an ocean and a continent away, dominates European and American markets. When the mangoes ripen, local people gorge themselves on this "food of the gods," and yet, with no way of preserving or selling the harvest, they can go hungry in the lean months. Although I'm neither an economist nor an entrepreneur, I believe that, with simple processing technologies and some good fair-trade connections, much of the poverty in this part of the world could be alleviated. Locavores might object, but, so long as we have globalization, shouldn't a small corner of it go toward connecting the world's poorest people to global markets? How this would happen is the question. I could see the wisdom of Colufifa's far-sighted strategy of promoting village food self-sufficiency.

For most of us in the wealthy countries, hunger is not an issue. Yet we are deeply embedded in a worldwide food web, a web that was woven during an age when cheap and abundant petrochemicals boosted crop yields and spawned a global transportation network. As I say to my students, "We put oil into our soil so we don't have to toil." According to the US Department of Agriculture, a century ago over 30 percent of the American workforce was engaged in farming; today, that number stands at less than 2 percent. My sense is that in the coming decades many more of us will be farming – and, like eco-villages, learning how to do so sustainably.

## Box 3.4 Collaborating with Bacteria

In Japan, a country that imports most of its food and grows less than 1 percent of it organically, Konohana stands out. This ecovillage is 100 percent organic and nearly 100 percent food self-sufficient. Farming is the economic basis for this community of fifty. Konohana's bountiful fields produce 260 varieties of vegetables and eleven kinds of rice.

One secret to its success is Konohana-kin (pronounced *keen*), the fermented bacterial brew that is applied to the soil, fed to the goats and chickens, and even ingested on a daily basis by the residents. Konohana-kin is based on Effective Micro-organisms (EM), a technique developed by Teruo Higa, a Japanese agricultural scientist, to maximize the production of beneficial bacteria. Konohana experimented with various proportions of molasses, brown rice amino acid, tofu refuse, bamboo leaves, and pine needles to develop its own formula. Konohana-kin serves simultaneously as a fertilizer, pesticide, cleaning agent, and preventive medicine.

Koichi Kitao, a 43-year-old resident who began farming organically during his years as a development worker in Ethiopia, led me to the community's chicken houses and goat pens to offer a visceral demonstration of the benefits of Konohana-kin. I've kept a few chickens in my life, so I know how they can smell. Standing among Konohana's 800 chickens, I detected only a vaguely sweet aroma. Ditto in the goat pen, where Koichi offered me some goat milk. It was fresh and delicious – milder than any goat milk I had ever tasted. Because Konohana-kin is a staple in these animals' diets, their excrement has no foul odor and antibiotics are unnecessary.

Koichi explained that Konohana-kin is a gift from the Divine. "We use it not only on our farms but also in our composting toilet. And we drink it every day. In fourteen years, nobody has had a major illness. Now and then, one of our members gets some conventional treatment, but this is rare. That, too, is a gift from God and may be used when necessary."

Later, I asked the community's 56-year-old founder, Furuta Isami (known as Isadon), about how Konohana-kin fits into the community's larger mission. Despite his pink Bugs Bunny T-shirt, I had no trouble taking this lively man seriously. His message was simply too compelling. "Our vision is that human beings will learn to live in harmony with nature," Isadon said. "Here in Japan, you see people wearing masks when they are sick and putting disinfectants in their toilets to kill the bacteria. The Japanese are a super-hygienic people, but it's a violent approach. They are at war with bacteria, but we need bacteria to live. At Konohana, we are finding ways to cooperate with bacteria to make life better."

Figure 3.6 At Konohana, farming supports the community economically while fostering social bonds and spiritual growth

## Transportation

Petroleum is the lifeblood of the global economy for good reason: it is a highly potent and mobile form of energy. No wonder, then, that our global transportation infrastructure relies upon the stuff – and increasingly so. Yet one principle of ecology is that there's no free lunch: it takes energy to get energy. Whether or not we've reached peak oil, we do know that its energy return on investment has declined precipitously in recent decades (see Box 3.5). And we also know that fossil-fuel combustion is the primary source of anthropogenic greenhouse gas emissions. In common parlance, petroleum-based transportation is unsustainable. In light of global trends, this is gripping information. In 2009, the United States had 800 cars for every 1,000 people, while China and India (comprising 40 percent of the world's population) had just 35 and 12 respectively. Now, car sales in both countries – and throughout the developing world – are booming. If America's car culture goes global, we can only wonder what kind of world we will inhabit.

---

### Box 3.5 "Peak Oil" Demystified

"Peak oil" refers to the bell curve of oil production over time, a phenomenon that occurs for specific oil fields, producing-countries' production, and globally. US oil production peaked in 1970, and other countries are now reaching theirs. Most analysts put the date for world peak oil somewhere between 2005 and 2015. Current oil production has indeed plateaued, lending credence to the idea that peak oil is on schedule.

A key consequence of "peak oil" is that more energy is required to extract the last half of the oil. Methods like steam injection, fluid injection, and hydraulic fracturing (fracking) are now being deployed to squeeze out the last bits of oil and gas. This has made metrics like EREOI (energy returned on energy invested) increasingly salient. An EROEI of 100 means the extracted oil has a hundred times the energy that was used to extract it. As EROEI declines, the payoffs dwindle – unless, of course, production is subsidized. Around 1900, EROEI for US oil was as high as 1,200. Today, EROEI for conventional oil ranges from 5 to 20, depending upon the source. Unconventional hydrocarbons and biofuels are less attractive: tar sands and shale oil are 2–5, while ethanol and biodiesel from conventional US agriculture barely break even.[8] All fossil

---

[8] For more on EROEI and peak oil, see the special issue of *Sustainability* (2011) 3(10); T. Butler et al., *The Energy Reader*, Healdsburg, CA: Watershed Media, 2012; and www.theoildrum.com.

fuels warm the planet but coal, the most abundant, also happens to be the dirtiest.

Practically speaking, "peak oil" means "peak cheap oil," which makes petroleum the Achilles heel of globalization. Today, most manufactured goods travel long distances from China and other low-cost producers. Plastics and fertilizer are made from oil and natural gas. Further, the world food economy is highly dependent on cheap oil. A typical US meal travels 1,500 miles from farm to fork. Most importantly, "peak oil" is occurring just as demand for "First World" lifestyles is skyrocketing among the 80 percent humanity living in the global South.

Barring a major technological breakthrough, renewables can only meet our needs if we radically downsize. Solar panels provide "clean" energy but require energy and scarce resources to produce; their lifetime EROEI is 5–10, depending upon placement. Wind power has a higher EROEI, but is intermittent and risky for wildlife. As energy analyst Ozzie Zeher argues. "We need to create the kind of society that *can* be powered by alternative energy"[9] – which means leveraging the remaining fossil fuels to build a low-energy infrastructure. For the global North, that means living smaller, slower, and closer. We can take our cues from ecovillages.

## Vehicle sharing

For those of us who want to find greener ways of getting around, our choices are usually highly individualized: ride a bicycle or take the bus. But there's power in numbers. Ecovillages, by virtue of their capacity for collective action, are able to ramp up their members' effectiveness. Both ZEGG and EVI, for instance, lobbied successfully for a bus stop at their doorstep. Some of the larger communities I visited, like Findhorn and Auroville, were experimenting with their own internal transit systems. In Auroville, plans were afoot to create an internal transit system of solar-powered electric bicycles. Even Damanhur, where nearly everybody owns a car powered by either biodiesel or propane, had its own characteristically fanciful transit system: Synchronic Rides. While the scheme is essentially a glorified version of hitchhiking, every time I stood by one of the quirky signs, I quickly got a ride to wherever I might be going – and often enjoyed an interesting conversation along the way.

[9] Ozzie Zeher, *Green Illusions: The Dirty Secrets of Clean Energy and the Future of Environmentalism*, University of Nebraska Press, 2012.

Sometimes, though, a car comes in handy. In most of the ecovillages I visited, members were sharing the responsibilities and benefits of ownership through car co-ops. The usual practice is for drivers to pay by the mile. Some insurance companies make car sharing easier than others by simply requiring the owner to give written permission to other drivers. At Svanholm, the community owns a fleet of cars and a task force handles the insurance, registration, and maintenance. When a major decision, like buying a new vehicle, needs to be made, the task force brings a proposal to the community.

The idea of car sharing is not new; carpooling is probably as old as the car itself. Today, companies like ZipCar are turning it into a growth industry despite – and, no doubt, partly because of – the recession. In principle, noncommercial car sharing could flourish in existing neighborhoods, but it would require two preconditions: first, a commitment to economic and ecological efficiency over convenience; and, second, strong relationships based upon trust and accountability. Like other ecological issues, the question of cars is very much about community.

### Thinking outside the car

The trick, though, is to find alternatives to the car, and here ecovillages have a distinct advantage. To the extent that an ecovillage is truly a village, it has its own internal economy that enables members to work close to home, thereby reducing their transportation needs. I found people in ecovillages working on site at just about every job imaginable: lawyers, farmers, therapists, builders, healthcare practitioners, beauticians, cooks, internet entrepreneurs, teachers, you name it. Again, the basic principle can be applied anywhere. Any neighborhood can begin to transform itself into a village by surveying the skills of the adults in, say, a three-block radius, putting them on a map, and then circulating that map to everybody who might want to participate. As we'll see in the next chapters, the social and economic benefits turn out to be just as important as the ecological ones.

Urban ecovillages have an advantage when it comes to reducing their car dependence – especially if they have access to a good mass transit system. UfaFabrik, for instance, is just a short walk from the Berlin subway station. When I arrived, the bicycle stand was full, despite the cold drizzle. Nestled between the community's organic grocery shop and its cozy café, I found UfaFabrik's Welcome Center, where I perused dozens of brochures for concerts, circus performances, social services, and classes of all sorts in the ecovillage. With only forty-five residents, UfaFabrik seems small, but it employs nearly two hundred people and attracts an astonishing 200,000 visitors each year to its plethora of public events. None of these people needs a car to get there.

Getting by without a car in a European city is one thing; living carless in Los Angeles is quite another. During my stay at LAEV, I struggled to tune out the roar of traffic. One block away was Vermont Avenue, an interminable row of old three-story buildings that had morphed into one strip mall after another, with signs in Korean, Spanish, and other languages I didn't recognize. The notoriously congested Hollywood Freeway was just a few blocks away, and so was a subway station. In this city, the epitome of car culture, LAEV is intent upon moving toward car-free living. With one car for every five members – about a tenth the average for the surrounding metropolitan area – this community is well on its way.

Several founders of the LA County Bicycle Coalition live at LAEV, so bicycle advocacy is a way of life here, but it's the homespun Bicycle Kitchen that most exemplifies the community's character. For Jimmy Lizama, the 34-year-old founder and "head chef" at the kitchen, teaching people how to repair their bikes is not just about ecology; it's about people power. Jimmy met me in the ecovillage apartment he was renovating. Sporting a black baseball cap, a tight black T-shirt with a white skull on the chest, and a military camouflage bandana around his neck, Jimmy was the picture of urban edginess. Yet his easy smile and contagious enthusiasm immediately set me at ease.

"My parents are from Honduras, both of them working class," Jimmy said. "I had no environmental background at all. I biked because having a car didn't fit into any kind of budget I could envision. When I came to the Los Angeles Eco-Village nine years ago, I had no skills. I wasn't educated. I didn't garden. I wasn't an activist. But I felt the need to contribute somehow to the community, so I decided to fix people's bikes once a week in the kitchen of an empty unit. People just started bringing their bikes and helping out."

Eventually, the operation outgrew the kitchen, moved to a nearly storefront, and spawned similar workshops around the city like the nearby Bike Oven and the Bikerowave in Santa Monica. Whether affiliated with an ecovillage or not, the basic recipe is the same: set up a conveniently located workshop with all the necessary tools, recruit a few bicycle enthusiasts to help, charge a nominal fee to cover the overhead, and make it fun.

For Jimmy, this last ingredient is the key. "Since I love to cook, I made pizza every Tuesday night for whoever came. That's how the Bicycle Kitchen was born. I'm not political. I don't want to tell people to get out of their cars because it's good for the Earth. I just say, 'Have a beer, have some pizza, take a ride, and you'll get it.' Bicycling, fuck, it's the easiest way to contribute. You put a wrench in someone's hand and it changes their life! And you get to see the city at the most democratic speed: fourteen miles per hour." Sure, I thought, in any other city. But his words planted a seed and the following day, I found myself touring Hollywood at a fairly democratic speed (see Box 3.6).

Half a world away, in Colufifa's West African villages, bicycle advocacy takes on a very different hue. Paved roads are in short supply, virtually nobody owns a car, and the few buses that run are packed. A trip into town can take a full day; children fortunate enough to go to school might walk hours each day to get there and back. So when Demba Mansare, Colufifa's founder, was studying agriculture in Brussels and saw perfectly good bicycles being thrown away, he asked his classmates, "What if some of Europe's unused bicycles could be shipped to Africa?" That question planted the seed for a new organization: Bicycles to Senegal. I happened to arrive at the village of Sinteth on the same day as a cargo container loaded with Danish bicycles. Seeing the excitement with which the villagers unloaded the bicycles – and sewing machines, cooking equipment, computers, and various sundry items – I marveled at the difference a simple device like a bike can make in a place like this. Somewhere between LA's car culture and Africa's privation, I thought, lies a happy, sustainable medium where bicycles are an integral part of everyday life.

In his provocative 1978 book, *Energy and Equity*, Ivan Illich estimates that the typical American driver devotes more than 1,600 hours a year to his car. That figure is probably not much different today. In other words, a driver spends four of his sixteen waking hours either in his car or working to pay for the cost of driving it. If he drives 7,500 miles in a year, then his average speed is less than five miles per hour – about the same as walking. A bicyclist, however, can go three or four times faster than a pedestrian while using five times less energy. "Equipped with this tool," Illich writes, "man outstrips the efficiency of not only all machines but all other animals as well."[10] Bicycles are perhaps the quintessential expression of appropriate technology.

[10] Ivan Illich, *Energy and Equity*, New York: Pantheon, 1978, p. 72.

## Box 3.6 Touring Hollywood at the Perfect Speed

I may be an avid bicyclist in Seattle, but it would never have occurred to me to ride a bike through Los Angeles traffic – not without LAEV's example. But I had that example before me, so I borrowed a bicycle, donned a helmet, steeled my courage, and joined the traffic on Vermont Boulevard. After pedaling over the thunderous Hollywood Freeway, I paused to dry my sweaty palms on my pants. Somehow, my fluorescent yellow jacket wasn't giving me the same sense of protection here that it did in Seattle.

Taking a side street, I realized that part of what was setting my nerves on edge was the noise. Words cannot convey the combined effect of the background roar of the freeway, horns blaring, and the intermittent blast of sirens. I was also adding to my anxiety by projecting a mental map of the gargantuan city onto my moment-by-moment ride. As I began to consciously breathe and relax, the sound became less oppressive. Moreover, it was a warm, sunny day in November – which I doubt was the case in Seattle – and the streets were wide and flat.

I rode most of the afternoon, taking in Hollywood and the surrounding neighborhoods. If I got too nervous on the busy streets, none of which had bike lanes, I rode on the mostly empty sidewalks. Every bus I saw had bicycle racks; when I stopped at a subway station, I found bicycle racks there as well. Gradually, it dawned on me that sun-drenched Los Angeles, with its wide, flat streets, could be the ideal bicycling city! And yet in my hours of riding, I never saw another bicyclist.

What prevents this vision from becoming reality? Bike lanes are scarce, drivers are not accustomed to seeing cyclists, and most people believe that cars are more efficient. Transforming LA into the bicycle heaven it could be would require a combination of infrastructural change and public education.

### Jet miles

A bicycle, however, could never have taken me to fourteen ecovillages around the world. For that, I relied on airplanes, an irony that at times weighed heavy on my conscience. My jet travel generated 17 tons of greenhouse gases – as much as fifty residents of West Africa would produce in an entire year – all for the purpose of learning how to live sustainably. Sure, I purchased carbon offsets to "neutralize" the harm, but that felt to me a bit like medieval nobility buying "indulgences" from the Church to "offset" their sins.

In his book *Heat: How to Stop the Planet from Burning*, George Monbiot set out to determine how the lifestyles of the world's affluent would need to change in order for us to have a shot at stabilizing the world's climate.[11] He concludes that, using available technologies and making significant behavioral changes, we could reduce greenhouse gas emissions by the requisite 90 percent and maintain most of the comforts of modern life. Only one practice would have to be eliminated: air travel. This made it especially hard for me to justify flying in the name of sustainability! As it turned out, some of the ecovillages I visited were faced with the same irony and some of their members had wrestled with this very question.

Findhorn's economy is utterly tied to a brimming schedule of conferences and workshops that attract visitors from all over the world, yet its residents pride themselves on their small ecological footprints. Those footprints, however, are only small if we ignore the air miles that make their economy possible.

I put this question to a community member, Jonathan Dawson, an Irish man in his forties and then-president of the Global Ecovillage Network. "Given the present system," he said, "where most air travel is for leisure and business, for us at Findhorn to say we will not fly feels self-indulgent. While corporate types are filling the air, it doesn't feel right for me to have a moral judgment that prevents me from maximizing my effectiveness. Still, I respect the decision not to fly that some people are making on ecological grounds, and I see a day when these resources will not be available. Until then, I want to be effective in helping us to make the transition." Jonathan's reasoning echoed my own: if I could write a book that would inspire people to transform their lives, then perhaps the jet fuel could be justified.

## Collaborative consumption

A natural consequence of our highly individualized lifestyles is that we have the luxury of making choices without considering who or what might be affected down the road or across the planet. From the constant barrage of advertising to more subtle forms of peer pressure, a host of cultural forces goad us into buying more than we need – indeed, into not even considering what we actually need. As a consequence, our lifestyles are threatening to unravel our home planet's life support systems – and, ironically, they're not making us any happier.

[11] George Monbiot, *Heat: How to Stop the World from Burning*, Cambridge, MA: South End Press, 2009.

Indeed, that's what Philip Slater means by "the pursuit of loneliness." We may own a car – even a fuel-efficient one – and a house with a fenced yard and a basement full of tools, but these often only intensify our sense of isolation. Most of us are hungry for a sense of connection, and connection requires sharing. In chapter 5, I delve into the social consequences of sharing. For now, suffice it to say that sharing materials is good for the planet and that ecovillagers are especially good at sharing.

Some of their ways of sharing materials have already been discussed: car sharing, shared-wall home construction, courtyards, common land (including farms), and energy and water infrastructure. Nearly every community I visited had a common house, a shared kitchen, or some other shared facilities. As a consequence, individual homes were anywhere from 25–50% smaller than the norms for their home countries, and yet their residents were not going without. These are some of the amenities I found in EVI's two common houses: laundry facilities, a playroom for children, a hang-out room for teenagers, a sauna, a recycled clothing room, a small gym, and several offices for professionals who work on site.

Jeff Gilmore, a former Silicon Valley computer engineer who had recently moved to EVI, described some of the benefits of sharing. He and his family had left their spacious ocean-view home in California for a shared-wall EVI home of less than half the size. I asked Jeff about the challenges of making that move.

He smiled. "You might think that moving five people and a dog from a 3,000-sq.-ft. house into a 1,260-sq.-ft. house would have been the hardest part," he said. "But it was surprisingly easy to adjust to having a lot less stuff. We had a massive purge before we left. We got rid of half of our stuff – furniture, clothing, half of our cooking gadgets, most of our books.

"Getting rid of most of our stuff felt good," he said. "Why should I have a whole collection of power tools in my own shop, for instance, when for five dollars a month, I can find anything I want in the community machine shop? I thought I needed so many things before, but when I came to see their impact, they just weighed me down." And for those of us who can't afford a collection of power tools – much less a gym, sauna, and miles of walking trails – it makes economic sense for us to share. We get more that way!

If we want to apply the lessons from ecovillages to our cities and suburbs, then sharing the everyday accoutrements of life is a good place to start. It doesn't require new buildings or infrastructure; nor need it entail a huge financial risk and deep social bonds. Much like asking a neighbor for a cup of sugar, which I suspect was a more common practice when I was growing up than it is today, sharing things can help to forge those social relationships – relationships we may count on in the future if the predictions of climate change and energy descent come to pass. And, in the meantime, does each of us really need a vacuum cleaner, a tent, a big-screen TV, a lawn mower, a fancy food processor, and a garage full of tools?

The idea is catching on. Sharing and shared ownership networks like GoLoco, NeighborGoods, ZipCar, and CitiBikes are cropping up all over.[12] The basic principle is simple: use social networks, especially via cell phones and the internet, to reduce consumption. But I can also envision low-tech forms of collaborative consumption. The transformational neighborhood map comes to mind. If my neighbors and I wanted to green our lives while building a sense of community, our skill-set map might also include whatever we would be willing to share. As our relationships deepened, we might eventually pool our finances and purchase some things together. We might even take down our fences, plant a neighborhood garden, grow food, and enjoy community dinners together.

During my visit to Sieben Linden, I was helping to prepare lunch in the Club 99 common house and was surprised to find myself using a VitaMix. How could these low-footprint ecovillagers let themselves have a 5-horsepower blender with a US$500 price tag? "I've been coveting one of these for years," I confessed to my fellow cook, "but it's hard to justify the expense and the ecological impact."

"Yes, none of us would have such a blender on our own, but sharing it with many people makes it easier to do." She caught my eye and grinned, adding, "You should get one because I'm sure you'll be living in a community one day."

Her comment caught me off guard, but she turned out to be right. Today, I live in a community, and we share a VitaMix.

## Wildlife conservation

So far, I've discussed ecological issues while barely mentioning any nonhuman species. Our people-centered world makes it easy to

---

[12] Rachel Botsman and Roo Rogers, *What's Mine Is Yours: The Rise of Collaborative Consumption*, New York: HarperBusiness, 2010.

forget that our clever species is just one node in the vast web of life that links untold millions of species into a planetary biosphere. We might learn on Discovery Channel that one third of those species are on the verge of extinction, and we might even send a donation to the Center for Biological Diversity. Yet the problem seems both daunting and far removed from our daily lives. For most of the ecovillages I visited, however, wildlife conservation is a vital part of everyday life.

Wildlife is in decline throughout most of the world, primarily because habitat is being lost. One of the most effective ways of restoring wildlife habitat is to plant native trees. A single tree can be home to hundreds of unseen species and billions of organisms. Restoring a whole forest, as Sieben Linden was doing in the monoculture pine plantation it inherited, will replenish the soil, which will in turn create a home for countless more creatures. Every rural ecovillage I visited was engaged in forest restoration.

In some cases, trees were a matter of human survival. Auroville's green oasis, for instance, was a barren, eroded plateau when the Mother founded it in 1968. The first order of business for the mostly Caucasian pioneers was to create shade, which meant harvesting rainwater, building soil, and eventually planting some three million trees. As one of those pioneers recalled, "Every tree was like a child. We had to water each one by carrying clay pots of water to it. Mother said that by planting trees, we could change the climate."

And so they did. Today, Auroville can be 20°F cooler than the scorching city of Pondicherry just ten miles away. More recently, the Auroville Forestry Group has ramped up its tree planting efforts with a new carbon offsets initiative. Residents and visitors coming from overseas can simultaneously alleviate their guilt and improve the local ecosystem.[13] Auroville's forest makes it one of the few places on Earth where biodiversity is *increasing*; every year, residents encounter insect and bird species that have not been seen for decades.

---

[13] We should not overestimate the ability of trees to mitigate global warming. Most trees in the temperate zones will sequester 50–200 lb. of carbon dioxide per year, depending upon their growth rate. A typical American's lifestyle emits about 20 tons of greenhouse gases in a year. In order to be carbon neutral, therefore, an American would need to plant 200 to 800 trees each year and tend them indefinitely. Still, planting trees offers other benefits.

## Box 3.7 Senegal's Charcoal Mines and the Man Who Plants Trees

Early one evening, I was walking along the main road outside the dusty village of Faoune. As usual, a dozen women were lined up with their old grain sacks full of charcoal; now and then, a car would stop and the driver would buy a bag. On this particular day, a government jeep pulled up and two policemen got out, sparking a ruckus. The women pleaded to no avail as the men loaded every bag into the jeep and drove off, leaving a trail of tears behind them. I looked on helplessly.

The next day, I asked my translator, Jiby, about the incident. "The men mine the charcoal, and the women sell it. It's illegal, but it's the only way for some people to eat," he said.

"And what will the police do with the charcoal?"

"They'll sell it in the city. People there have no firewood." Jiby said a bag sold in Faoune for the equivalent of US$1 could fetch five times that much in the city.

I had seen coal mines, but what was a charcoal mine? Jiby led me about a quarter mile into the forest to a desolate clearing with dozens of charred tree stumps and a pile of ash. The "charcoal mine" is an oven made from dried grass and wet sand. After creating his oven, a man fells nearby trees with hand-tools and, over the course of several days, burns the trees inside the oven. He must tend the oven constantly to ensure that neither too much nor too little air gets in. A large oven and perhaps fifty mature trees will yield a hundred bags of long-burning charcoal.

The local forests are pocked with such mines. "Two years ago," Jiby said "the forests were coming back because women were cooking with gas. Gas is much easier than either wood or charcoal. But now gas has become costly and people are returning to wood." This was a troubling perspective for me. I'd always thought that higher fuel prices were good for the environment because they drive down consumption. Now I envisioned innumerable charcoal mines like this one dotted across the developing world like a virulent rash.

Fortunately, there are also those in Africa who plant trees. From the charcoal mine, it was a short walk to the home of a full-time tree planter, Séckou Bodian. Ten years ago, Séckou left his job as a biology teacher in the city to return to his family's village and plant trees. "If I stayed in Dakar," Séckou said, "I could write books and talk. I came here because I want to create something real. I plant edible trees so people will have food, and I plant some trees for firewood." Séckou's nursery, a protected clearing around his home, was packed with hundreds of saplings in plastic bags.

In the beginning, villagers uprooted Séckou's trees. "They didn't understand why a civil servant would not just sit down and collect his salary," he said. "But once they started eating the fruits, they stopped spoiling my trees."

How many trees has he planted and tended so far? Séckou looked up into the towering tree canopy overhead for a long moment before he replied. "Probably 300,000." And at 47, he probably has a lot of planting time left.

Trees are a vital element of permaculture design, but they're nothing new. For centuries, people have planted trees around their homes to provide food in the growing season, to give shade in the summer, to provide protection from wind in the winter, and for cooking and heating fuel. Every ecovillage I visited enjoyed an edible landscape that also modulated heat and light. Even inner-city LA Eco-Village enjoys a lush courtyard full of trees that bear fruit and provide a habitat for songbirds. But ecovillages can plant only so many trees. Large-scale tree planting programs sponsored by governments and nonprofits are far more effective. These programs will become increasingly more important in our urban-heat islands as global temperatures rise and the need for local food production increases.

Another key element of permaculture design is the wild zone, an uncultivated area of land set aside for wildlife. Again, most of the ecovillages I visited have a wild zone, but the principle can be applied anywhere. At the household level, a backyard wildlife sanctuary can be certified through the National Wildlife Federation. For most people, the biggest hurdle in creating a backyard wildlife sanctuary is carnivorous pets.[14] A conservative estimate puts the number of birds killed by domestic cats each year at one billion in the United States alone. The ecovillages I visited have the predictable range of pet policies: no pets, no outdoor pets, free-range dogs and cats, dogs on leashes, etc. In some cases, the issue was debated for months before being resolved.

Of all the communities I visited, Crystal Waters, which prohibits dogs and cats, had the most impressive display of wildlife. Home to more than two hundred residents who share 640 reforested acres, this undulating landscape near Australia's eastern shore is also home to a plethora of nonhuman residents. Each day, I awoke to an astonishing symphony of birdsong and saw dozens of kangaroos and wallabies as I bicycled through the community, which is, in effect, a park.

In the minds of many, concern for wildlife is merely an aesthetic

---

[14] We might also consider the ecological footprint of our pets. In the United States, a dog on the standard diet of industrially farmed food requires as many resources as three Africans.

or ethical matter for those who have the luxury to think about such things. Yet it turns out that certain life forms – some of which, no doubt, are still undiscovered – are essential to our survival. Among these are the bees that pollinate our crops. Before my ecovillage journey, I was dimly aware that bee populations were being decimated by a mysterious phenomenon called colony collapse disorder. There is no organized movement to promote beekeeping in ecovillages; rather, the impulse comes from the "can-do" attitude that pervades ecovillage life. Rather than waiting for someone else to "save the bees," ecovillagers simply become beekeepers. Koichi Kitao, a Konohana farmer, reported that, while local nonorganic beekeepers lost most of their bees in the previous year, Konohana's organic hives produced more than a thousand pounds of honey. "It's a partnership," he said. "We feed them, and they feed us."

Wildlife conservation deserves conscious pursuit, but it also comes as a natural consequence of green living. Every dimension of ecology entailed in ecovillage life – everything we've discussed in this chapter – is also good for other species. Small, sustainable homes preserve wildlife habitat. Water conservation safeguards this precious substance for other life forms. Organic farming not only eschews pesticides and herbicides that kill indiscriminately, it also builds the vibrant microbial networks that constitute healthy soil. Decreased consumption of energy and materials means less pollution – not just for us but for all creatures. As ecovillages demonstrate, wildlife conservation need not be something we learn about on television or delegate to others. It can be woven into the fabric of our daily lives, wherever we may be.

## Living in the circle of life

The *eco* in "ecology" is derived from the ancient Greek term for household, *oikos*, and at first glance seems to have nothing to do with nature. Yet, just as the key to a healthy household is harmonious exchange among people fulfilling various roles, the key to a healthy ecosystem is harmonious exchange among the various species. Both household and ecosystem depend upon an integrated network of interdependent relationships. The ancient Greeks made a sharp distinction between the *polis*, the public arena where landholding Greek men debated the issues of the day, and the *oikos*, the private realm of family life. Today, however, when driving a car in California sends out fossil-fuel emissions that melt Antarctica's ice shelves, this distinction has dissolved. Our *oikos* is now as big as the planet. Whatever merit the distinction between *polis* and *oikos* may have had historically, it is now untenable. Now, our everyday choices – how we move about, the homes we build, and even what we eat – are suitable matters of public concern.

In his 1971 bestseller, *The Closing Circle: Nature, Man, and Technology*, Barry Commoner described the environment as "a house created on the Earth by living things for living things" and ecology as "the science of planetary housekeeping."[15] This science seeks to understand the cyclical life processes that ceaselessly consume and replenish our home planet's air, water, and soil. In other words, ecology seeks to understand the circle of life. When we convert the self-regenerating cycles of life into linear events leading from extraction to consumption to waste, we are essentially placing ourselves outside that circle. Forty years ago, it was not so apparent that the circle was closing. Terms like "globalization," "climate change," "the mass extinction of species," and "deepwater drilling" had not yet entered the lexicon. Today, however, our global technologies and their planetary effects are compelling us to find our way back into the circle of life. We must translate the limits of our planetary household – its finite resources and its finite capacity for absorbing our waste – into the limits of our personal households.

As ecovillages are demonstrating, we can do this with existing technologies while at the same time honoring our desire for comfort, beauty, and enjoyment. Technologies are available for natural and green building, clean energy and water systems, local and organic food production, and energy-efficient transportation. Some ecovillage practices can be applied at the household level, others require a larger area and community, and still others require infrastructural change – the kind of change that necessitates our acting as citizens in the *polis* and not just consumers in our households. The point is that we don't need to join an ecovillage in order to situate our everyday lives within the circle of life.

The twelve permaculture principles listed earlier provide excellent guidelines for how to live within the circle of life, and they can also be distilled into the basic premise of ecology: everything is connected to everything else. In this deep interdependence, there is no waste; there is only replenishment. The reality of interdependence runs contrary to our individualistic notions, but the core question that follows from it

---

[15] Barry Commoner, *The Closing Circle: Nature, Man, and Technology*, New York: Random House, 1971.

refers powerfully back to our sense of self: how are my actions replenishing the circle of life that sustains me? When we bring this question of enlightened self-interest to our everyday choices of consumption, we find ourselves asking some challenging questions: Where does it come from? Where will it go? Who is affected? If, as thousands ecovillagers have done, we join with others to transform our lives as we answer these questions, then we encounter more personal questions: What am I willing to share? With whom am I willing to share it? In taking these questions to heart, we discover the synergistic possibilities that emerge when we take an integrative approach to E2C2. Most importantly, we find ourselves consciously joining the Earth community and living within the circle of life.

A circle is both *finite* in terms of what it can hold, and *infinite* in that it goes around endlessly. Respecting the finitude of the circle of life, we might ask about the consequences of our actions for others: other people, both near and far, as well as other creatures. Respecting the circle's continuity, we might ask how our actions nurture the regenerative capacity of life itself. In a global era, our circle of influence spans the circumference of Earth, which means that we must widen our circles of vision and compassion commensurately.

# — 4 —

# ECONOMY: PROSPERING IN THE CIRCLE OF LIFE

With everything else he had to do, Brian Love could talk with me only at 9 p.m. and on a construction site. It wasn't ideal, but I'd heard enough about his work at Earthaven to jump at the opportunity. This is someone with a wide reach: sustainable forestry, construction, farming, and more. At the appointed hour, I found a young man bringing in sheep and turkeys from the field of his farm, the Gateway Farm described in chapter 3. Brian and I had our conversation in the shell of what will by now be his family's home. His after-hours project was building a state-of-the-art eco-home for himself, his wife, and their soon-to-be child.

Now the picture of a committed family man and entrepreneur, Brian arrived at Earthaven in 2005 as a high-school dropout with US$20 in his pocket. "I was bored to tears in high school so I ran away from home at sixteen and learned to forage and hunt," he said. "I wanted nothing to do with money."

I smiled. It's not an unusual stance for people who move into ecovillages, but, as it turns out, no one gets to keep a no-money stance for long. It takes financial balance to live anywhere on this planet, even if you're trading fish for deer pelts. An ecovillage is no exception.

Brian was building a home for his future family at the time, and he and his business partner shared the working apparatus and livestock for the farm as well as a construction and forestry business. Quite an achievement for a 22-year-old!

Earlier Brian had been describing himself as anti-civilization, taking a rage-against-the-machine stance that I've seen in my own students, and yet his economic position didn't come close to fitting the model. I asked him about this.

"I've come to see the value of economic exchange," Brian said. "The problem comes when you don't have relationships with the resources you're acquiring or the people you're dealing with. The beauty of the village model is that you have real relationships with the people and the resources."

The village model is nothing new and it's not limited to ecovillages. Indeed, human cultures all over the world began to thrive in village-size groups. The image of "the global village" is appealing, but it does not replicate the benefits of small-scale economies. We may be able to travel and communicate globally, but our ability to engage in an authentic way with far-flung people and resources is necessarily limited. In a village, farmers know who mills their wheat, who eats it, and if these farmers dump sludge into the local river or burn off the stubble from their fields, it's their neighbors who can no longer fish or who have trouble breathing. The neighbors know precisely who caused the problem and why. There is greed and deception in villages, just as there is anywhere, but they aren't invisible, and the community has more power in the equation. I like to think that economics is the intersection between ecology and community, the place where the common good has an opportunity to figure in the bottom line.

In an ecovillage, the purpose of the economy is to promote human wellbeing within the limits of finite ecosystems. The point of ecovillages, however, is not to return to the villages of the past. Every ecovillage I visited draws from the village model while simultaneously engaging in national and global scales. This is what it takes to establish viable economies in the twenty-first century. As Brian puts it, this means cultivating real relationships with people and resources.

Brian Love and others like him have acquired economic assets as a direct consequence of the impressive skill sets they've developed in ecovillages. Brian's skills include carpentry, masonry, plastering, insulation, concrete casting, excavation, grading, logging, lumber processing, setting up renewable energy systems and wastewater systems, as well as construction management and building design. In addition, there are the skills in law, accounting, and financial management that are necessary to handle any project that interfaces with a larger community and the communication skills – verbal and emotional – necessary for living in a community. Part of an ecovillage economy is the education that comes along with it.

Brian acquired this inventory of skills in his five years at Earthaven – quite an education! I asked him what his most important on-the-job lesson had been.

"Now I know that radical change is possible," he said. "The potential is beyond imagination, but you won't know what you can do till you try. You just have to go out and do it. You're going to make mistakes. Whatever you might read in a book won't necessarily apply. But one thing is definite: you've got to do it because it's not going to do itself."

Brian was roughly the age of my students, so I couldn't help but make a comparison. Even with a college degree from a top research university, only a small minority of my students will find deeply satisfying work in the way Brian has. Most students graduate heavily in debt, with limited job opportunities and no prospect of owning a home in the foreseeable future. Most importantly, few of them feel as hopeful and empowered as Brian.

This man's personal journey from neo-primitivism to green capitalism represents just one response among many to the issue of economic necessities. Ecovillages are laboratories for economic experimentation. In the fourteen communities I visited, I saw everything from private property to communalism with many permutations in between. I also encountered all manner of innovative financing and investment strategies, and even alternative monetary currencies. Yet issues of money and property can be challenging and divisive in an ecovillage, just as they are for the rest of us. Most of the communities I visited have a two-class society comprised of owners and renters; in some, rising real-estate prices have kept young people from buying in. The fact that ecovillages are not isolated enclaves but are subsets of regional, national, and global economies only intensifies the challenge. Ecovillagers might be able to feed themselves, employ one another, and even print their own internal currencies, but most of them still have jobs on the outside. Even those who have artfully downsized have bills to pay.

No matter what scale is involved – from village to worldwide – whenever people deal with the biophysical world, what comes into play is economics. No wonder, then, that the words "economy" and "ecology" share the same root: *oikos*, the Greek term for household. Both terms refer to a system of exchange, whether it's material or energetic. Ecology is the household's management of natural resources, and economics is its management of its financial resources. The idea that my household can save money by buying inexpensive goods created through the plunder of faraway lands is no longer viable. The upshot of the global economy is that my household is now operating on a planetary scale. There is no "faraway," no frontier save those fantasies of space colonization. We must, therefore, harmonize our resource extraction, production, consumption, and waste with our best understandings of the circle of life. In other words, we must reinvent our economies.

In a quiet and often homespun way, ecovillages are marrying economics to the other four dimensions of E2C2: ecology, community, and consciousness. In practice, this means revamping the basics of economic exchange: consumption, production, property, currency, and the fulfillment of needs. This chapter investigates how ecovillages approach each of these five basic dimensions of economic life.

The first principle of ecovillage economics is full-cost accounting. Essentially, this means that, rather than buying cheap products at the expense of distant people and ecosystems, consumers pay prices that reflect a living wage for the workers and a responsible approach to natural resources. As we'll discuss, this is more complex than it first appears.

The second principle of ecovillage economics is right livelihood. Here, the question becomes: How do I promote human wellbeing, *including my own*, within the limits of Earth's ecosystems? Not surprisingly, the ideal place to answer this question is where people have firsthand contact with one another and the material resources upon which they depend.

Third, ecovillages are rethinking ownership. While private property is the norm in today's individualistic societies, throughout history common property has been far more prevalent. Ecovillages are finding innovative ways of blending these two styles of ownership, but they are not immune to the snarls that ownership can provoke. Every community has its haves and have-nots, along with the tensions this dichotomy brings.

Fourth, all post-barter economies entail a social fiction that most of us take very seriously: the dream of money. Currencies, as they are aptly called, foster flow. In today's global economy, money flows ever faster, farther, and more furiously. Our interest-driven monetary system *requires* extracting resources to churn out ever more goods for ever more distant consumers, who generate ever more waste – hence the growth *imperative*. But, as the rebellious economist Kenneth Boulding quipped, "Anyone who believes that infinite growth is possible on a finite planet is either a madman or an economist." The need of the times is, therefore, to re-localize money in the service of people and ecosystems. Ecovillages are doing this, and several have even invented their own currencies.

The fifth and final component of an economy brings us to the question: what do I need? Under the logic of consumerism, the inexorable answer to this question is "more." For ecovillagers, the implicit answer is, "more time, more intimacy, more integrity – and less stuff." Their needs, they are finding, are best met in community and substantially outside the cash economy. In the affluent countries, many ecovillagers are living comfortably on incomes that place them well below the poverty line. Their secret? A combination of self-sufficiency, sharing, and elegant simplicity.

This chapter takes up each of these dimensions of ecovillage economics with the aim of distilling key lessons for the majority of us who will never live in an ecovillage.

## Full-cost accounting

Among my students, who in many ways represent the public at large, I find a common misconception that sustainable living must be expensive. According to this line of thinking, we can only become concerned about nature after we've reached a certain level of material comfort. As a political ecologist, I find this idea disturbing. If high levels of consumption are a precondition for ecological care, then our collective goose is cooked. As Gandhi pointedly asked, if British affluence required colonies all over the world, how many planets would India's affluence require – and, we might add, the other 50 percent of humanity living in the developing world?

Still, it's easy to understand why people believe that green living is a luxury. Just look at the price of organic produce or an electric car! Even considering efficiency gains over the long haul, many green technologies are pricey. A friend recently retrofitted her home with double-pane windows to the tune of US$20,000, and I doubt she'll ever recoup the cost in lower utility bills. Solar panels, the emblem of green living, are more efficient than they used to be, but in some climates their payback period can be twenty years. We may want to green our lifestyles, but how many of us have the upfront cash for this kind of long-term investment?

Psychologists tell us that people are innate "discounters," meaning that we tend to value near-term benefits over gains in the less certain future. We tend to favor the bird in the hand, including the current economic order – even if that bird is pecking our planetary household to bits. And yet we also make long-term investments, from the big ones like our home, our car, where we go to college, and our retirement funds to the seemingly small ones like our food and exercise choices. Very often we're willing to pay more if we foresee a likely benefit down the road. Even so, we can be surprisingly irrational. We can predict with a fair degree of certainty, for instance, that our capacities will decline as we age, but a disturbingly large number of us are not particularly good at planning for that eventuality. People, it turns out, are predisposed toward assuming that the future will be more or less like the past.[1]

From day to day (which is how most of us live), that assumption may be a good bet, but what if the coming decades are not like the past? What if the price of petroleum, the lifeblood of the global economy, goes through the roof and production declines just when demand in the developing world starts exploding? What if climate, that backdrop of ecological constancy taken for granted since the dawn of civilization, is destabilized? This is the future that most ecovillagers foresee. Given the data, they're probably right. And if they're right, paying a bit more for a well-insulated, passive-solar home with rainwater catchment and renewable energy systems is a no-brainer. Banding together with others who are making similar choices is eminently sensible. Jonathan Dawson, a resident of Findhorn and then-president of the Global Ecovillage Network, summed up this prudent ecovillage logic nicely: "Better to plan for the future that's coming rather than just let it land in our laps."

In the short term, however, the easy route is to perpetuate the status quo by basing our purchasing decisions on that time-tested maxim: the greatest value for the lowest price. This would be fine if the prices we paid reflected the actual costs associated with our consumption. The problem is that our global economy is amazingly proficient at displacing costs onto distant ecosystems and people – especially people not yet born. The pollution, habitat destruction, occupational hazards, and so on associated with our products are not reflected in market prices. Hence, the economists' term for them: "externalities." In the United States, we might complain about paying US$4 for a gallon of gasoline, but economists estimate that if the social, health and environmental costs as well as government subsidies were internalized, we might be paying as much as US$15.[2] And that doesn't include costs not so easily quantified. What is the price tag on the social alienation associated with a speed-obsessed culture, for instance, or the beauty of wilderness lost to mining?

On the whole, ecovillages are adept at full-cost accounting and valuing what may not be reflected in prices, but they face the same challenges as the rest of us – with the important difference that they do

[1] On the psychology of risk perception, see Paul Slovic, *The Feeling of Risk: New Perspectives on Risk Perception*, Earthscan, 2010.
[2] "The Real Price of Gasoline." International Center for Technology Assessment, 1998. This estimate neglects the substantial portion of the military budget devoted to ensuring access to global petroleum supplies.

so in community. When I questioned residents about their willingness to purchase solar panels and other renewable energy systems, they offered two basic reasons, one pragmatic and the other ethical. For sure, they are preparing for an energy-descent future. In some cases, government tax incentives and buy-back plans made their choices easier, but their strongest motivation was conscience. Recognizing that the true cost of this nonrenewable resource is not reflected in its price, they are setting the right price.

Asked about his family's decision to go solar, a resident of EVI spoke about tax credits and selling excess power to the local utility, but he also said, "The costs from our local coal or nuclear plants might be borne by people we'll never meet, but they're still real costs. If we don't pay the real cost for our energy, then we're essentially thieves, aren't we?"

Prices are probably most distorted in regard to agriculture. On average, Americans spend just 9 percent of their income on food – far lower than the global average of 35 percent.[3] This figure is one of the little-known secrets of American affluence, but once again, that wealth is a chimera. The hidden costs of our cheap food are passed onto the healthcare system, small farmers and farm workers, depleted aquifers and ecosystems, and the horrors of industrialized meat production. Government subsidies are another hidden cost. In the United States, that means dairy, wheat, grain-fed meat, and high-fructose corn syrup. If the true costs of the American diet were registered at the checkout counter, I suspect that most of us would quickly change our diets.

Ecovillages have their own ways of equalizing food inequities. Just as governments subsidize the diets – and the farmers – they want to promote, so do ecovillages. They do this primarily by offering their farmers heavily discounted access to land, low- or zero-interest loans, and free labor in the form of community work parties and infrastructural support for interns and WWOOFers.[4] The result is low-cost, high-quality food. EVI residents pay only US$2.50 for community dinners because much of the food comes from their own farm, and the cooks and clean-up crew are generated by the community's internal labor requirement of 2–4 hours per week.

Every rural ecovillage I visited was growing a substantial portion

[3] Nathaniel Jones, "Mapping Global Food Spending (Infographic)" at http://civileats.com/2011/03/29/mapping-global-food-spending-infographic, accessed June 20, 2013.
[4] World Wide Opportunities on Organic Farms is an international organization that matches travelers, usually young people, with organic farms looking for help. See www.wwoof.org.

of its food, in some cases virtually all of it. This means that most ecovillagers have something that's rare in the industrialized world: a personal relationship with the people who grow their food and the soil in which it grows. Even urban ecovillages have forged strong relationships with local farmers. UfaFabrik's popular café, for instance, sources most of its produce from a rural farming community outside Berlin, and the Los Angeles Eco-Village, whose edible courtyard landscape supplies only a tiny portion of the community's food, had, when I visited, just launched two new food initiatives. The first, the Food Lobby, was a buying club that provides LAEV members and their low-income neighbors with healthy, more sustainably produced food at a discount. The second initiative resembled a cut-rate personal-delivery farmers' market.

Yuki Kidokoro, a resident in her late thirties, described LAEV's special relationship with two farmers, an arrangement that enabled her to increase dramatically the fresh fruits and vegetables in her diet. "Every Sunday, they deliver fresh produce on their way from the market. It's organic, it's local, and it's *so cheap*! Now I can buy high-quality food fresh from the farm, and I pay less than half what I would at the farmers' market." Clearly, I surmised, these two farmers were more interested in expressing their solidarity with LAEV than profiting from it.

So long as food prices do not reflect actual costs, sustainable farming can only make business sense if consumers base their choices on factors besides price – factors like health, ecology, or social justice. In a rural ecovillage, one of those factors would presumably be solidarity with one's own farmers, and in most cases, this is what I found. Crystal Waters, however, was an instructive exception. During my visit, the proprietors of all three farms – vegetables, poultry, and dairy – were in the process of leaving. They couldn't support themselves.

One of the departing dairy farmers, Julie Shelton, explained, "It really came down to a lack of support from the community members. If price is your priority and you're in town anyway, you'll buy the non-organic milk there." The departing vegetable farmer told me essentially the same thing: too few residents were willing to pay slightly higher prices in order to support Crystal Waters' internal businesses. Why so? Max Lindegger, a Swiss engineer-turned-permaculturalist and one of the community's founders, offered a simple explanation. "We have a long way to go," he said. "The problem is we're not hungry enough yet."

So it seems that as long as we have the luxury of displacing costs onto distant peoples and ecosystems, the village model – an economy based upon real relationships with people and resources – will likely remain elusive. The experience at Crystal Waters inspired me to do some serious thinking about the intangible factors that differentiate an ecovillage from a green subdivision. Some of the qualities I came up with were a shared sense of purpose, solidarity, reciprocity, and trust. Max's comment "we're not hungry enough" made me wonder about the relationship between these qualities and material factors. If he is right, then village life under conditions of affluence is an oxymoron. Yet that is precisely the point of ecovillages: to forge a sense of solidarity through a shared commitment to sustainable living – before we are hungry.

## Right livelihood

One of my favorite classroom experiments is to ask my students to imagine what work they would choose if they could meet their needs while doing work they love. I then ask them to compare their current career ambitions with their imaginary world. In the real world, most of them (being political science majors) hope to go to law school – though few will have the grades and test scores to do so. In their imaginary worlds, virtually none of them want to be lawyers. Instead, their most common fantasy careers involve working with children, helping people (very often in developing countries), and working outside. Of course, my job is to help prepare them for the "real world," but I also want them to enter that world aware of their own deeper values and able to think outside the box – especially because that box is looking increasingly flimsy.

In the mainstream economy, small farmers and others who are doing vitally necessary work struggle to eke out a living while the big bucks go to CEOs and stockbrokers. All too often, our jobs are the compulsory drudgery we must endure in exchange for a paycheck. "TGIF," we say at the end of the workweek, though when we hear the news reports about high unemployment rates, we're also inclined to feel grateful just to have a job. At the same time most people, I find, have a deep longing for meaningful, life-enhancing work – what the Buddhists call "right livelihood." The concept also has deep roots in western thought. As Aristotle put it, "Where your deep joy meets the world's great hunger, therein lies your vocation." If the purpose of an economy is to promote human wellbeing within the limits of Earth's ecosystems, then right livelihood must be an integral part of it.

Quite a few of the ecovillagers I encountered had left high-paying jobs because their longing for right livelihood was not being met. Werner Wiartalla, for instance, was managing UfaFabrik's physical infrastructure in the heart of Berlin when I met him. Twenty years before, he had been working as a physicist at Siemens by day and playing samba music at UfaFabrik by night. Werner became so intrigued by the possibilities for the community's energy infrastructure that he quit his job and joined UfaFabrik full time.

"The structure at Siemens felt too small," Werner said. "It was too one-sided, too much about money. A system can only survive when ecology, economics, and culture are in balance. If one thing is dominant, it goes the wrong way. I didn't understand this then, but I felt it without knowing it. You can't eat money, and it doesn't feed your soul."

Yet, when he came to UfaFabrik, Werner's first impulse was economic: he hoped to save the community money by creating synergies across the electrical, heating, and water systems. One of the things he did was to design a system of green roofs where the condensation cools the solar panels, causing them to generate more electricity. Largely because of Werner's work, UfaFabrik became an international sustainability demonstration site.

"For me," he said, "Ufa is like a giant laboratory. I had a big concept for many systems in one place, and here I could do that."

Werner, a self-possessed man in his forties, said that the most rewarding aspect of his life at UfaFabrik is "to work in a relatively free way with people who share that life. Here, I organize the gardening and the systems, but I also do Thai massage." Gesturing to his heart, he added, "Here, I can live what's inside."

Nearly every person I spoke to felt freer, more fulfilled, and more socially engaged since joining an ecovillage. In the words of Petra Hepburn, a founding member of EVI, "Even though I have less money, I feel richer here. There's so much support."

In our workaday world, the quest for integrity might seem idealistic, but it need not be an unobtainable goal. When money and work are put at the service of community, integrity follows naturally. I was surprised to find that most of the jobs within ecovillages were not at all exotic. They were exactly what you would expect to find anywhere: cooks, housecleaners, carpenters, plumbers, electricians, web designers, beauticians, writers, farmers, lawyers, accountants, teachers, and so on. The distinguishing feature of these ecovillage occupations is that, in contrast to their counterparts on the outside, they are pursued with an ecological vision and within the context of a dynamic community. Unlike the distant and anonymous relationships that typify the mainstream economy, most work relationships in ecovillages are characterized by proximity and personal contact. And, in a more practical vein, working from home not only fosters community, it makes economic and ecological sense.

Observing the range of small businesses in ecovillages, I decided the road these communities have taken is one most of us will be compelled to travel in the not-too-distant future. The convergence of rising fuel prices, changing climate, and intensifying ecological disruption means that economies will necessarily become more local. If more of us embark upon that path sooner rather than later, we're likely to find ourselves living in a better world. An economy characterized by distance and anonymity tends to cause environmental damage and undermine social cohesion. In the more vibrant ecovillage economies I encountered, the circulation of money and skills through the pursuit of right livelihood actually strengthened social bonds. In the larger communities, like Damanhur and Findhorn, the same money can circulate for quite some time. The yoghurt maker, for instance, buys milk from the dairy farmer, who buys vegetables from the crop farmer, who gets her hair cut by the community hairdresser, who pays an accountant in the community to keep her books, and so on. When money circulates through many hands before it leaves the community and each pair of hands is practicing right livelihood, the consequences can only be positive.

For those of us outside an ecovillage context, how might we apply this principle in our daily lives? On a very basic level, by supporting local businesses – even if that means paying a bit more. But what if the practices of those businesses are not life-enhancing? In that case, we might find ourselves joining with our neighbors to facilitate positive change. For instance, a loose-knit movement is springing up to persuade corner stores in US inner cities to supplement their alcohol and junk-food inventory with fresh produce purchased from local farmers. Or what if existing local businesses do not offer the services we need? In this case, the neighborhood skills-sharing map comes to mind (see chapter 3). If our neighbors turned out to include a good hairdresser or a reliable handyman, would we so easily resort to the Yellow Pages?

Ecovillages have internal economies, some more dynamic than others, but I don't want to create the impression that they are self-sufficient enclaves. The economic boundaries of ecovillages are quite porous. Money flows in from jobs, cottage industries, visitors, and even, in a few cases, grants; and money flows out for many purchases. Most of the ecovillagers I interviewed earn at least some of their income from outside jobs, and a few – like UfaFabrik's energy systems designer – received outside funding for their innovative work within their communities. Far more common than grants are cottage industries, and I found quite a range: renewable energy companies, organic nurseries and seed suppliers, handcrafting herbal supplements, glass blowing, furniture making, ceramics, weaving and knitting, just to name a few.

Auroville's cottage industries stand out for their size and their impact on the local economy. Thousands of local Tamil villages work in Auroville rolling incense, dying cloth, sewing clothing, and making everything from handmade paper to jewelry and soap – much of it for export. At first glance, the arrangement looked to me like neo-colonialism dressed up as New Age spirituality. But after considering the paucity of opportunities available to these Tamil villagers and comparing Auroville's relatively comfortable work environments with village conditions, I concluded that the overall socioeconomic impact of Auroville's cottage industries is positive – for Auroville *and* for the surrounding villages. All of Auroville's food products are organic and most of its cottage industries subscribe to fair-trade principles. In some cases, the impact is spectacularly positive for both people and the environment. For example, women working at WELL Paper (Women Empowerment through Local Livelihood) earn a living wage and become socially empowered while transforming garbage into attractive jewelry and practical household items.[5] The basic idea of creating useful products from waste is one that can be applied anywhere.

While most jobs in ecovillages are not so different from what we might find in the mainstream economy, some are extraordinary and serve as demonstrations of what becomes possible when we pursue our dreams collectively. UfaFabrik, for instance, got started in the heart of Berlin when the Cold War was still a hot topic. Intent upon promoting a "third way" beyond capitalism and socialism, the community's political strategy was to poke fun at both sides. To that end, they started a circus, complete with clowns, jugglers, tightrope walkers, and trapeze artists. They had no business aspirations, but their circus became so popular that parents from all over the city wanted to send their children to these performers to learn their skills. So UfaFabrik started a circus school for young people. Within a few

---

[5] An Israeli sociologist-turned-Aurovilian started WELL Paper as part of the community's extensive tsunami-relief effort in 2005. The project was so successful that it turned into a larger sustainable development project. See www.welllpaper.org.

years, the adults were clamoring for a school of their own. What began as political activism and pure fun evolved into a thriving business and a shining example of right livelihood.

Every ecovillage I visited sponsors some kind of educational event for the public, but one, Findhorn, has created a workshop economy. Findhorn captured media attention in the 1970s for its stupendous results in growing food on a blustery ridge with sandy soil, but today its focus is on "growing" people. In practice, this means that tens of thousands of people participate in the Findhorn Foundation's calendar of personal growth events every year. Between the events themselves and all the requisite food and lodging, this workshop economy constitutes Findhorn's primary source of employment. Foundation staff salaries are minimal – the equivalent of US$320 a month plus food and lodging. Until recently, this workshop economy made Findhorn the number-two source of employment in the region, second only to the Royal Air Force base next door. With the recent closure of the base, which employed thirty times as many people as Findhorn, the ecovillage now finds itself at the center of regional economic planning. This means that right livelihood, rather than being just the idealistic pursuit of several hundred ecovillagers, may become the economic foundation of a region of northern Scotland. It also means that this corner of the world may be better prepared for the slower, simpler, more localized economy of the future.

Right livelihood is about putting our labor in the service of our dreams while forging high-quality relationships with people and resources. Ecovillages, where people have firsthand contact with one another and the material resources upon which they depend, are ideally suited to this pursuit, but the basic principles can be applied anywhere. First, consider what you love to do and how you might make a living doing it. "Follow your bliss," as they say. Second, find like-minded souls – preferably ones who live nearby – whose dreams are compatible with your own. Third, understand that the economy is a subset of the ecosystem, not vice versa. This means keeping your work and your consumption as local as possible. Organizations like the BALLE network (Business Alliance for Local Living Economies), which represents over 22,000 businesses all over North America, can offer guidance. Fourth, be open to new possibilities. Some people might start a circus school; others might transform garbage into beauty. The paths to right livelihood are many, but their destination is the same: a world where self-fulfillment is a corollary to social and ecological wellbeing.

## Box 4.1 A Gambian Life Boat

For Lamin Camara, a lanky young man putting his ecology degree to work for Colufifa, the path to right livelihood entailed remaining in his village when he could have earned far more in the city. Most men of his age had left Sinteth, a village along the Gambia River. When I visited, Lamin and a group of villagers took me through drought-parched rice paddies to the crocodile-infested river. "People eat crocodiles," Lamin said, "and they eat us, but only rarely because they are shy. It's a relationship." On a wistful note, he added, "When I was growing up, a hippo lived in the river. A villager killed it because it could eat a full rice paddy. Now the hippos are protected by law, but they are gone."

Our group walked purposefully toward a long wooden boat under construction. The village men were clearly proud of the boat, none more so than the quiet boatbuilder who showed me his tools: two pieces of sharpened steel he had attached to handmade wooden handles. I gazed at the hand-carved boat, perhaps 12 meters long, and marveled at the man's skill and fortitude, and the vision behind the project. When it goes to sea many miles downriver, this boat will carry a 15-horsepower engine, nets longer than a football field, and ten young men. For most of them, it will be their first glimpse of the ocean.

"Once we had river fish, but for many years the rain has been too small and the salt comes in from the sea," Lamin explained. "The trees in the forest are cut, and the freshwater has gone, so the mangroves are dying. Our young men leave for Spain because there is nothing for them here, but many of them die crossing the ocean. We have built this boat so they can go to the ocean for fish – a boat for life instead of death." For desperate young men, right livelihood might mean finding a heroic way of feeding their people.

A discussion of names followed. I laughed when someone suggested Karen, but that was the choice. Lamin handed me a pencil and asked me write my name on the stern. Momentarily overpowered by the image of ten young men who could not swim navigating a boat named Karen in the ocean, I struggled to hold back tears. The older men looked at me with concern, as if to ask "have we offended you?"

Lamin put my sudden emotion into context: "Sometimes white people cry when they are happy, especially the women."

I printed my name on the rough wood and expressed my wishes for the men's safety and a bountiful harvest. "What color should we paint it?" one man asked me, and I replied that I like all colors. Lamin suggested green, the color of life, and that was the choice.

The boatbuilder offered me a small piece of the enormous tree from which he had carved the boat, and that ruddy memento now sits on my desk even as I write. Months later, I received an email from Lamin, reporting that the boat had made her maiden voyage and that the young men had returned safely to Sinteth with several tons of fish. My mind traced the steps along the path of right livelihood in Sinteth, from Lamin to the boatbuilder to the boatload of young men.

Figure 4.1 Jiby, my translator, in front of his hand-built mud home
in Faoune, the village where Colufifa is headquartered

Figure 4.2 Lamin Camara stands with me on a hand-carved wooden
fishing boat, with the boatbuilder on the left

## The snarls of ownership

As we saw in chapter 3, one of the primary ways ecovillagers reduce their resource consumption and waste is through collaborative consumption. This is also one reason that ecovillagers can live on a fraction of what their fellow citizens spend: they are meeting their needs through innovative forms of co-ownership. When it comes to the big three – housing, transportation, and food – ecovillagers spend less, often dramatically less, because they share more. Take the ubiquitous practice of car sharing. When you consider that transportation accounts for nearly 20 percent of US consumer spending (second only to real estate, with food a distant third), car sharing makes economic sense.[6] And because the fossil fuels that literally drive our current economy will only become dirtier and more expensive over time, more sharing – including the large-scale sharing we call mass transit – must surely be the wave of the future.

For most of us, housing is the big ticket item and is what first comes to mind when we think of private property. My sense is that in tomorrow's energy-descent world, we'll be sharing more even with this bastion of private property: real estate. Again, ecovillages can give us some clues. In those I visited, most of the land and community facilities were held in common. Even at Crystal Waters, which has no common house and where private homes are sold on the open market, 80 percent of the land is co-owned and can be licensed for sustainable farming, forestry, and recreation. Though full-fledged communes are rare among ecovillages, I visited two communities where *all* of the real estate is held in common: Svanholm in Denmark and Konohana in Japan.

For those of us raised in single-family homes, common property might sound like a strange concept, but sizeable tracts of common land were the norm throughout most of human history. Even when homes and farmland remained within the family, pastures, forests, and fresh-water sources were traditionally shared. Despite today's emphasis on private ownership, common property continues to be widespread: think public parks, national forests, roads, and schools. Yet many of the relationships entailed in these government-mediated arrangements

---

[6] For a good analysis of US transportation economics, see "Driven to Spend" at http://transact.org. US consumer debt, which excludes real estate debt, tallies up to US$2.4 trillion – about US$8,000 for every man, woman and child, with car loans accounting for about 67 percent of the total. Low-income people spend a far higher portion of their income on transportation than those with average incomes.

are characterized by distance and anonymity. Consequently, most of us have few meaningful experiences of common property outside our own families.

While private property is the norm today, ecovillages have a range of legal options for sharing property. Under EVI's co-housing model, for instance, 80 percent of the land is owned and maintained by a *homeowners' association* to which members pay annual dues of about US$4,000. This fee covers real-estate taxes and maintenance of the community sauna, pond, roads, and common houses. Residents have title to their own homes and the land beneath them. In contrast, the tenements at Los Angeles Eco-Village are owned by a nonprofit corporation and units are rented cheaply to residents. During my visit, LAEV was looking toward a housing cooperative that would enable members to co-own their apartments. Other possible financial structures for communities include condominium associations, limited liability partnerships, and community land trusts. Without going into detail about the panoply of available legal and financial structures, suffice it to say, there are many.[7]

Some of these options permit more flexibility than others for change and expansion – accepting new members, for instance. In many countries, including the United States, fair housing laws prohibit homeowners who sell on the open market from being very selective. Earthaven, for example, wanted to choose their members. So they created a membership process in which provisional members must live and work at Earthaven for at least six months before being granted full membership, a decision that requires the consent of every community member. Full members pay a nonrefundable joining fee of US$4,000, which entitles them to membership in the organization and the right to choose a homesite on which to build their homes.

During my visit, Earthaven was rethinking its legal and financial structure because any lawsuit against the community could put everyone's property at risk. Martha Harris, a retired lawyer, was helping the community think through these issues. Earthaven's founders were divided, she said. Some didn't believe in private property and others did, so they ended up with a risky compromise: a homeowners' association that grants 99-year leases. "If one person does something wrong," Martha said, "everybody here could lose their homes. As an

---

[7] For information on legal entities for owning property in the United States, see Diana Leafe Christian, *Creating a Life Together: Practical Tools to Grow Ecovillages and Intentional Communities*, Canada: New Society, 2003.

educational center, we bring in the public, which makes for more risk. We're working on it. It's complicated."

I observed during my travels that, as a rule, the more a community's membership is determined by market forces, the weaker is its social fabric. At Crystal Waters Permaculture Village, where there is no membership process, one of my big questions was whether it actually was a community. First-rate hydrology and free-range kangaroos help to boost real-estate values, but they do little to create robust social bonds. Many people, especially younger ones, have been priced out of the market. As a consequence, the average age of the residents was fifty and rising. One member put it bluntly: "We're not a community; we're a green subdivision – and moving toward becoming a retirement village!" Even if Crystal Waters is a green subdivision, though, I felt a far greater sense of community there than I ever experienced in suburbia. Neighbors knew each other, families cared for one another's children, and the Saturday market was fun.

Most of the younger residents I met at Crystal Waters were renters, yet the benefits of this economic diversity were partially undercut by the fact that they were excluded from key aspects of decision-making. Rightly so, perhaps: renter-ship does not entail the same level of responsibility as ownership. Still, a two-class society stands in sharp contrast to the democratic culture of ecovillages. As one woman in her thirties said, "There's a hierarchy of ownership here, and I'm at the bottom. I'm just a renter." I heard similar comments in many of the communities I visited.

Having lived on both sides of the renter–landlady divide, I am poignantly aware of the issues. As a renter, I lived with the constant sense of someone looking over my shoulder. As a landlady, I was forever cleaning up after my tenants. Pride of ownership, I've learned, is a real phenomenon – even, as it turns out, among ecovillagers who have embraced the notion of common property. One comment sums up the problem nicely. Frustrated with the dirty counters in her living group's common kitchen, a Svanholm resident remarked, "It's owned by everybody, which means that it's owned by nobody." Private property, for all its shortcomings as an individualistic socioeconomic institution, can foster a sense of accountability.

Both of the ecovillages that found an alternative to private ownership did so in the context of cultures that support other priorities. Konohana, for instance, operates as a family in Japan, where the traditional culture reveres family ties. Konohana even has *family* in its name – Konohana Family. It is officially listed with the Japanese government as a family for tax purposes, and its members relate to one another as family. They live in close quarters, work side by side in the fields, eat their homegrown food cheek by jowl at one incredibly long table, and discuss the day's activities each night after dinner. New members pay a joining fee of US$2,600 and most, although this is not required, contribute all of their assets.

Like a close-knit egalitarian family, Konohana disburses the earnings from its collectively owned farm equally. Michiyo Furuhashi, a former supervisor in a technical lab for Unilever Corporation, reported that her annual income was the equivalent of US$7,000 and her living expenses came to US$3,000. For Michiyo, leaving Unilever for Konohana meant an 80 percent pay cut, but she has no regrets. "Our income is so low that we never need to pay taxes," Michiyo said. "I can save US$4,000 each year in my own account. I have never lived on so little, but it is amazing how rich I feel!"

Svanholm, on the other hand, operates within Denmark's strongly communitarian culture, which offers a distinctive venue for testing alternative models. Svanholm calls itself a *kommune*, which in Danish means not only "community" but also, as it sounds, "commune." "We're proud to be one of the last surviving communes," said Birgitte Simonsen, a sociology professor and one of Svanholm's founders. "We don't want to be just a community, where people come together as separate units. In Denmark, to be a commune is not negative because people associate it with freedom – especially freedom of ideas."

I paused to let her words sink in. To be *proud* of being a commune – what a contrast! In the United States, most ecovillages struggle to distance themselves from the baggage associated with communes: the hippie culture, communism, and so on. But in Denmark, an ecovillage can be proud to be a commune.

Birgitte went on to explain how Svanholm's economy works. When members join, their assets and earnings go into the common pool. If they leave, those assets are returned. More than half of the members work outside; the rest work for Svanholm's farms and shops or its building and lumber companies. Everybody receives a minimum salary decided at the annual budget meeting. In 2009, it was 240,000 Danish kroner, or about US$47,000, making Svanholm the most prosperous ecovillage I visited. In the early years, everybody received the same salary, but they had recently decided to give more to those who earn more.

"It's because we're between worlds," Birgitte said. "If things get too equal, some people think it's unfair. If they get too unequal, there's poverty."

I was dubious. Don't those who earn more still find the arrangement unfair? And what about the lazy ones?

Birgitte, whose university salary surpassed the community average, told me that she gladly supports the people she loves rather than just her "lonely existence." She also assured me that Svanholm's arduous membership process, which can take years, weeds out anyone who might be lazy.

"We probably turn down 80 percent of the people who want to join," she added. "We get suspicious when people are overwhelmingly positive or dreamy, or when they're in a big life transition. People here need to be able to work and relate well. If you can't make it in the regular world, you definitely won't make it here. We need a lot of trust to make Svanholm work, so people need to show they're trustworthy."

And that, I began to see, is the key to Svanholm's collective economy: not ideology but trust. Again and again, this theme emerged in ecovillages: trusting, earning trust, discerning when to trust.

The following day, Kirsten Høngsmark, Svanholm's accountant, cheerfully answered all of my questions – plus some I would not have dared to ask. Svanholm is co-owned by all the members as a registered commercial organization. Two-thirds of the annual budget comes from members' outside salaries; the rest comes from Svanholm's businesses. What a strange mix: a commune that doubles as a well-run business! In this case, however, "well run" does not necessarily mean revenue generating. If this were a conventional business, Svanholm would have long since abandoned its 440-acre organic farm. Their common economy allows them to focus on other values besides profit.

After showing me the ledgers for Svanholm's taxes, debts, and assets, Kirsten made a simple statement that lodged in my mind: "Everybody's salary is known by all." To my mind, one's salary is a fairly private matter, so the thought of eighty adults knowing one another's salaries was a bit unsettling. Yet if sharing is essential to community life, I reflected, why not also share this vital information?

Kirsten must have seen the wheels of my brain turning. "Would you like to see the list of everyone's salaries?" she asked, handing me the list. The numbers were revealing. The range was large, running from less than US$20,000 for pensioners up to one professor's earnings of nearly US$200,000. The average salary for professionals on the outside was about US$58,000. Since everyone was guaranteed US$47,000, this meant that those with outside jobs were subsidizing those working inside. Was this level of financial transparency normal in Denmark? Kirsten assured me it was not. It was, I surmised, what fosters the trust that makes Svanholm so successful.

While very few of us would ever consider joining a commune, even a well-heeled one like Svanholm, we can still glean an important lesson from this flourishing ecovillage. Common property arrangements work best when there is trust, which in turn must be earned through responsible action. At Svanholm, I found myself pondering whether I would ever consider joining a commune. Upon reflection, my answer was not so different from what I saw there: perhaps, but only with the right people.

For many Americans, communal sharing implies a loss of freedom. Yet *freedom* is precisely the value that Svanholm holds most dear – a freedom of ideas, social interaction, and creative expression. When I compared the ambient anxiety of American life to the social cohesion I experienced at Svanholm, I had to wonder how so many of us came to associate freedom with consumerism. The values enshrined in our Declaration of Independence – life, liberty and the pursuit of happiness – were in abundant supply at Svanholm, but this was clearly not the American Dream!

We may have no attraction to entering a legal agreement to share our property, but surely we can glean some relevant practices from ecovillages for our own lives – and we need not sign a contract to do this. We can simply expand our ideas about ownership and devise our own experiments. Does every household in my neighborhood, for instance, really need a lawn mower? Or, if I have a water-hungry lawn, why not simultaneously put my land to good use and forge meaningful ties with enterprising young urban farmers? Imagine our cities and suburbs becoming increasingly food self-sufficient through a network of backyard farms. The social benefits would likely be as great as the ecological benefits. If food prices rise with climate instability and declining oil reserves, these homegrown experiments would become increasingly profitable.

If we are wary of offering our own land, why not take advantage of the common property we already co-own? We could, for instance, band together with our neighbors to plant fruit trees in our local schoolyard or an edible landscape in a nearby park. We might pool our resources to hire one of our neighbors to tend our plantings and harvest and distribute the produce. Whether or not we live in an ecovillage, when we revise our individualistic notions of ownership and integrate property into a network of social and ecological relationships, we increase our capacity for generating real wealth.

## Box 4.2 When Everything Isn't Equal

Over time, Findhorn has experienced a trend common among ecovillages that trace their roots to the 1960s and 1970s: a shift from "all for one and one for all" to private ownership. Almost all of the dozens of businesses and nonprofits associated with Findhorn began under the auspices of the Findhorn Foundation and eventually became independent. Robin Alfred's Findhorn Consultancy Service, a now-private firm that exports Findhorn's social and spiritual practices to the corporate world, is a perfect example of this trend.

"We pulled in a lot of revenue," Robin said, "but we got the same allowance as everybody else. That was fine for a while, but after a few years, I was spending more and more time outside the Foundation. With so much travel, I had to leave the choir and couldn't attend all the community meetings. It felt like a different relationship with the community, so we proposed a division of profits – 30% to the Foundation, 30% to those of us who earned the surplus; and 40% to go back into the business. The Foundation was unable to agree this – and a few years later, we took the Consultancy Service completely out. Now we tithe back to the Foundation 5% of what we earn. I think everybody's happy with the arrangement."

I was dubious. Wouldn't this inequality tend to foster envy and resentment?

"In communities," Robin said, "there's often this notion that everything needs to be equal. Some good comes from that, but the downside is that it can squelch the kind of resourcefulness people need in order to be more in the world."

I asked several of the modestly paid Findhorn staff members how they felt about the Foundation's arrangement with what are called its "independent centers of initiative." One woman, who nicely summed up the responses, said, "Sure, I'd like to make more money. But their income doesn't take anything away from me, and their work does a real service to Findhorn. I'd say it's a win–win."

## The dream of money

If you have ever traveled abroad, then you've experienced that strange moment when, after exchanging your currency, you look at your new wad of bills as something genuinely foreign. The strange slips of paper seem unreal, like play money. In time, however, you grow accustomed to them, and the slips of paper assume real value for you. If you're away for a while, you have the same experience in reverse when you come home. That moment of strangeness reveals a truth we seldom admit to consciousness: money is a fabrication. A uniquely human invention, money rests upon our capacity for symbolic thinking and a social agreement to honor something with no inherent worth as a representation of the value of our goods, our services, and our time. This paradox is all the more stark when our currencies are not backed by something tangible like gold.

Ironically, in a money-driven culture, it is considered the height of realism to be fixated on this collective fiction. Yet socially constructed reality is still . . . well, reality. Werner, UfaFabrik's physicist-turned-energy-expert, puts it this way: "You can't eat money and it doesn't feed the soul, but I need it." No matter how fervent our idealism, very few of us can escape the need for money. Money is the warp and woof of our everyday lives: the reason we go to work, the source of just about everything we own, our personal and collective measure of success. Like fish swimming in the ocean of money, few of us ever stop to ask ourselves what the stuff actually is, how it comes into existence, or whom it chiefly serves. We know only that we need it to survive and, all things being equal, the more we have of it, the better.

Because I have a steady salary and live modestly, for most of my life I've been able to turn my mind to larger thoughts. I may be a political scientist, but when I read the newspaper, I steer clear of the finance pages. It wasn't until I observed ecovillage economies that I became deeply curious about the nature of money. To my great surprise, some were minting their own currency, and one had built a thriving economy on that basis. Who wouldn't be curious about funny money that seriously works!

The idea behind *complementary currencies*, as these local economic trading systems are called, mirrors a basic principle of right livelihood: the more circulation money has locally, the stronger the social and ecological relationships. Complementary currencies take this principle one step further by introducing a local medium of exchange. When Bernard Lietaer, one of the architects of the euro and author of *The Future of Money*,[8] began studying complementary currencies in 1984, there were only two in circulation. As of 2010, Lietaer found 5,000 complementary currencies operating in towns, cities, and even among businesses all over the world. This explosion of local currencies is facilitated by the internet, but its primary

[8] Bernard Lietaer, *The Future of Money: Creating New Wealth, Work, and a Wiser World*, London: Century, 2002.

impetus is a growing distrust in the dominant money system.[9] Several ecovillages I visited had their own internal currencies: Earthaven's *leaps* and the Findhorn's *eko*, for instance. But by far the most dynamic and lucrative complementary currency I encountered was Damanhur's *credito*.

The *credito* has enabled this federation of communities, with a membership approaching one thousand and a constant flow of visitors, to increase its wealth while at the same time strengthening social relationships and moving toward a sustainable economy. The *credito* began as a system of internal vouchers among Damanhur's members in the late 1970s, when commercial interest rates were high. The purpose was to free up Italian currency for purchasing necessities and building the community. At one point, in order to strengthen its internal economy, Damanhur declared the lira "illegal," a move that precipitated an upsurge of entrepreneurial activity. Residents generated new *creditos* through promising their labor, investing existing funds, inventing new products, and starting new projects. I tried to imagine what I would do if the dollar completely collapsed and I found myself thinking like the residents of Damanhur: I would use my creative abilities to produce what others valued. The *credito* is essentially a social fiction that motivates the people of Damanhur to do this – plus it enables the community to invest their "real" money elsewhere.

Over time, Damanhur created a central treasury with two capacities: (1) oversight for new *creditos* involving the community's real-estate cooperative (co-owned by all Damanhur citizens), and (2) the operation of what amounts to a bank, Damanhur Economic Solidarity (DES). Depositors, including nonmembers, receive a nominal interest rate (1.5–2.5%) on their euros, which are guaranteed to support ethical investments and entrepreneurial initiatives within the community. Today, both euros and *creditos* circulate within Damanhur, and members with outside jobs are encouraged to exchange a portion of their euros for *creditos*.

On my first day at Damanhur, I found a currency exchange machine just outside the café, bookshop, and clothing shop – all selling Damanhur goods. Macaco Tamerice, the German woman with impeccable English who shepherded me through my ten-day visit, explained, "You can also use euros anywhere in Damanhur, but if you

---

[9] Lietaer's elaborate website, Currency Solutions for a Wiser World, is an excellent source of information on complementary currencies. See www.lietaer.com, accessed June 20, 2013.

want to use *creditos*, you can exchange your money here: one *credito* to the euro. Whatever you don't spend, you can exchange for euros when you leave."

A one-to-one exchange, I thought, so nothing to lose. I deposited €20 and out came a handful of silver- and gold-colored coins, each emblazoned with Damanhur's symbol, an eight-pointed star, and an assortment of mysterious figures. The ritual seemed pointless, even silly.

"If it's a one-to-one exchange," I asked, "what's the point?"

"The *credito* has two purposes," Macao said, clearly accustomed to this question. "Philosophically and spiritually, it is clean money. Because it's not based on violence and greed, we can use it to create a sustainable world. The second purpose is very practical. It allows us to keep the money inside a circuit and so helps to develop our professions and services."

While Damanhurians pay Italian taxes on their transactions in *creditos*, complementary currency frees up euros for outside investment. I was beginning to see how Damanhur was able to revitalize this economically depressed valley in the foothills of the Italian Alps.

The next day, Macaco brought me to the community's primary commercial and cultural center, the Damanhur Crea (Italian for creativity), where some of the material consequences of the credito were on display. The Crea, housed in an old Olivetti factory abandoned during the recession of the early 1980s, is a powerful symbol of Damanhur's economic prowess. Besides a middle school, an art gallery, and a performance hall, the Crea houses the community's organic grocery store and a plethora of high-end shops and services, all cooperatives owned by the community. I found everything from jewelry, textiles, and Tiffany glass shops to a well-appointed beauty spa and a solar energy consultancy. Many of these workshops required expensive materials – precious metals and gems, fine silk and cashmere. This is one of the secrets of Damanhur's prosperity: use skilled labor to transform high-value raw materials into *very* high-value goods.

"In Damanhur, everyone works for the cooperatives, businesses, and associations and gets a salary – the equivalent of €1,000–1,600 per month – and some work outside as well," Macaco said. "From this, we pay all living expenses. We are not so rich individually, but we are very rich collectively."

Damanhurians pay for their own food and lodging, Macaco explained, and they can use *creditos*. Salaries are on a par with the

Italian average, but they go farther because the cooperatives keep internal prices low.

"For instance, when our cooperatives build our homes, they submit bids just like any business," Macaco added. "But since they make money on the outside, they don't have to charge so much inside."

It took quite some time for this concept to sink in: a complementary currency is literally a way of making money out of thin air – or at least out of something as ephemeral as social trust. "In God we trust," US dollars say, but when we use them as a medium of exchange, we are implicitly trusting our economic and political order. Money can be *anything*, so long as it is generally accepted as payment. We use terms like "currency," "liquidity," and "the flow of money" for good reason: money is like a boat that moves goods and services across the waters that separate us. When enough people begin to suspect that the boat is unsound, they create alternatives – as many communities did during the Great Depression. Complementary currencies are nothing new, but their growing popularity seems to indicate a perception of a leaky boat.

With this image in mind, I began to ask how "real" money is created. Most money, I was surprised to learn, is not minted by a government. Rather, it comes into existence through bank loans. It's thin air with interest – or, more accurately, compounded interest, or interest on interest.[10] And there's the rub. An interest-driven economic system *must* grow, and a system driven by compound interest *must* grow *exponentially* – hence the growth imperative. Such a system requires extracting ever more resources to churn out ever more goods for ever more consumers who generate ever more waste. According to this system's logic, the only sensible response to an economic downturn is to stimulate growth, which political leaders all over the world are frantically trying to do as I write this book. In the biophysical realm, however, exponential growth can only be short-lived. A cancer either subsides at some point or else it kills its host; an exploding population of a species either levels off or else it starves. A sustainable economy, it stands to reason, cannot be premised upon a compound interest-driven monetary system. For that reason, complementary currencies like Damanhur's *credito* are trial runs for a new dream of money.

---

[10] For an eye-opening overview of this process, see "Money as Debt," www.youtube.com/watch?v=jqvKjsIxT_8, accessed June 20, 2013.

Figure 4.3 Damanhur's complementary currency, the *credito*, fosters prosperity and community solidarity

## Box 4.3 Toward a Gift Economy

In *The Wealth of Nature*, John Greer enumerates three dimensions of economic life. The primary economy comprises Earth's biophysical processes; the secondary economy conjoins human labor with the primary economy to generate goods and services beyond what raw nature supplies; the tertiary economy constitutes the monetary flows that facilitate the exchange of goods and services.[11] Mainstream economists and the politicians they advise believe that money drives the secondary economy, but the primary economy is actually the irreplaceable basis of all the rest. Environmental economists have made valiant attempts to calculate the monetary value of all of the primary economy. Suffice it to say that the dollar amounts are astronomical: nature turns out to be, literally, a priceless gift.

Indeed, what most of us think of as "the economy" – the secondary and tertiary economies combined – actually rests upon a multilayered gift economy of symbiotic ecological and social relationships. Those relationships run the gamut, from the biotic food web that makes up soil to

---

[11] John Michael Greer, *The Wealth of Nature: Economics as if Survival Mattered*, Gabriola Island, BC: New Society Publishers, 2011.

freeware available on the worldwide web. The modus operandi of a gift economy is "pay it forward." Unlike goods, which can be bought, sold, and possessed, the nature of the gift is that it must be kept in motion.[12] Like a river, the logic of gifts is one of flow and reciprocity, whereas scarcity emerges when wealth is disengaged from the flow and becomes concentrated in pools. Gift economies are marginalized in today's world, but anthropologists consider them to be the fundamental bedrock of human cultures.

Ultimately, my sense is that a truly ecological economy would operate according to the logic of gift flow. What that would mean in concrete terms I cannot say, but I did find some intriguing experiments in this direction among the ecovillages I visited. Sarvodaya, as we know, is premised upon *shramadana*, or the gift of labor. And Auroville hopes to someday have an all-for-one-and-one-for-all nonmonetary economy. While it is very far from this goal, I found some intriguing innovations there. At Indus Valley Restaurant, customers pay whatever they wish for their wholesome vegetarian meals – which means that some pay nothing. After three years, the restaurant is still in business. At Pour Tous ("for all" in French) Distribution Service, Auroville residents pay a modest fee for the right to simply take whatever food and household goods they need. Everybody I interviewed praised the new system.

For those tied to the market economy, which is most of us, a gift economy may sound quite foreign. But if we pay attention, we see that we are the unwitting beneficiaries of a mind-bogglingly complex gift economy provided by Earth's biosphere. As recipients of this gift, the question then becomes "How do we offer our own gifts to sustain the flow of gifts from the primary economy?" This, of course, is far more than an economic question.

## Sufficiency: enough is plenty

In an economy that valorizes limitless growth, contentment is a subversive emotion. Critical reflection upon our true needs, as opposed to what a constant barrage of advertisements tells us we need, seems to require almost an act of heroism. Yet if we can come together with others who share our vision of a different kind of abundance, then we can view this critical reflection not as a moral burden but a reciprocal adventure. This is a vital aspect of what ecovillages are doing.

[12] See Lewis Hyde, *The Gift: Imagination and the Erotic Life of Property*, Vintage Books, 1983; and Karen Litfin, "The Sacred and the Profane: The Politics of Sacrifice in an Ecologically Full World," in J. Meyer and M. Maniates, *The Ecological Politics of Sacrifice*, MIT Press, 2010.

One of my favorite classroom exercises is to ask graduating seniors what salary they would be content with in their first year out of college. Putting aside tuition and books, most of them have been living on less than US$12,000 per year for the past four years and very few have dependents, so I am always intrigued to see the range of responses. Invariably, the answers range from US$10,000 to US$70,000. When we probe a bit, most of them discover that their "needs" are determined far more by social expectations than by physical necessity. "Enough-ness," it turns out, is a culturally mediated phenomenon. There's nothing wrong with this. We are, after all, social creatures. The problem arises when whole societies go about meeting their needs in ways that cannot be sustained – or, worse, even failing to meet their authentic needs while wrecking the planet.

In our economically polarized world, where the average per capita income is roughly US$7,000 but extremes of overconsumption and destitution persist, the down-to-earth prosperity of ecovillages demonstrates the possibility of a happy medium that is globally viable. A few forward-thinking economists have laid out the process for getting there: contraction and convergence. In other words, *downsizing* for the global rich and sustainable *upsizing* for the poor, converging upon a sustainable middle way. Ecovillages are hewing the path toward this goal. At Earthaven in North Carolina, residents live comfortably on US$8,000 per year. At Sieben Linden, in the heart of pricey Germany, members subsist with pleasure on the equivalent of US$12,000. In industrial countries, frugality, I found, can be quite consistent with prosperity.

In developing countries, where most people are only a generation away from village life, the collective dimension of needs is more apparent. In these once self-reliant villages that have endured a recent mass exodus, the need for sustainable upsizing is particularly acute. With few economic opportunities at home, young people in search of work are migrating to the cities, including those of Europe and North America. In some of the African villages I visited, 90 percent of the men were gone. However sustainable these villages may have been in the past, they have been eviscerated by modernization. Small-scale farming, the backbone of traditional rural economies, cannot compete with modern industrialized agriculture. As a consequence, the social structures of countless families and communities are crumbling. The key to revitalizing village life in the global South, therefore, mirrors the ecovillage vision: to link local economies to the wellbeing of people and ecosystems. This is precisely what Colufifa

105

and Sarvodaya are doing through participatory initiatives, ranging from organic farming and aquaculture to microfinance and women's literacy. Here is good economy: prudent "household" management marrying ecological conservation to the satisfaction of basic human needs.

In Sri Lanka, when villagers face a development need that they cannot meet on their own, they often turn to Sarvodaya. Unlike most aid agencies, Sarvodaya works only with villages whose people are committed to a democratic process of discovering their true needs and working together to meet them. Gandhi coined the term *sarvodaya* from Sanskrit, signifying "the welfare of all," to describe a new social order beyond capitalism and communism. The organization's full name, Sarvodaya Shramadana Movement, literally means "a movement for universal wellbeing through the sharing of labor."

Sarvodaya insists that villagers first decide upon a concrete project that will benefit everybody – perhaps creating a road, a school, a well, irrigation canals, public toilets, or a community center. The villagers then hold a *shramadana* camp where they supply the labor and Sarvodaya supplies the materials. When success generates further projects, the village forms a Sarvodaya Shramadana Society with its own bank account. The local society is then eligible for Sarvodaya assistance in microfinance, organic agriculture, conflict resolution, computer literacy, legal services, and women's empowerment. Once a village achieves financial self-sufficiency, it helps other villages to organize their first *shramadana* camps. By working together, the villagers simultaneously build a cooperative spirit and enhance their material wellbeing. As one Sarvodaya activist told me, "We build the road, and the road builds us."

I traveled to Gunambil, a Sarvodaya village in the rugged hill country near Kandy, to see these ideals put into practice. Even though rain is plentiful, remote villages like Gunambil lack clean water because the rain runs off and the government will not plumb such steep terrain. In 1980, Gunambil held its first *shramadana* camp to build a gravity-fed system. Six months later, thanks to the backbreaking work of fifty volunteers, most households were receiving fresh water. Each family pays less than a dollar each month to the caretaker, the Shramadana Society's only employee, who services the system.

The society president, a young carpenter, beamed as he showed me the community's bank. Outside, women were spreading cloves on plastic tarps to dry under the hot sun. "When we came to Sarvodaya, we only wanted water," he said. "But once we had our bank, we built a preschool. Now 180 people have taken loans for housing, school-ing, small businesses, and water tanks." The bank, a tiny concrete hut with a corrugated metal roof, was unlike any financial institution I had ever seen. Two stout middle-aged women, the bank's manager and assistant manager, served us tea and cookies in a space barely larger than their makeshift desk. The bank's ledger hung on the wall, a sprawling yellowed sheet of butcher paper with handwritten rows and columns recording every loan. Most loans, I could see, equated to between US$10 and US$30. Like most microfinance operations, the bank enjoys a nearly 100 percent repayment record.

What do downsizing in European and American ecovillages and upsizing in Africa and Sri Lanka have in common? A sense of suf-ficiency rooted in meeting real human needs with an eye toward long-term viability. Unlike the artificial needs generated by the growth economy, these needs are determined through personal introspection and collective discernment. During my ecovillage travels, I came to believe that the first step in creating real wealth is to inquire into our authentic needs. And because no man is an island, that inquiry is most fruitful when pursued in and supported by a social context.

Why should those of us in the affluent world be concerned about rejuvenating village economies in the developing world? For three good reasons. First, in a global economy and a changing climate, our social context includes distant others. This interconnectedness has practical consequences. As the Bangladesh representative told delegates to the United Nations climate talks, "We'll come with our wet feet to your doorstep." Second, 80 percent of humanity lives in the so-called developing world. For those of us in the affluent world, the point is to live simply so that others can simply live. Third, if *we* don't develop a sense of sufficiency, why should *they*? In the end, the upshot of globalization is that we're all in this together.

## Box 4.4 The Haves and the Have-Nots: Two Approaches

Taken as a whole, per capita incomes in the European and American ecovillages I visited were less than those of their host countries, but where ecovillage homes are sold on the open market, incomes were higher. At EVI, for instance, two-thirds of the residents had postgraduate degrees and the median income was higher than the county average. That's why Elan Shapiro, an educator working with Sustainable Tompkins County, believes that EVI cannot be replicated everywhere.

"I work in minority neighborhoods because these communities are under-served by the sustainability movement," Elan said. "To the extent that ecovillages are refugees from the privileged cultures, they can't really offer a model for the whole world."

Today, EVI prides itself on being a middle-class ecovillage, but this trajectory was not clear early on. EVI's first major crisis came in 1992, soon after the land was purchased. A split developed between those who wanted to create low-income housing and those who wanted to build a model for Middle America. After six painful months of internal debate, the majority opted for the middle-class model. A sizeable, disgruntled minority left. Even fifteen years later, I found disparate interpretations of that turning point. One participant recalled, "We either had to go forward or give up the project completely." Another regretted the outcome. "That's when we decided to ignore the issue of class in America."

The dichotomy between the haves and have-nots is present to some degree in most ecovillages, and sometimes the polarity serves as the basis for a mutually beneficial arrangement. I saw some wonderful examples of this sort of symbiosis during my travels, such as the "unlikely friendship" (as they both called it) between Martha Harris and Brian Love.

Brian, who opens this chapter, built a state-of-the-art eco-home for Martha, a retired attorney. The passive solar house, built almost entirely from Earthaven timber, is a model of efficiency and comfort. Even in the dead of winter, it requires virtually no heat. "Per square foot and over time, this is the cheapest house at Earthaven because it will last for many generations," Martha said. The cost for this beautiful, Earth-friendly home? Close to US$140,000 – expensive for Earthaven but a bargain by market standards.

A young builder working for a retired lawyer sounds like one more example of a two-class society. Yet both Martha and Brian saw the project as an opportunity to forge the kind of positive interdependence that makes a community work.

"Brian's probably my best friend here," Martha said. "Here I am, a middle-aged woman from the privileged class with big dreams about sustainability but very limited in my physical abilities. And here's Brian, who comes along at nineteen with no assets. He had all the skills and excitement to manifest the things I wanted."

Brian said, "Martha's support has given me the staying power I might not otherwise have had in the face of adversity." He's been able to apply what he learned from building Martha's home to his own dream house, and he is also immensely grateful for her investments in his Gateway Farm.

Martha and Brian's unlikely friendship unleashed a cascade of thoughts in my mind. I, too, am a middle-aged professional woman with big ideas and far smaller capacities for manifesting them. Like Martha, I would gladly share my wealth with young people who share my vision and have

108

the skills to implement it. So long as my basic needs were met, I would *enjoy* investing in a sustainable community much more than earning higher dividends. Suddenly the term "socially responsible investment" took on a whole new light.

## Prospering in the circle of life

As I reflected upon the ecovillage experiments I encountered in the global North and South, I saw more deeply into *both* the fault lines in our prevailing economic models *and* the emerging principles of alternative models. In the global economy, consumers and producers are distant from one another, both geographically and psychologically. Anonymity undercuts accountability as unfathomable quantities of matter are propelled on a one-way trip from resource to waste. The name of the game is growth, which entails social and environmental externalities – or, more bluntly, exploitation. This growth-based economy is very good at producing stuff, but not so good at producing viable societies. The metaphor that comes to mind is a cancer that grows uncontrollably until it eventually destroys its host.

In a healthy economy, the goal is the furtherance of life: the creation of real wealth rather than the illusion of wealth. Ecological, economic, and social resources circulate for the maximum time possible, entwining themselves in a symbiotic network of relationships that mirrors the abundance of a mature ecosystem. Indeed, every act of production and consumption contributes to the welfare of both the individual and the larger community. Money literally comes down to earth and serves its rightful purpose of connecting human needs with human gifts.

People might imagine that the hottest issue in community life is sex, but my observations suggest that it's economics. Unresolved tensions around money have unraveled many a community. Even relationship conflicts – say, divorce – quite often play themselves out most contentiously on the economic stage. Consequently, every economic experiment in an ecovillage is simultaneously a social experiment. In general, the deeper and wider the trust, the more successful the experiment.

The key to the trailblazing efforts of ecovillages is that they are *collective*, not solitary, endeavors. If we can enhance our sense of solidarity in our own neighborhoods, many ecovillage success stories can be replicated at home. Wherever you live and whatever your level of affluence, there are two key questions that can guide your efforts. First, what do I need in order to lead a full and productive life? Second, how can I get what I need in ways that deepen my relationships with others? – including unborn and nonhuman others. One of the most important lessons I learned from my ecovillage journey is that, if we take these questions seriously, then prosperity within the circle of life becomes a possibility.

While none of the ecovillages I visited has achieved a fully sustainable economy, each of them offers glimpses into what one would look like. The basic principles are simple and can be applied wherever we might find ourselves:

- Consider your true needs and how you might meet them in ways that feed both belly and soul while benefiting others – including nonhuman and unborn others.
- Find like-minded souls and forge a common vision to invest and circulate money and resources within the community, perhaps through a skills-sharing network.
- Pursue possibilities for sharing property and consumer goods, including existing common spaces in your neighborhood.
- Prioritize local food production and intergenerational synergies.
- Engage in exchange outside the cash economy, including the use of complementary currencies.

Each of these principles ensues from one powerful shift: from narrow economic rationality to a broad-minded relational thinking. When we make that shift, the synergistic possibilities inherent in E2C2 kick in and seemingly disparate pieces fall into place. In creating economies of solidarity, as ecovillages are doing, we are literally reinventing ourselves, our societies, and our future. If the modern story of humanity's separation from nature is at the end of its tether, then so too is its corollary in the realm of economics. The new story will be written with our lives as we transition from living as separate, acquisitive individuals into recognizing ourselves as vibrant nodes in a vast web of human and ecological relationships.

# — 5 —

# COMMUNITY: RELATING IN THE CIRCLE OF LIFE

What would you guess an affluent family of five – six, counting the dog – would miss the most in moving from a 3,000-sq.-ft. ocean-view house in Northern California to a 1,260-sq.-ft. garden-view house in Upstate New York? The sun? The sea? The living space? You'd be wrong. What Jeff Gilmore and Kirsten Nygren most missed in their recent move, they said, were their friends.

And what did they gain? You have to understand that they made this move on a totally voluntary basis, deciding they would leave their home and their well-paid jobs – he as a computer engineer in the tech industry, she as a psychiatrist – so that they could live an ecologically sustainable lifestyle at EVI. Unlike most affluent suburbanites, even before the move they had already greened their lives substantially. They had solar panels on their house and organic, locally grown food on their table. But, still, they felt powerless to halt the steady accumulation of "stuff" in their lives, Jeff made a daily commute of fifty miles, and they were disturbed by the tension between their own yearning for sustainability and the culture of affluence in which they were raising their children – a culture in which, as a norm, parents would lay out US$500 for a child's birthday party.

"We had educated ourselves on climate change, world energy supplies, and the deteriorating basis of civilization," Jeff said. "We would have been more complacent if it wasn't for our sense of urgency and the kids. But even with all we knew, it was still an agonizing decision. We talked about it for hundreds of hours."

The deciding factor was what would be best for the children. "The main thing was that we wanted to put our kids in the best possible place to learn the skills they'll need to live in the world – skills that involve working with their hands, living close to the Earth, and

111

getting along with people. We both felt the hypocrisy of our wealthy liberal lifestyle. Already we can feel, as difficult as it was, that it was the right decision."

Asked what experiences affirm their decision, green living did not top Jeff's list. Rather, he cited the high quality of social interaction. "The most important thing," he said, "is that people here are willing to talk honestly and look for the best solution for everybody – not just themselves. We've been in several hot meetings, and we're always impressed by people's ability to find the best solution. It's self-reinforcing: when people set the tone for honest communication, there's less need to be self-protective, so trust grows."

So, in moving to an ecovillage, they most missed old friends and their greatest gain was a sense of community. "Human beings are hard-wired for community," Kristen said. "In California, we talked a lot about how our isolated lives were part of the problem: driving, overconsumption, working for a big multinational corporation. Community was the next step for us."

Jeff outlined EVI's basic protocol for dealing with conflict, a commonsensical approach mirrored in most ecovillages. First, go to the person directly in order to avoid gossip. Second, call on the mediator list. If that fails, bring the dispute to the steering committee. He added that everyone in EVI is trained in facilitation (to be able to run meetings and group discussions) and in Nonviolent Communication (to avoid getting into conflicts). "Ecological goals are important, but the real gift an ecovillage offers is to show the world how people can live together."

Jeff said that his engineering training has helped him understand the frailty of systems on which our modern lives are based. "It feels like we're headed en masse for a cliff. In light of that, I have two responsibilities: to help create a viable alternative and to keep my family safe." He added that living in EVI addresses both of these goals and, as well, puts him and his family ahead of the curve. "When the Roman Empire collapsed, it broke into little villages."

Kristen interjected that they are not survivalists, not "me first at any price." "There is both ethical and strategic merit in community," she said, adding that, since she is a psychiatrist with a background in anthropology, "my main interest in this is human happiness. I believe that people evolve better in places that look more like ecovillages than they do in suburbia."

I did feel royally welcomed to their home at EVI. Kristen greeted me at the door, and I was put so at ease by her warmth that, only minutes after my arrival, I admitted I was facing a wardrobe problem.

I was scheduled to speak on global atmospheric politics at Cornell a few days hence, and I'd packed only jeans and hiking boots. "Visit the recycle room in our Common House," Kristen said with an easy smile. "You'll find something to wear." She was right; I did. I gave my lecture wearing a green tailored blouse, linen pants, and a pair of black dress shoes that fit just fine for one afternoon. And there it was – yet another reason for living in community: the astonishing support that's available from those who share what they have with others.

Joining a community is, however, still a huge act of faith and, as Jeff admitted, it's a little scary at times. "My job ends this month," he said, "and I feel some anxiety about having no salary. Stepping out of the rat race may be a powerful act, but I don't yet know what will be accomplished by it." In 2012, Jeff was a stay-at-home dad. "It has worked well for us," he told me. "I've enjoyed learning about gardening, canning, pickling, cooking, etc., and Kristen, who's a very good psychiatrist, earns enough to meet our needs. I do miss the high-tech intensity of my old career, but I have replaced some of that by tackling complex projects here, like running the network and implementing solar projects. On the downside, I never get paid for any of this, and that feels less OK as time goes on."

How many unsung heroes, I wonder, have stepped out of the rat race in an attempt to create an authentic life for themselves and their families? During my interviews with roughly 150 ecovillagers around the world, one of the questions I always asked is "What do you experience as the *most challenging* aspect of community life?" The most common answer was some version of "the people." When I inquired about the *most rewarding* aspect, these same ecovillagers often chuckled as they gave their answer: "The people."

Successful community living requires enormous skill – the kind that often comes only through the school of hard knocks. As author and longtime Earthaven resident Diana Leafe-Christian says, "Community living is the longest, most expensive personal growth workshop you'll ever take." Virtually everybody I spoke with agreed that this full-immersion workshop was well worth the price.

When I set out on my ecovillage journey, as curious as I was about things like passive solar design and rainwater catchment, I was far more interested in how ecovillagers manage to live together. Intellectually, I had long before come to Benjamin Franklin's conclusion: "We must hang together or we shall most assuredly hang separately." Personally, however, I was painfully aware of the challenges of hanging together. I wanted to learn how ecovillagers accomplish all the aspects of a community: how they share a vision, agree to self-governance, resolve conflict, work with each other (and with the outside world), raise their children, engage in cultural expression, and take part in each others' joys and sorrows. This chapter takes up each of these dimensions of ecovillage life with the aim of teasing out some basic principles and skills to help people anywhere weave that all-important web of human ties that constitutes the heart of community.

## Sharing a vision

While every ecovillage shares a commitment to sustainability, the wider vision that informs this commitment and what it means in practice vary wildly. In Auroville, for instance, sustainability is not an end in itself; rather, it stems from the township's overarching spiritual objective of realizing human unity. Auroville's lofty aim would have little or no meaning in the both-feet-on-the-ground culture of Svanholm. And the pioneering methods of Sieben Linden and Earthaven look very different from the middle-class lifestyle of EcoVillage at Ithaca and village life in Sarvodaya and Colufifa. When the going gets rough, as it inevitably does, clarity of intention can help a community put aside factionalism and personality conflicts in service to a larger vision.

A community's core purpose can change over time, as it did for LAEV even before it got off the ground. Lois Arkin, the 72-year-old founder, recalled how the 1992 Los Angeles riots were a pivotal event in that community's inception. That year, she and several others were in the process of purchasing from the city an 11-acre parcel on a former landfill. "We had a great architect and I have a big mouth, so we got lots of publicity," she recalled. Their intention was to serve as a model of sustainable living and farming on the city's outskirts – and then came the wave of violence that swept Los Angeles in reaction to a police brutality case involving a young black man named Rodney King.

"Several of us were living near here," Lois said. "We had fires all around us for three days. The whole time I sat at my computer and wrote up a plan for an inner-city retrofitted neighborhood that would be a demonstration for how to live so this would never happen again. Until that moment, I had never committed to my own neighborhood."

After the riots and a subsequent earthquake, LA real-estate prices plummeted, enabling the nascent ecovillage to purchase two apartment buildings at the bottom of the market. "They were slums," Lois said, "which made them the perfect place to start an ecovillage based on diversity." Fifteen years later, LAEV was the most ethnically diverse ecovillage I visited.

When a community combines green living, which until recently was avant-garde, with an unconventional social or spiritual intention, it runs the risk of being ostracized. As a consequence of their mystical beliefs, both Findhorn and Damanhur were, in their early years, accused by conservative neighbors of being cults. By the time I visited, both of these ecovillages had become respectable sustainability demonstration sites, though Damanhur still has detractors.[1]

I found nothing I would call a cult among the ecovillages I visited. What I mean by "cult" is that, in addition to an enclave holding views that are divergent from the norm, the leadership exercises an element of psychological coercion over other members. Yet for some, a cult is simply a group with unorthodox practices and beliefs. Of the core intentions I encountered in ecovillages, ZEGG's "quest for new forms of love and sexuality" was, for me, the most unsettling. Before my visit, I could not grasp why a community that hopes to be, as its own literature claims, "an international meeting and research center, creating models for a socially and ecologically sustainable life" would throw itself into the muck of free love. Upon closer inspection, I found that there is, not surprisingly, a grand theory informing ZEGG's heterodoxy. Dieter Duhm, the sociologist who founded the community that eventually became ZEGG, posits that the primary cause of violence, including ecological destruction, is the patriarchal suppression of sexuality. This, he claims, manifests most strongly through the institution of monogamy. I didn't meet Duhm on my visit to ZEGG; he had long since left Germany to start Tamera, a more radical polyamorous ecovillage in Portugal.

I took my questions about the connection between ecology and polyamory to Achim Ecker, ZEGG's chief resident ecologist. "The obvious link," he said, "is that when people can't live their full potential, they do violent things," he said. "Underneath, violence comes from a lack of honesty about love and sex. For me, 'sexuality' means something very broad. It's about the life energy that flows through everything." Several of the older ZEGG members I interviewed echoed Achim's expansive reading of sexuality as sensuality, but I

---

[1] Through online research, I was aware of the accusation before my visit and even attempted to interview disgruntled former members. The only evidence I found for the accusation were some highly eccentric beliefs and a charismatic leader. I found, however, no coercion.

could see that unfettered sexual expression continued to command the attention of many members.

While everybody I interviewed expressed great admiration for Dieter Duhm, I harbor some doubts about the years when, as one member put it, "he ruled as a benevolent dictator." Though I never met the disaffected academic, I detect a penchant for grandiosity both in his book, *The Sacred Matrix*,[2] and his legacy at ZEGG. I asked one member, for instance, about the cement amphitheatre, which struck me as an ecological boondoggle, at the top of ZEGG's land. Without any apparent sense of irony, he recounted, "Dieter Duhm said this would put us on the map as a real university." So while I cannot draw any conclusions about ZEGG's early years, I did note that ZEGG was the only ecovillage I visited where not one of the children raised there has returned to live. And were it not for the dedication of a few members, ZEGG's ecological achievements would hardly be worth mentioning. What most impressed me was ZEGG's open, trusting, and cohesive culture. And because ZEGG, unlike most ecovillages, shares most meals, I enjoyed three fascinating conversations each day of my visit.

Sustainability is itself a multifaceted objective and most ecovillages pursue this shared goal in a multiplicity of ways, so tensions are inevitable. Consider the potential conflicts between serving as a demonstration site and raising children or between farming and forest preservation. The most successful ecovillages are the ones where the tensions implicit in a complex mission are openly acknowledged and harnessed in the service of a larger vision. Earthaven, as we explore in the next section, faced a crisis when competing perspectives on sustainability threatened to unravel its decision-making process.

## Deciding together

Most ecovillages in affluent countries operate by consensus, making them as much experiments in participatory democracy as they are in green living. As a political scientist, I found myself perplexed at why people from the most individualistic countries would bind themselves to a potentially time-consuming group process. I also wondered whether there was any relationship between consensus governance and ecology. I came to see that, when it works well, consensus decision-making expresses a deeper individualism than is possible

[2] Dieter Duhm, *The Sacred Matrix*, Belzig, Germany: Verlag Meiga, 2008.

in one-person-one-vote representative democracies. The basic logic is that when minority views, rather than being overruled by the majority, are incorporated into better proposals, better decisions will emerge. And when each individual can block any decision, the level of personal responsibility is very high. As I watched the give-and-take in ecovillage meetings, I also came to see that consensus decision-making can mirror how healthy ecosystems operate. In both cases, each individual offers a unique and essential contribution to the collective intelligence of the whole.

Whatever their resemblance to the village economic model, though, ecovillages are clearly *not* resurrecting the village model of politics. Consensus governance bears little resemblance to the patriarchal models that typify premodern village life. Historically, representative democracy took root in the modern nation-state, which itself emerged from a long process of urbanization and the breakdown of village societies. Whether modern democracies will rise to the challenges of global interdependence remains an open question. In the meantime, ecovillages in the global North are experimenting with small-scale postmodern models of governance, including consensus.

Consensus does not mean that everybody agrees on everything; it only means that people must be sufficiently satisfied not to block decisions. A legitimate block must be about principle, not personal preference. How often should a person block? Most trainers believe an appropriate number over the course of a person's lifetime would be three to six blocks – and, as one consensus trainer quipped, "then only after a sleepless night and a shedding of tears." When it works well, as it did in most of the ecovillages I visited, consensus yields high-quality decisions and stronger relationships. When it doesn't, welcome to the flipside of democracy: tyranny of the minority.

In 2006, Earthaven had sixty residents and was running twenty workshops a year. On my visit three years later, membership was down to about forty and overnight workshops had been discontinued. Back in 2006, the North Carolina State Health Department tested Earthaven's spring-fed water system and, despite finding no serious pathogens, closed the ecovillage down to overnight guests and required Earthaven to install a well for future guests. All the associated jobs – teaching, cooking, lodging, promotion – evaporated. For an economy dependent upon outside visitors and hoping to grow itself to a membership of 300, this was a major blow.

At the epicenter of the ensuing conflict was Patricia Allison, a permaculture instructor and owner of Earthaven's primary guesthouse.

By the time I got there, Patricia had moved away from Earthaven after being asked to refrain from speaking in the council until she could be "more collaborative." She spoke to me by phone about the conflict, which she described as "devastating and heartbreaking."

"You bet I used inflammatory language!" Patricia said. "These people were not willing to just take what our Mother gave us from the sky. They wanted to dig into her tissues to get it. So I used the word 'rape.'" I might not agree with Patricia, but her objection sounded like a principled block to me. Or was it?

Chris Farmer, whom we met at Gateway Farm in chapter 3, was on the other side of this issue. In the drought conditions at the time, he felt that a backup well would keep creeks flowing and ensure the survival of aquatic life. Since there is scientific dissent over the sustainability of wells, Farmer believed that neither perspective qualifies as a principled block. The bigger issue, therefore, was the nature of a principled block. His response to Patricia was "Why are you not amending the proposal before it comes to council? Why are you being so adversarial?"

By the time I came in 2009, a committee had been working for two years on "The Consensus Document." The gist of the twelve-page document was that a proposal can only be blocked if it can be shown to violate Earthaven's mission or if it represents "a grave, catastrophic endangerment to the community." According to the document, a block is unprincipled if it relates to a member's *personal* values. A personal conviction that wells are a form of rape would not be the basis for a principled block.

When I spoke with him, Farmer was hoping that Earthaven would adopt a "pressure relief valve," some way of resorting to a supermajority vote, say 75 percent. "Consensus is going to die hard here," he predicted. "We're a very idealistic community. That's the number one thing I'd say to anyone starting an ecovillage: name your ideals, then step back and be real. Because sometimes, to get to your ideals, you need to *not* be a purist. If you grasp your ideals too hard, they'll slip right through your fingers."

During the turmoil of 2006, Patricia Allison and Kimchi Rylander composed what came to be known as "The Threats Document." Despairing over the "unraveling of the community's social fabric," they listed their grievances and demanded action. If they were not satisfied, they threatened to block *all* community decisions. The responses and counterresponses erupted into what some referred to as "our civil war." Even two years later, some relationships had not been restored beyond civility.

Kimchi, a 49-year-old bookkeeper and artist, recalled the anguish that led her to co-author the controversial document. She had lost her livelihood with the collapse of the workshop economy and several people she loved had left as a consequence of this conflict and others. "After 'The Threats Document,' my social bank account went to zero," she recalled. "The reactions to the document were just as heart-wrenching as the document itself. We were hurting each other, and we were desperate for another way of relating."

So Kimchi and seven other residents started a practice group on Nonviolent Communication (discussed in the next section) with representatives from all sides of the conflict. When I arrived, the group had been meeting for over a year. A big part of their work was rereading "The Threats Document" and the ensuing controversy in light of NVC. They were even planning a theatrical performance for the full community based on their shared work.

"Because of all this, we'll never have somebody threaten to block like this again," Kimchi said. "We're going to make sure we can trust our consensus process. We're fine-tuning it and really defining what it means to have a principled block. What a gift 'The Threats Document' turned out to be! I made a big mistake, but I was doing the best I could. I felt like I lost everything, but I really didn't. Tincture of time is an incredible healer." Tincture of time, I thought, plus an earnest desire to collectively learn from mistakes.

In her book on community life, *Creating a Life Together*, Diana Leafe-Christian writes about structural conflict, the built-in tensions associated with how a community defines itself. As an Earthaven member, Diana was surely speaking from firsthand experience. Like many ecovillages, Earthaven has a twofold mission: to live sustainably and to serve as an educational center. People who are building homes, growing food, or raising children will likely have very different concerns from those running classes. Beyond that, because Earthaven was established on 320 acres of jointly owned forest, every decision to build or farm requires the consent of several dozen diehard environmentalists to kill trees. Essentially, this contingent has tied a dynamic, proactive vision to a conservative, time-consuming governance process.

Another social distinction Diana describes is the contrast between *strategic* and *relational* people. Strategic people are goal-oriented and focused, energetic, and often blunt in their manner. Relational people are process-oriented; for them, the strategic movers and shakers are like bulls in a china shop. To strategic thinkers, relational people are self-indulgent wimps. True, relational people can be effective and

119

strategic people sensitive, but I think the distinction holds. Ecovillages attract two kinds of people: those who feel a sense of urgency to build another world and those who crave a deep sense of community. In other words, ecovillages are magnets for the extremes of the strategic/relational spectrum, and communities furthest from the mainstream (like Earthaven) tend to attract the greatest extremes. Stir in consensus governance and you have a recipe for disaster or – as Earthaven experienced in the aftermath of its civil war – an incredible personal growth workshop.

Striking a happy balance between efficacy and sensitivity doesn't happen overnight. Nearly every community I visited had undergone years of training in consensus, meeting facilitation, and relationship building. Far from being tedious exercises in interminable debate, most of the community meetings I attended were surprisingly enjoyable. Generally, in their comments people were succinct yet friendly; they took obvious pleasure in being together. As communities mature and trust grows, they tend to decentralize decision-making, which makes for shorter general meetings and more specialized subgroups.

Not all ecovillages operate by consensus. Some, like Damanhur with its elected "king guides" – one male and one female – are plainly too large. For others, like the traditional patriarchal villages working with Sarvodaya and Colufifa, gender equality and simple majority rule are already enormous concessions to democratic self-governance. And a few that once used consensus are experimenting with variants like super-majority voting (where a prescribed majority is needed for action) and sociocracy (a decentralized form of governance with feedback loops within and among a community's subgroups).[3]

Whenever we come together with others to accomplish something, we must decide how we will decide. Whether or not we make our decisions by consensus or another method, we will face certain basic questions. How do we transform division into symbiosis? How can strategic and relational people join forces? How do we, like Kimchi and her friends who are reworking "The Threats Document," use crisis and conflict to deepen our insight and compassion? How do we cultivate the kind of leadership that empowers others? How do we temper our idealism with pragmatism without compromising our

---

[3] Rooted in complexity theory, sociocracy views social organizations as analogous to ecosystems: self-organizing and self-correcting through feedback loops. See John Buck and Sharon Villines, *We the People: Consenting to a Deeper Democracy*, Sociocracy.info, 2007.

larger vision? Here are a few basic principles of self-governance that I gleaned from the ecovillages I visited.

- Cultivate group mind without sacrificing individuality. Decisions might take longer, but they'll be better decisions because they'll have been reshaped in light of many ideas.
- Practice decentralized forms of leadership as trust and competence allow.
- Be aware of structural conflicts and minimize their negative effects.
- Balance efficiency and sensitivity. A short check-in at the beginning of a meeting to see how people are doing, for instance, can deepen relationships and make meetings go more smoothly.
- Most of all, keep learning.

## Becoming free together

From strategic planning to the casual dinner conversation, communication is the lifeblood of community. Ecovillages are hotbeds of learning in this department – particularly in individualistic cultures where personality differences are not so tempered by customs and established roles. In contrast to the mainstream, where many of us don't even know our neighbors, community problems are not easily swept under the rug. Small complaints, like how he doesn't put his dishes away or how she uses the clothes dryer even in July, can fester and grow into thinly disguised hostility. Ecological values might bring people together initially but, as we saw at Earthaven, ideas about green living are themselves potential fodder for conflict.

Some ecovillages have developed their own unique communication practices. For instance, much like a traditional family, Konohana Family discusses the day's events each evening after dinner. When a tough issue comes up, the conversation might last for hours. In the meetings I attended, Isadon, the community's founder, presided as a judicious patriarch, offering his perspective without seizing the limelight. The members seemed fully engaged; one-on-one, they praised these tell-all sessions. I, however, after the first hour found them unendurably tedious.

A few ecovillages have devised communication techniques and exported them. ZEGG invented its Forum in response to the inevitable emotional intensity entailed in its no-holds-barred approach to sexuality. The ZEGG Forum is a fusion of group therapy,

121

improvisational theater, and collective meditation in which people gather in a circle with one or more of them at the center with their "hot issue." A trained facilitator guides that person through a dramatization of their issue. The aim is to evoke the underlying emotional dynamics while fostering a greater sense of clarity and compassion in both participants and observers. When conflict arises, each person is encouraged to take responsibility for their own part in it. The Forum worked so well at ZEGG and its Portuguese sister ecovillage, Tamera, that it is now used in hundreds of communities to address all sorts of hot issues – not just sexuality. Every European ecovillage I visited had incorporated the Forum into its communication toolkit, and the practice is spreading to the United States and Latin America.

Damanhur has developed a range of communication skills as part of its commitment to "personal refinement." The community believes that eventually, when each member lives by his own "individual law," external rules will be obsolete. Falco, Damanhur's founder, describes the goal: "We need to create a superconductive system where there is no resistance to the energy that circulates between people."[4] Members of the College of Justice, the community's internal court and mediation system, help Damanhur citizens discover their individual law through a set of practices known as Technakarto.

Technakarto cannot be exported wholesale to other ecovillages because it is thoroughly embedded in Damanhur's idiosyncratic culture. Still, some practices might work for a group that has already developed a degree of trust. Imagine asking fifteen people who know you well and whom you respect to tell you what they appreciate and what bothers them – about you! Their perceptions, of course, would be filtered through their own psychological makeup, but, if a number of them agreed on something, then you might want to take it seriously. Imagine delving into your findings with a group of wise elders with the aim of refining your personality. And now imagine hundreds of people adopting this practice. This is a window into Technakarto as it works in Damanhur's culture.

Macaco Tamerice, one of Damanhur's international liaisons, described how this practice worked for her. "The point is," she said "to see what you can't otherwise see. We are all mirrors for each other. For instance, people didn't like me playing with my hair. It bothered everyone. I looked into this with the people from Technakarto and

---

[4] Jeff Merrifield, *Damanhur: The Story of the Extraordinary Artistic and Spiritual Community*, Santa Cruz, CA: Hanford Mead Publishers, 2006, p. 121.

saw that it came from a basic insecurity. So I worked on it. When I understood its cause, the habit disappeared."

I found myself wondering: Do I know fifteen people I could trust this much? Yes. Would I have the courage to ask them for a critique of my personality? Perhaps – particularly if I belonged to a community and this was a part of it. It could even be fun, as it seems to be at Damanhur.

In most of the ecovillages I visited, the social skill set of choice is nonviolent communication.[5] NVC is a compassionate approach to communication devised by psychologist Marshall B. Rosenberg. It has been applied in many contexts, from corporate boardrooms to war-torn countries, and it seems ideally suited to intentional communities. The gist of NVC is to foster empathy, both for others and oneself, by speaking to the underlying needs and feelings of all parties. When the life-alienating language of shame and blame gives way to the life-enhancing language of honesty and compassion, conflict becomes the gateway to a deeper sense of connection. It's an impressive practice, but it's not a silver bullet. The basic formula is: "When I observe X, I feel Y because I need Z. So I'm asking you to do Q." While leaning on this formula might be better than "You're an idiot for doing X and I demand that you do Q," it's unlikely to work if it's applied formulaically. Rather, it's the spirit of nonviolent communication that ecovillages seek to cultivate.

At LAEV, which had been studying NVC for several years prior to my visit, that spirit was taking hold. Several members told me how the practice was enhancing their relationships. Yuki Kidokoro, a Japanese-American environmental activist in her thirties, described how NVC was helping the ecovillage to "create a space which allows for and embraces different personalities." She offered a story as illustration.

"There is an individual here who is an alpha male. He barks a lot. His job seems to be pushing everybody's buttons. It was a big problem in the past. Recently, he was very rude to a guest speaker – definitely not respectful communication! A community member confronted him afterward, and they got to the point where they were on the verge of a physical fight. We were all terrified. They were literally in each other's faces, and the other guy just kissed him. Everyone burst out laughing, and the alpha male grabbed this guy and hugged him and said, 'That's why I love you, man!' This is an indication of how far we've come."

---

[5] See Marshall B. Rosenberg, *Nonviolent Communication: A Language of Life*, 2nd edn, Puddledancer Press, 2003.

Again and again, it was apparent that play and work can be wonderful partners. The UfaFabrik Circus, with its penchant for political satire, is a case in point: its spinoff, the circus school, is a thriving business whose mission is to help people have fun. Likewise, at Findhorn, Jonathan Dawson described how the community helped him to break the dichotomy between work and play. He arrived at Findhorn feeling burned out from years of development work in Africa. "I was so badly in the need of play," Jonathan said, "that I spent a lot of time dressing in drag my first year. The woman I eventually married thought at first that I was gay! I've worked harder than ever these past few years, but I feel happy and balanced."

When it comes to turning ecovillage play into serious business, Damanhur takes the cake. Each citizen engages in prolonged introspection before assuming an animal name and a plant name that express his or her connection to the natural world. Whatever the spiritual benefits, the outward result of this exercise is hundreds of people with some of the silliest names you'll ever find – like Rattlesnake Sesame, Locust Licorice, and a large scholarly man named Anaconda Papaya. Community buildings are painted with enormous insects and plants, which makes for a festive atmosphere while conveying a larger point about humanity's place in nature. And Damanhur is bursting with practical jokes. During my visit, the gatekeeper rewired the central gate and posted the instruction to open it by saying, "Open sesame." When drivers uttered these words into the microphone, he would open the gate remotely from his office. People thought their own words – that magic incantation from the story of Aladdin and his lamp – were the power opening the gate until later that day, when the gatekeeper revealed that the secret power was mechanical, and everybody could have a good laugh.

Damanhur's focus on play follows from its convictions about the role of play and promoting creative change. Here is a sampling from the book containing the Damanhur Constitution:

> In nature, children (like young animals) play to experiment with themselves and the world around them, to learn and find new models in a safe way. . . . Joy and imagination are the most powerful allies of play. They make it possible to break the rigid patterns of the mind that often confine us and make us believe that situations are unchangeable.[6]

Damanhur has institutionalized the habit-breaking power of play under the rubric of "The Game of Life." These "games" have

---

[6] Damanhur, *Constituzione della Federazione di Damanhur* (with English translation), 1999, pp. 178–9.

included months of adventurous travel, survival exercises in the forest, and "battles" between different factions of the community.

Capra Carruba (in English, Goat Carob), a German Damanhur resident in her thirties, described her first battle as a "huge learning experience." The rebellious younger members were pitted against the older residents, who felt that these headstrong novices should learn from their elders. The goal was to capture the other side's flag. Everyone wore white T-shirts and had squirt guns filled with red paint. Anyone judged by the referees to have more than two-thirds of their shirt red was out of the game. The battle, originally slated for three days, ended on day two.

"We were the Milk Drinkers (or the babies) and they were the Seniles. These things sound funny now but they were dead serious then. We were trying to prove ourselves, to put our best into the game and see what we were made of. It was very hard for me to see who I really was, who *we* really were."

Even before the battle commenced, the Milk Drinkers felt besieged. Each side was required to supply the referees with a list of everything they brought into the game. The first embarrassment came when Capra's team neglected to declare their underwear and had to publicly hand it over. Years after the fact, Capra recalled these events with a pained expression. "We were terribly unprepared. It was winter and raining, and we were freezing under thin plastic tarps, with no hot food! The other side had great food, warm fires, even a tractor! They offered to help us, but we (especially the younger men) had too much pride to accept their offer."

In the end, a lot of tension was released and the younger members had more respect for the older ones. "And everyone had some great stories to tell!" Capra added, managing to smile.

From NVC to Technakarto, I found a smorgasbord of novel communication techniques in ecovillages – everywhere, that is, except in the rural villages of Africa and Sri Lanka. The villages of Colufifa and Sarvodaya were democratizing by encouraging participation by women and youth, but consensus was nowhere to be seen. Why the difference? I cannot say for sure, but perhaps the communication and governance techniques that emerge from highly individualistic cultures are neither necessary nor appropriate in premodern villages facing the onslaught of modernization.

An exchange with Bandula Senadeera, the amiable young agronomist serving as Sarvodaya's international liaison, offers a glimpse into the cultural differences between these traditional villages and postmodern ecovillages. On one of our excursions to the Sri Lankan countryside, Bandula mentioned having lived at the Nature-Spirit Community in South Carolina, where he taught rice farming. Having heard of this fleeting experiment, I wondered why it fell apart.

Bandula shook his head. "Even minor things became major issues. If someone didn't wash the plates properly, we had long meetings. In Sri Lanka, our elders wouldn't allow this. They would intervene. Sometimes I wished that Dr Ari [Sarvodaya's founder] could help Nature-Spirit. Their dream failed in less than a year. It was very sad."

What did Bandula find most surprising in his eight months at Nature-Spirit?

"They had complete equality between men and women. I had never seen this! Here the men just eat; we never cook and clean! And here it is very rare for a woman to drive. If a family buys a car, they also hire a driver. In the US, many women drive."

Staring into the distance, he continued, "I learned about different cultures. In Sri Lanka, we never ask for anything directly. In the USA, you are so frank. We are always concerned about hurting the other person. We come to the point through a meandering road; you take a straight road."

"It sounds like Nature-Spirit could have benefited from the curvier road," I observed, and we both laughed. How much simpler life would be, I thought, if age carried automatic authority, if gender roles were clear and distinct, and if people were trained to be more concerned with others than themselves. But would I trade my life for such an existence? Not in a heartbeat! For better or worse, I am a product of an individualistic culture. Yet I was fascinated by the smorgasbord of communication techniques I found in ecovillages.

If I could distill the basic principle behind these practices, it would be something like: take personal responsibility for your thoughts, feelings, and actions, and then express yourself with honesty and care. Throw in a splash of humor and an enduring passion for experimentation, and you're likely to learn a lot and enjoy the journey. It is one thing, though, to make a personal commitment to this way of communicating, and an entirely different thing to live alongside dozens or even hundreds of others who share your commitment. When an entire community dedicates itself to effective communication, the result is powerful and appealing.

## Box 5.1 Architectures of Intimacy

The built environments of ecovillages are not just about saving energy and water. They are about people. Common houses, courtyards, pedestrian walkways, off-leash pet areas, and small alcoves in doorways: all of these are natural gathering places. I recall a wonderful conversation I had in a hand-sculpted window box at Sieben Linden: the soft cob edges seemed to soften the edges of discussion. Each time I left an ecovillage and found myself in the sterile anonymity of an airport, train station or hotel, I felt jolted into a visceral awareness of how much physical structures influence social interaction.

One thing I rarely saw in an ecovillage was a fenced yard designed to keep neighbors out or children and pets in. In contrast to the dissecting lines of cities and suburbs, ecovillage landscapes have a sense of fluidity. Children run freely from house to house across one giant "backyard." The primary exception was an oversized fence at LAEV, a consequence of several incidents of vandalism. The metal fence, constructed from brightly painted bicycle parts, was actually a work of art. Every time I walked by, I lingered to admire the intricacies of this multipurpose fence, sculpture, and bicycling ad.

When it comes to ecovillage gatherings, the most ubiquitous physical structure is the human circle. A circle, that magical shape that enables everybody to see everybody else, lends itself to open sharing and an egalitarian disposition. Everywhere I went I found myself sitting, dancing, singing, and playing in circles.

Most of life, however, happens not in public spaces but in the privacy of our homes. In individualistic cultures, communities that do not respect people's needs for privacy generally don't last – hence the failure of most communes of the 1960s and 1970s. This need for a balance between privacy and sharing is the rationale for the co-housing model: people share common spaces but live in private homes. Even at the Danish commune, Svanholm, every adult and child has their own room.

With so many common spaces, do ecovillagers ever crave privacy? The short answer is yes. At EcoVillage at Ithaca, a retired airline pilot admitted, "All my life, I was frustrated with the lack of relationships with my neighbors. Now I'm frustrated with the intensity of relationships with my neighbors!" He was only half joking.

Co-housing communities have a slang term for the spontaneous interactions that come with living in close proximity: *ratcheting*. Another EVI resident addressed this issue head-on. "Sometimes you just want to walk from your car to your house without having to greet everyone along the way," she said. "If that's what you want, you can just say so. We place a high value on honesty here." When spaces are designed to facilitate human interaction, good communication skills are crucial for striking the right balance between contact and solitude.

## Working together

A primary bonding experiences is the simple act of working together. When we spread compost, chop vegetables, and lay bricks, we get our bodies into the action. And when we join together with like-minded souls to realize our ideals, the earthy pragmatism and nonverbal communication entailed in shared work can help us overcome discord, whether it's personality- or ideology-based. Meaningful work can also be profoundly healing. In every ecovillage I visited, this sense of collective delight in work well done was almost palpable. Yet I never had the sense that anyone wanted to rest on their laurels. On the contrary: ecovillages are, by definition, places of work.

Findhorn, which began in the 1960s by growing vegetables on the advice of nature spirits, now prides itself on "growing people." I expected it to be a hippie haven, and, while I found a smattering of this, Findhorn turned out to be one of most well organized workplaces I've ever encountered. Every Findhorn project – the farm, the kitchens, the college, and so on – has a team leader called a focalizer, someone who knows that project inside out and who functions almost in the capacity of midwife. Through attention and application, while healing rifts and applying pressure where it is needed the focalizer brings a project into being. Part of Findhorn's genius is that a good chunk of its work is done not just by volunteers but by people who enroll in its personal development and green-living workshops. I myself paid for the privilege to work on the Findhorn's 7-acre farm, Cullerne Gardens, as part of a full-immersion course called Experience Week. That work I paid to do turned out to be a highlight of my journey. At Findhorn work is considered to be love in action, and that was what I experienced in it: love in action.

Perhaps because Peter Caddy, one of the founders, is a former military man, every Findhorn activity, from meditations to meals, begins precisely on time. Work is no exception. Each morning at 9.00 on the dot, I found myself in an "attunement circle" with about ten people, half of them guests, half residents. Dürten Lau, the middle-aged German woman serving as the farm's focalizer, would explain what was to be done that day, and those of us who had gathered would "attune" to our specific task. For each person, the point was not to choose what we *wanted* to do but rather what we felt *called* to do. Somehow there was always the right number of bodies on each task. Whenever possible, we were encouraged to work in silence and to feel ourselves working together as one body. My senses alive to the sights, sounds, and scents and the rising heat of the day, I found

128

myself reveling in the companionship of my wordless co-workers as we harvested beans and tomatoes and shoveled compost. We worked like this for three hours each day, with the obligatory British tea break at precisely 10.30. Each day, I was astonished to see how much we accomplished, even with a tea break. I don't know whether it was many hands making light work or the focus.

I am always curious about women who do manly things like driving tractors so, on one of those tea breaks, I asked Dürten how she came to focalize the Findhorn gardens. She said that when the position first opened up, she had no interest in it. She had never farmed, even though as a child she had lived on a farm in East Germany. "My father's family farmed the same land for 300 years," Dürten said. "When he had to move us from the land for political reasons, it was a huge grief to him. It became a family scar."

Just before the attunement circle for the decision, a friend encouraged Dürten to step forward. "Even though he knew nothing of my family," she said, "he told me, 'You can do it. It's in your blood!' His words hit me hard, and at that moment I knew that this work was for me. It was for my own and my family's healing."

And that's just what happened. Dürten said that for many years it felt as if she and her mother were in different worlds. "Now we can talk about growing flowers and vegetables." She added, "For my brothers and sisters who visit, the garden has been healing. For myself, it's helped me integrate different parts of myself."

Among ecovillages, Findhorn is not alone in placing a high value on work. Sarvodaya's foundational principle, *shramadana*, means "the gift of labor." The villagers say, "We build the road and the road builds us." Members of Sieben Linden and Earthaven who build their own homes using local materials could just as easily say, "We build the house and the house builds us."

It is one thing, though, for ecovillagers to labor together for the sake their own happy green lives, and another to work for the benefit of others. For Jonathan Dawson, president of the Global Ecovillage Network, the difference between escapists and activists is a primary tension in ecovillages. "Many ecovillages are about social transformation," he said, "but some just want to say, 'Stop the world, I want to get off.' The isolated enclaves are always in danger of collapsing. What I've noticed over time is that the success stories are the ecovillages that find a way of being of service." Having selected for success, I missed the isolated enclaves. Even beyond their efforts to educate the larger community about the principles of ecology, I met plenty of ecovillagers who were serving on local school boards, town councils, and volunteer fire departments. Others were involved in national political movements, international humanitarian relief, and Third World development. Damanhur residents have started a political party, and one of their members is the local mayor. For these ecovillagers, broad-scale social change and personal change are two sides of the same coin.

Yet the impulse to serve need not be purely altruistic. Ecovillages generally find it good public relations to be of service – especially when their neighbors are distrustful. Jonathan Dawson told me a story that hammered this point home. Before Rob Hopkins published his widely acclaimed *The Transition Handbook*, he lived in a small ecovillage in Ireland where he spent years building his own cob house. Just as he was putting the finishing touches on his home, it was destroyed by arson. For the first time, Hopkins understood how deeply suspicious the local people were of his lifestyle. Recognizing that his deepest passion was social transformation, he left his cob-house dream and began helping cities and towns prepare for peak oil and climate change, founding the Transition Town concept and the Transition Network. Today, Transition initiatives – which are essentially scaled-up versions of ecovillage living – are cropping up all over the world.

In Jonathan's view, and I tend to agree with him, ecovillages will need to be of even greater service in the future. "If we have a graceful transition to a new order," he said, "ecovillages will be excellent training centers. They already are that. If the transition is more catastrophic, ecovillages could be models – but only if they're not devoured by hungry hordes. They will need to be perceived by people as helpful to their own survival. So it's critical that they have strong local relationships."

In the hyper-individualized world we've inherited from the petroleum age, we've not had to know our neighbors – much less work with them. Work was a place we drove off to each morning. Machines did our physical work, and petroleum was so cheap that we could fritter it away on leaf blowers and throwaway plastics. Our primary food-related human connections were at the checkout counter with a cashier and a bagger. In the energy-descent world of the future, people will work closer to home, do more physical work, and do it in groups. I came away from my ecovillage journey believing that we might actually be better off in such a world because human relationships would come first. The sooner we start working together and building those relationships, the better.

Starting near home, a first step might be to gather with our neighbors and devise a project that would make a positive difference in our local community. That could be any number of things: build a pleasant gathering place like a corner tea stand, beautify a traffic circle, construct a covered shelter for the bus stop, or replace lawns with community gardens. Our deliberations alone would develop our relationships. Whatever the tangible results of our collaboration, the most significant end would likely be a growing sense of community. From that fertile soil, many fruits can grow.

## The power of example

Education is one of the greatest responsibilities of any community, and ecovillages are no exception. As living laboratories, ecovillages are places of learning, and the knowledge they produce does not stop at their gates. Ecovillages aim to send out shoots and branches. Nearly every resident I met was at least as committed to changing the world as to changing their own lives. Consequently, ecovillages turn out to be fabulous classrooms – albeit utterly different from the ones I've been accustomed to. The hands-on teaching methods of an ecovillage diverge sharply from the intellectual guidance offered in our schools. Likewise, ecovillage education has a different aim from standard classroom learning. Rather than trying to pass exams in order to find a niche within the status quo, students are learning the skills necessary to create viable models of living. As a schoolteacher who has for years questioned the status quo in my classes, I know that lectures of this sort generally offer only critique and not constructive alternatives. What kind of impact can this possibly have on young people? And looking at myself and my colleagues, I made the disheartening discovery that those who lob the sharpest critiques are usually living entirely conventional lifestyles.

I embarked upon this journey because I could no longer tolerate the yawning gap between what I knew and how I was living. I needed to know – not just theoretically, but with my whole being – that another world is possible. For this, I needed the visceral experience of working together with people as one body, living in places where I never flushed a toilet and never turned on a heater against the winter cold, and spending alternative currencies that foster resilience. Most of what I learned in ecovillages came from day-to-day life: the ease of conversation, the wholesomeness of the food, the freedom of children to play outdoors after dark. I suspect that this kind of full-bodied

learning makes the strongest impression on the hundreds of thousands of ecovillage visitors each year.

For those who study at one of the Global Ecovillage Network's
Living and Learning Centers, the ecovillage literally becomes their
classroom. The most popular course is the EDE (Ecovillage Design
Education); the curriculum is available for free at http://gaiaeducation.
org. A grand finale of the EDE is a hands-on project designed and
implemented by the student under faculty supervision. In essence,
the project imports ecovillage practices into existing communities.
Past projects have included creating community gardens, transforming sewage systems in urban slums, and establishing environmental
education programs for children. I spoke with several EDE graduates
and, to my surprise, not one of them lived in an ecovillage.

I asked Jonathan Dawson, author of the economics module of the
curriculum, about GEN's educational mission. Along with the other
Global Ecovillage Educators for a Sustainable Earth (GEESE) from
GEN, Jonathan assumed that the EDE would generate ecovillages.
"But that's not what happened!" he said. "There was a glass ceiling:
the price of land. Today, fewer new ecovillages are being built, even
though our courses are more popular than ever. People are taking our
courses into their own communities rather than starting new ecovillages. That's fine with us. The point is not for ecovillages to replicate
themselves; the point is to build a sustainable world."

Jonathan said that, from its very inception, GEN had a twofold
mission: information exchange among ecovillages and education for
social change in the larger world. Some of its offerings fulfill both
missions. Its online Community Sustainability Assessment tool, for
instance, can help any community (not just an ecovillage) measure
how well it meets the criteria for ecological, economic, and social
sustainability. Jonathan emphasized that GEN has served its member
ecovillages in many ways.

"Internally, the primary benefits have come through sharing best
practices," Jonathan said. "For example, the export of the Forum
from ZEGG has sent teams of trainers throughout Europe. Less
tangible but perhaps more important is decreasing the sense of isolation, especially for rural communities. At every annual meeting, I do
a PowerPoint presentation on the year's greatest successes. It is very,
very inspiring. Externally, I would say that our greatest impact has
come through the Gaia Education courses and the United Nations
work."

At the UN Habitat Conference in 1996, GEN was the largest
nongovernmental organization presence, and since then several

132

ecovillages have won the UN's Habitat Award. At the 2002 World Summit on Sustainable Development in Johannesburg, GEN hosted several programs on ecovillage development. GEN's Living and Learning Centers have been endorsed by the United Nations Institute for Training and Research (UNITAR). More recently, GEN has been a significant player in the UN Decade for Education on Sustainable Development (2005–2014).

In terms of political action, opposition to economic globalization serves as a rallying point for many ecovillagers. Yet, even in their opposition, they move beyond the politics of protest. During the 2005 G-8 Summit in Scotland, for instance, a core group from Findhorn led thousands of activists in creating a temporary ecovillage as a counterpoint to the unsustainable policies being promoted at the summit. The fully functional demonstration ecovillage included composting toilets, graywater systems, solar panels and wind turbines, and thirteen kitchens serving fair-trade and local organic food. This photogenic village was the darling of the news media. Similarly, at the international climate negotiations in Copenhagen (2009) and Cancun (2010), GEN promoted positive solutions, rather than simply protesting the existing order.

Far from being exclusive enclaves of escapists, ecovillages tend to be dynamic nodes of global engagement. Sarvodaya, for instance, was an active peace broker in Sri Lanka's long-term civil war. Both Sarvodaya and Auroville assisted in tsunami relief work. Damanhur participated in several humanitarian relief operations. During my stay at ZEGG, several members were visiting Jerusalem to promote peace efforts between Israelis and Palestinians. Peace activism and international solidarity pervade the ecovillage ethic.

Yet most of the ecovillagers I met were wary of the scale and complexity of global social and technological systems. For them, responsible action entails building a positive alternative from the ground up and then sharing this example with as many people as possible. In our tightly networked world, who knows what possibilities we might generate if we start at home and branch out!

## Raising the children

When I asked people what they most valued about living in an ecovillage, one of the most common answers was, "Raising my children here." Being a single mother, I could appreciate this response. The social support for ecovillage parents is enormous: daily contact with other parents, a ready pool of babysitters and friend groups, a relatively safe yet stimulating environment for playing and learning, and the peace of mind that comes from raising one's children with the values and skills that will prepare them for the future.

While University of Washington research (which is what my ecovillage project is) cannot by policy include interviews with minors, I was free to observe. In most cases, what I saw verged on the idyllic: by and large, the children were more confident, more creative, and more positive than children I've encountered elsewhere. And I was free to interview young adults who had grown up in ecovillages. Reflecting on their childhoods, every one of the nine I spoke with was immensely grateful. In particular, they valued being exposed to a wide range of adult perspectives. When their parents didn't seem to understand them, they could usually find an adult who did, and sometimes this was crucial. Yet each of these young adults admitted that, as adolescents, they had chafed under the perceived limitations of ecovillage life. Like children from small towns, nearly all left as soon as possible. And then many of them returned. What most struck me about these ecovillage graduates was their competence and confidence.

At Svanholm, where self-governance is a high value, every common meeting begins with "news from the children." This seemingly trivial ritual, I came to see, offers a window into Svanholm's philosophy of child rearing. As a counterpoint to the Danish mainstream, childhood at Svanholm is consciously structured as a training in self-governance. While Denmark's welfare state offers day-care arrangements that would be the envy of many American working parents, this system has its drawbacks. Extended day care alongside compulsory schooling means that Danish children's lives are highly institutionalized. For most of their waking hours, they are segregated (save for their teachers and caretakers) into a world apart from adults. Nor do they have time to play freely. Svanholm, by contrast, integrates children into the everyday lives of the adults. Rather than being regulated by externally imposed schedules, children become self-regulating – they're exposed to many possibilities and encouraged to make their own choices. Some might play computer games or build forts in the forest, others might ride horses or raise chickens, and still others might learn to paint or build. The children make choices, and, at the same time, they're expected to keep appointments and follow through on commitments. It is true self-governance.

Birgitte Simonsen, the Danish sociologist introduced in chapter 4,

134

explained that even though Svanholm's children may live with their parents, it is the larger community and not the family that is the primary social structure. "This has many advantages," she said. "A good example is divorce. Even though they may divorce, both parents can continue living with the children because there's no house and property to sell! Many couples have done this here. When they separate, they simply put in a request to the Moving Group." Both parents get accommodations large enough to include the children.

At Damanhur, children are a focus as well, although, according to one of the teachers in the community's elementary school, "they are not considered children; they are small people. They participate in regular debates, group processes, and decision-making." This teacher, the Anaconda Papaya mentioned earlier, added, "And they still get to be kids – to be noisy and get dirty." Anaconda said that education at Damanhur is not a job but a mission, and so self-education is the primary work of every resident, young and old alike.

I spent a morning in Damanhur's elementary school, which has an enrollment of seventy-five children. Classes were small – no more than eight pupils – and the project-driven curriculum integrates language, math, science, and the arts. One class of 9–11-year-olds had just returned from helping to build a rainforest ecology school for a sister village in Nicaragua. Some children were writing letters to their Nicaraguan friends, while others sat with their teacher, scrutinizing the school's blueprint. The noisy room was ebullient yet orderly.

Damanhur has moved even further from the nuclear family model than Svanholm. Marriages are renewable contracts (usually three to five years in length) and each nucleo takes full psychological and financial responsibility for all of its children, including for their college education. While children know their biological parents, they also have, in effect, twenty to thirty parents. So far as I could see during my two-week stay, Damanhur's children were flourishing.

## Box 5.2 "I Decided to Be Crazy Too"

Growing up in Damanhur, leaving, and then choosing to return is the path of one 19-year-old, a young woman with the demeanor of someone a decade older. Unlike other Damanhur residents, Arianna Santanera is keeping her given name because, she said, she loves its mythological meaning: it's Ariadne's thread that links everything together. Like many ecovillage children, Arianna was grateful for knowing many adults and, as the youngest of fifteen children in her nucleo, never lacking playmates. But she said she often resented her parents for focusing more on Damanhur than on her, and she sometimes wished she belonged to a "normal" nuclear family.

Damanhur has no high school, and so this is when the community's teenagers must confront just how unusual their lives are. Arianna recalled her sense of isolation in the public high school. "The Damanhur school brought out our individuality," she said, "but this school tried to make everybody the same." She found she didn't share her peer's obsession with fashion and conformity, and then, most painfully, her first boyfriend broke off with her when he learned she was from the ecovillage.

"I was bored in high school," Arianna said, "but actually I didn't fit in anywhere then. I didn't feel at home on the outside, but I didn't feel at home at Damanhur either because I didn't choose it. So I found an exchange program to Chile where I could be part of a family and go to school. I loved this experience. The people were very warm. They helped me to refine parts of myself that were pushed down in high school. And the landscapes really fill you!"

After returning to Italy and graduating from high school, Arianna realized she didn't really know Damanhur. "When you don't take a decision, you live on the surface," she said. "So I decided to get to know it better. I entered into the meditation school and asked to become a citizen." When I met Arianna two years later, she was still taking the citizenship course even as she was studying medicine at the University of Turin and helping to spearhead a residential learning center for Damanhur teens.

I asked Arianna what she was learning from going back and forth between Damanhur and Turin. "That I am never alone, that I can always feel the strength of others. This sense of belonging to the people and moving toward an ideal makes us go beyond the egoism that is so common on the outside. When I am in Turin, I see people on the bus who are physically close but worlds apart. So I decided to be a Damanhurian to change this egoism that is so toxic for humanity and the Earth. When I was in high school, I used to think Damanhurians were crazy because the world is already too far gone. But I decided to be crazy too. Thank God for humor – this is what saves us!"

I laughed with Arianna even though I was so moved by the wisdom of this 19-year-old that I had to suppress my tears. Once again, I found myself thinking of my own students and wishing that mainstream culture could offer a suitable channel for the idealism – even heroism – that so naturally emerges at this age. Instead, most of their energy is channeled into getting a degree, getting drunk, and getting laid.

All the same, every ecovillage is not a childhood paradise. As I mentioned, ZEGG's children from the early days rarely return. At LAEV, lying awake at night as police helicopters beamed their spotlights into the tenement windows, I knew in my gut why this ecovillage has no children. Every member I interviewed, including the founder herself, said they would have serious reservations about raising a child there. Still, in most of the ecovillages I visited, I found myself heartened by the child-rearing practices I found. It's hard to grow up in an ecovillage without learning how to live simply, make compost, consider divergent perspectives, and, most importantly, have a sense of hope.

Many of the child-friendly practices found in ecovillages can be applied anywhere. Some, like hands-on learning, conflict resolution, and children's gardens, have been incorporated for years in schools and community centers. One of the most inspiring practices I encountered was Auroville's Awareness through the Body (ATB), a subtle yet powerful set of exercises for honing the human capacity for concentration. When it comes to self-awareness and kinesthetic intelligence, Auroville's children are exceptional – largely, I believe, because they learn ATB from an early age. During my visit in 2008, hardly anyone

Figure 5.1 Local village children enjoy hands-on environmental learning at Auroville's Aikyam Bilingual School

outside of Auroville had ever heard of it. Two years later, I found ATB online, purchased a book about it, and attended a first-rate ATB workshop in Seattle. Interestingly, the other participants were teachers bringing ATB into their classrooms.

We don't have to travel to an ecovillage to find what our children need. As I took in the range of innovative child-rearing practices in ecovillages, I kept returning to Jeff's and Kirsten's primary reason for uprooting their family from Half Moon Bay and moving to EVI: "We wanted to put our kids in the best possible place to learn the skills they'll need to live in the world: skills that involve working with their hands, living close to the Earth, and getting along with people." We can teach these skills to our children wherever we might live, but we must first learn them ourselves. If there is any truth in the adage that it takes a village to raise a child, then we need to create village conditions in our own neighborhoods.

## Cultural expression

Being a pragmatic social scientist, I imagined that ecovillages would be too focused on sustainable living and conflict resolution to indulge in the arts, but I was hugely mistaken. Cultural enrichment is as vital to ecovillages as eating and composting. I took in more performances and exhibitions during my ecovillage tour than in any other year of my life, and I certainly sang in more groups than ever before. I saw that in ecovillages hardly a meeting, mealtime, or celebration goes by without some kind of song. Most communities I visited either had their own singing group or were integrally involved with a local choir. Some, like Findhorn, have regular dances. Others, like UfaFabrik and ZEGG, organize huge cultural events for the wider public. In every case, the point is to strengthen community bonds through shared aesthetic experiences and rituals.

For its emphasis on social change – especially cross-cultural exchange – through the arts, UfaFabrik stands out. Ever since its origins as a squatter camp in Berlin's old Universal Studios, UfaFabrik has been building relationships with artists in war-torn countries. I happened to arrive on the first day of the South Korean Festival. Sigrid Niemer, a founder of UfaFabrik and the woman who arranged my visit, invited me to the evening performance and met me at the theater.

As people flowed into the 300-seat hall, Sigrid explained how this dance and drumming concert fit into UfaFabrik's mission. "We believe that art and culture, not words, are what hold people together," she said. "When the Ethiopian and Cambodian circuses come here, we practice and perform together with no common language."

UfaFabrik is unusual among ecovillages in that its members share neither ideological beliefs nor spiritual practices, and yet its urban cultural center has flourished since 1979. Sigrid chalks this longevity up to the nonverbal communication made possible through the arts. She said, "We can interact and have fun together beyond words and community issues. This gives us a bigger perspective. I might argue with someone in a meeting, but when I play music with him later, I see another side to him."

My concern about falling asleep in the dark theater because of travel fatigue was completely allayed by the performance. For two hours, my senses went into overdrive as fifteen brilliantly costumed dancing drummers leaped and somersaulted and flipped across the stage, all the while beating out rhythms of mind-boggling complexity. After the grand finale, I jumped to my feet applauding along with the rest of the audience. In hindsight, I cannot explain what this spectacular performance had to do with sustainable living. I only know that I grasped Sigrid's words viscerally: it is culture, not words, that holds us together, and sharing that music with the performers and others in their audience, I felt profoundly grateful to be human. It's possible that when we explore the creative heights of our humanity, it's then easier for us to navigate its narcissistic depths.

And every ecovillage has its annual rituals and celebrations that build social cohesion. Most celebrate their country's primary holidays, as well as key dates in the community's history, like its birthday. And there's usually somebody's birthday just around the corner. One afternoon at EVI, I pitched in at the common house to make dinner. Of the dozen people in the kitchen that day, half were teenage girls who had gathered to bake six cakes for the celebration of a child's birthday party. "When you have thirty kids in your family," one girl said with a smile, "you bake a lot of birthday cakes!" Then there are the idiosyncratic events that reflect an ecovillage's unique culture. EVI, for instance, convenes several gender-specific annual events: Guys Baking Pies, Oafs Baking Loaves, and Women Goin' Swimmin'. Over time, shared memories from these occasions help to weave the community's social fabric.

Because every culture represents an assemblage of life skills that has endured the test of time, one of the saddest effects of globalization is its tendency to undermine people's cultural pride. Auroville, despite being an international township, runs the risk of exacerbating this tendency. Many thousands of visitors flock there each year, making it the strongest globalizing force in this part of India. The ensuing socioeconomic instability has returned like a boomerang to Auroville: land prices have soared, motorbikes and tacky shops have proliferated, and – most ominously – gang activity has escalated. In response, Auroville has built Tamil cultural centers in two adjacent villages with the aim of fostering people's cultural pride while meeting their practical needs. The centers offer kindergartens and after-school programs during the week, South Indian dance and martial arts classes for children on the weekend, and ongoing employment programs and cultural activities for young people.

The latter are vital: adolescent men in developing countries are often the weak link in their cultures.[7] The combination of violent media images, high unemployment rates, and easy access to alcohol, drugs, and fast motorbikes is a heady mix for a testosterone-charged young man. Consequently, the "stick dance" performance I enjoyed at one of Auroville's Tamil cultural centers struck me as pure genius. Eight men were simultaneously executing extremely difficult feats, preserving a cultural tradition that would otherwise be lost, and earning some money for their efforts. Like the Korean dancers, the Tamil men combined tightly choreographed acrobatics with fast-paced, thunderous rhythms. These men were not, however, beating drums; they were striking one another's sticks with such force that one false move could prove lethal. It had been so many years since the dance was performed that the dancers received their instructions from an old man in a chair.

Cultural preservation is also a concern for ecovillages in the industrialized world. At LAEV, for instance, Julio Santizo, a 58-year-old Guatemalan activist, told me about the annual EcoMaya Festivals he started in the city in 1995, a Mother Earth Day celebration to connect environmental concerns and cultural heritage. "We are 500,000 Guatemalans in LA, but we have no real identity," Julio said. "I'm not Chicano, I'm nothing. I never identified with the environmental movement because I wasn't white, but, in Guatemala, we were losing a lot of trees. I wanted to help my people. I needed an identity and so

---

[7] This may be true wherever traditional rites of passage have been lost. In the United States, for instance, where driving a car and drinking alcohol mark the entry into adulthood, the largest population of prisoners is young men. Historically, the passage to manhood required a courageous display of skill and strength that benefited the larger society. Think of the young Gambian men in chapter 4 who went to sea to feed their people. Many of the strong, able-bodied young men I met in ecovillages, I suspect, were devising their own rites of passage.

did my daughter, so we agreed that we're Mayan. EcoMaya is about bringing our culture back."

Living sustainably means creating a life-sustaining culture. In our technologically and linguistically mediated world, this might sound like a tall order, but it can be pretty simple – and, as I have learned, gratifying. We can create the kinds of aesthetic experiences that hold us together as a people – in our neighborhoods, our workplaces, our schools, our places of worship. We might start or join a choir, or hold a talent show or a sketching day or a jam session or an ethnic dinner or a monthly movie night . . . The possibilities are limitless, and who can say what new synergies will grow from the deeper bonds forged from these shared experiences.

Modernization has been the death knell for many traditions. Why dance or tell stories when you can watch television? Why learn to grow and preserve food when you have a refrigerator and year-round access to Safeway or Walmart? In the United States, the epicenter of novelty and technological progress, the loss of farming traditions is particularly acute. Composting, animal husbandry, food fermentation – all of these were vital aspects of traditional cultures, which interwove artistic expression and ecology into the fabric of everyday life. As a consequence, most American ecovillages find themselves combing through old books or relying on others who have done so in their efforts to live sustainably.

Earthaven, however, happens to be in Appalachia, where the older generation retains many traditions that are vital for survival. Most of their children and grandchildren have left the area, but a new generation of ecovillagers has moved in and is hungry to learn about clearing land, growing food, repairing tractors, welding, and so on. When Earthaven had its first hog feast, they invited the local elders to show them how to slaughter, butcher, and roast a hog – helpful information for survival!

"If it weren't for these old-timers," Chris Farmer said, "I don't think Earthaven would be here today! Take Reed Murphy. He's taught me so much. He fixes things – *anything*. If you've got something that's broken, you just take it to Reed. He'll fix it and won't take your money. And there's John McEntire. He knows about wood and heirloom corn, and he'll soon be growing feedstock for biofuels."

These elders are living treasures for Earthaven – and the ecovillagers are themselves a boon for the elders. "We've joined the local fire department and fought fires side-by-side with them," Farmer explained. "Plus, they love to laugh at us. We're a constant source

141

**Figure 5.2** Music, dance, and ritual are vital to ecovillage culture. Here, Findhorn residents form a human spiral

*Source*: Painting by Shunsuke Shimura, photograph taken by Isao Yoshikoshi

of humor! At the same time, we're doing things they could never imagine, so they're also learning."

## Sharing the passings

Deep community is akin to marriage. While no vows are taken in an ecovillage and everyone there has an exit option, there is a sense of being together "in sickness and in health." When I asked ecovillagers about the experiences that brought the community together most strongly, many of them spoke about standing together in the face of serious illness and death. Some communities were grappling with questions that come with an aging population and a few of the more established ones (like Findhorn and Auroville) had created their own cemeteries and rituals surrounding the dying process.

Julio Santizo described how LAEV rallied to his support when he had colon cancer. "Everyone helped me," he said. "Esfandiar cooked for me and took me to appointments. Lois also took me for chemo and radiation. Ann helped me with the bag I carried for nineteen months. Arisha, Summer, Jimmy, Yuki, Joe – they all did things for me. In a normal apartment house, I would never get that kind of attention." Every community I visited had similar stories.

It was at Sieben Linden, however, that I learned firsthand how times of human vulnerability can reveal a community's depth. On my first morning in this rural German ecovillage, I learned that just a half-hour earlier one of the members had died – Milan, a 64-year-old who had left a successful career as an architect of skyscrapers to become the ecovillage's horseman and master composter, was Sieben Linden's first death.

Later that day, the residents came trickling into the dining room, silent or speaking in hushed tones. I ate my lunch alone, hoping to be as unobtrusive as possible. Since Milan's death coincided with St Martin's Day, a mid-autumn festival popular in Germany, a notice was posted after lunch: the evening celebration would include a walk to Milan's wagon.

At sundown, the meager warmth of the day gave way to a frigid evening. Everybody gathered outside the main house, the children swinging handmade lanterns. We walked in silence to the blue wagon where we were each handed a lit candle in a small glass jar. Although I hadn't met Milan, my life had been touched by his death and so, without hesitation, I took a candle. We formed a semicircle around the wagon as a lone candle burned in the window. People began singing, "All I want is that forever you remember me as loving you." The song was in English, so I joined in, thinking of my own loved ones a continent away. With the song's end, we placed our candlelit jars around Milan's wagon.

We proceeded around Sieben Linden, stopping at several specially decorated places to sing traditional St Martin's Day tunes. When we circled back to the common house, the children's mounting enthusiasm made it apparent that the evening's culmination would take place there. Eventually, a half-naked man came limping across the snow. The excitement grew, and the crowd began to chant, "Come, St Martin," until a well-dressed man, mounted atop a hefty workhorse, materialized out of the darkness. The woman next to me kindly translated as events unfolded: St Martin was so generous that he cut his own cloak in half to save a poor half-naked man from freezing. My teeth chattering, I felt vicarious gratitude for the saint. To everyone's applause, St Martin emptied a burlap sack full of treats onto the snow and the children made a wild dash for them. A bonfire was rising behind the crowd. I was offered a cup of hot cider and stood in the circle of firelight, savoring the drink and the warm faces glowing all about me. The murmur of German conversation was indecipherable for this foreigner who arrived only yesterday – yet I felt bathed in a sense of intimacy and belonging.

Milan's body remained in the blue wagon for three days as a steady stream of visitors, young and old alike, flowed through. One man played guitar and sang for hours at a time. At the end of the vigil, Milan's body was laid in a plain pine coffin (built by one of the residents), and the coffin was placed under a canopy of rounded willow branches. People came to the *globalo*, as it was called, whenever they wished. Many residents commented upon the fortuitous weather: the Arctic front lingered through the week, making it possible to keep the body outside. I asked if the local authorities had approved. They had not, though they were aware of Milan's death as the burial was to be in the local village cemetery. The community members had decided to do what they felt was right and no one had objected. People also commented upon the timing of Milan's passing, just a week before the community's annual *Intensiv*. Milan's death, they told me, was bonding them together strongly just before they would be addressing some major interpersonal and strategic planning issues.

Beginning with St Martin's Day and throughout the week, I was constantly impressed by how the community integrated Milan's death into its everyday life. One afternoon as I sat in the seminar room, for instance, a group of exuberant children dressed in colorful capes made from silk scarves burst in. The children careened about the room, their arms outstretched as if flying, shouting, "We're milans!" Milan, whose birth name was Hennig, had renamed himself after the kite, a large European bird known for its broad vision and graceful flight. The afternoon before the funeral, one of the residents gathered several mothers and their children in the library where I was working. "Milan loved flowers," she said, "but mid-November is not the time for flowers. So we're going to make flowers." I closed my laptop and joined in. Two hours later, several boxes were overflowing with bright tissue-paper flowers.

On Saturday, my last day at Sieben Linden, about 150 people gathered after lunch for the funeral procession to Poppau village. Enfolded by a freezing fog that pierced the lungs, I walked alone, conscious of my status as an outsider. I allowed myself to be carried along by the mourning throng, which was so long that from my vantage point at the back, the front was out of sight. This image of a whole village walking along a desolate gray road to the cemetery seemed both archaic and novel. For untold centuries past, this was

the customary funeral procession: a small village walking together to
bury a loved one. But we were in the third millennium: where were
the cars? Earlier that morning when I pictured the funeral, I predicted
that Sieben Linden – world renowned for its ecological values –
would surely walk to the cemetery, despite the miserable weather. I
imagined Milan's body being driven in a black hearse, followed by the
entire community on foot.

As I recalled this image, the procession up ahead turned left onto
the main road, and I could finally see the front: the coffin was being
pulled by two draft horses. How simple and natural! Milan, the
master composter who had helped to bring draft horses to Sieben
Linden, was now being carried to his final resting place by these same
horses. But what did my morning imaginings say about my own
conditioning? Even as an avid ecologist, I was so deeply ensconced in
the car culture that I pictured a motorized hearse at the head of this
convoy! But why would a community that plows its fields with horses
drive the corpse of their brother into town? My mind resettled into
an expansive intimacy as we traced the long, flat road into Poppau.

We arrived at a wooden chapel, too small to accommodate us all.
I stayed outside with about fifty others. Unable to comprehend the
eulogies, which were all in German, I listened with my other senses. I
felt drawn to a small table at the chapel's entrance. A candle, its flame
defying the wind, sat between two photographs. One showed Milan
in the garden, his face deeply etched with what looked like a permanent scowl. The other, which captured my attention utterly, was taken
after his death. It showed the lines on his face melted into a beatific
serenity and, on his lips, a subtle, unmistakable smile. What surprises,
I wondered, might await us on the other side of this life?

The congregation flowed outside, and those of us who were not
weeping once again sang, "All I want from you is to forever remember me as loving you." Our song seemed to rise up in the cold, gray
sky as, in the face of death, we offered an affirmation of life. Several
people then spoke about Milan. The woman who translated for me
on St Martin's Day happened to be by my side again. She gave a rough
translation of the stories about Milan's intensity and ferocity, his gratitude for simple things, his transformation from an urban architect to
a gardener in love with the soil, and his returning now to the soil. As
the coffin was lowered into the ground and people took turns with the
shovel, the community choir sang in an exquisite four-part harmony.

Toward evening, the gray sky darkened and a pallid moon struggled to penetrate the fog. Our journey back to Sieben Linden was
less formal than the morning procession. Small interspersed groups

ambled in conversation. For the first time in hours, my aching fingers and toes captured my attention. I was chilled to the bone. Solid ice along the road showed that the day's temperature had never gone above freezing. Suddenly, the thought of sharing hot tea with these ecovillagers in their bright wooden dining room was irresistible. Quickening my pace until I was nearly running, I felt warmth returning to my body: glad, strong, and generous.

## Relating in the circle of life

As I reflect upon the darkening clouds on our planetary horizon, I am increasingly convinced that our relationships with one another will be absolutely pivotal in determining the evolutionary viability of our species. The issues at hand are fundamentally about how we live. We might even say that there are no environmental problems: there are only human problems. And while viable communities are needed at every social scale, most of us are best equipped to contribute in our own neighborhoods. The more we can come together, the better we'll be able to weather the coming storms.

Despite being an outsider during my year of ecovillage living, I often had the distinct sense of witnessing and, at times, participating in a culture of belonging. Belonging, I believe, is the psychosocial counterpart to sustainability: we feel that we belong when our lives contribute to and are nourished by the greater whole. When we relate not as individualistic particles that bump and clash, but rather as integral parts of a greater whole, we automatically experience a greater sense of belonging. Yet while we each have it in our power to make a unique contribution to the whole, we are powerless to create a culture of belonging by ourselves. For that, we need one another . . . and for that, we need trust.

As I traveled from one ecovillage to the next, I found myself increasingly fascinated by this nebulous yet utterly essential quality called "trust." What is trust? How can it be created – and destroyed? It's well and good to say that sharing is the essence of ecovillage living, but so long as we have a choice in the matter, sharing only makes sense in the context of trust. If I were to assemble a list of best ecological and economic practices in ecovillages, it is quite likely that every one of them would require trust. Car sharing, co-ownership of land and housing, every form of collaborative consumption, even community-wide composting and food production – without trust, none of these can work. And if I were to assemble a list of reasons

146

why many communities fail, the breakdown of social trust would surely top the list. So far as I know, no community has ever collapsed for want of solar panels or composting toilets, but many have been torn asunder when trust wore thin.

Trust, I've come to believe, is the soil from which true community grows. Like all good soil, trust is built upon a gift economy of symbiotic relationships, with the key nutrients being honesty and compassion. This is especially critical during times of conflict. As they say, shit happens. Fortunately, we can make some beautiful soil from it if we know the secrets of composting. This, I suspect, is why, for nearly every ecovillager I interviewed, social relations were simultaneously the most challenging *and* the most rewarding aspect of their lives. Building trust can be a messy process, but when we come together authentically, something is born that is far greater than the sum of its parts – something that we seem hardwired to want. We could call that something a "culture of belonging."

Wherever we live and at whatever depth of community engagement we find ourselves, we can glean some helpful tips from ecovillages for cultivating that all-important generative ground of trust. When joining with others in a community endeavor, there are certain ground rules that support success:

- Be clear about your shared vision and your intentions. In a group endeavor, embracing a larger purpose can help people to set aside personality differences. Even if that purpose is as simple as creating a community garden, the very process of deliberating and working together can forge lasting relationships.
- Agree to a decision-making process that maximizes the contribution of each individual, balancing inclusiveness with the need for efficiency.
- Develop communication skills, drawing from practices like Nonviolent Communication, the Forum, Appreciative Inquiry, and Compassionate Listening.
- Foster nonverbal communication, including song, dance, celebrations and collective work. To the greatest extent possible, make it fun for everyone!
- Incorporate the children. If there's any truth to the adage, "It takes a village to raise a child," then we and our children will all be better off if we start behaving more like villagers.
- Share the joys and sorrows of life. Relationships grow from celebration as well as traversing dark times together.
- Most important, keep on learning and embodying what you learn.

147

The evolutionary need of our time is to find ways of "hanging together." In order to live within the circle of life, we must therefore make an epic transition from living as separate, acquisitive individuals to living as conscious participants in a vast web of biotic and social relationships. In other words, we must create a culture of belonging, one community at a time. And if authentic community is the longest personal growth workshop we'll ever take, then we will, no doubt, be transformed in the process. After all, we can have the community of our dreams only if we are willing to become the kind of person that community needs.

# — 6 —

# CONSCIOUSNESS: BEING IN THE CIRCLE OF LIFE

To live in an ecovillage is to inhabit an evolutionary laboratory where people are running collective experiments in every realm of life, from how they build their homes to how they communicate. These applied scientists, however, are not disinterested observers. On the contrary: every ecovillager I interviewed reported having experienced extraordinary personal growth through their shared experiments. Their accounts suggest that when we set out with others to transform our material and social landscape, we simultaneously – often unwittingly – enrich our inner landscape. The journey may not be an easy one, but it is a path of integrity and growth.

As much as we might crave the sense of belonging that comes from living as an integral part of a greater whole, becoming such a person requires unpeeling layer after layer of cultural conditioning. This is why community living is the longest, most expensive personal growth workshop you'll ever take. Whether you call yourself secular, religious, or spiritual, that journey will entail much the same effort: the work of moving from being me-centered to social, ecological, and even cosmological relationships.

Like everyone else, ecovillagers are divided in their beliefs about God, spirit, or nonmaterial reality. Of the ecovillages I visited, five are organized around a cohesive spiritual worldview, three are eclectically spiritual, five are secular but tolerant of religion and spirituality, one is interreligious, and one (Sarvodaya) is both interreligious and spiritually focused[1] (see Table 6.1). I was intrigued to find that the largest

---

[1] I distinguish between *religion* as an organized institution and *spirituality* as a less structured approach to matters of the spirit. Among the people I interviewed, I found Buddhists, Christians, Hindus, Jews, and Muslims. While a few ecovillages are organized around a single religion, this is not the norm and I did not visit any of them.

and most dynamic communities I visited (Sarvodaya, Auroville, Findhorn, and Damanhur) each subscribes to a cohesive spiritual worldview. Their spirituality is embodied and relational, aiming not for *liberation from* this world but rather for the *transformation of* it. As you'll see in the table below, in my tally I place Sarvodaya in both the first and fourth categories. I do this because, while most of the leaders are Buddhist, this nontheistic worldview does not conflict with the religious beliefs of the organization's millions of Hindu, Muslim, and Christian members.

Table 6.1   Ecovillage Worldviews

| | |
|---|---|
| Spiritually focused | Auroville, Damanhur, Findhorn, Konohana, Sarvodaya |
| Spiritually eclectic | Earthaven, Sieben Linden, ZEGG |
| Secular | Crystal Waters, EcoVillage at Ithaca, Los Angeles Eco-Village, UfaFabrik |
| Interreligious | Colufifa, Sarvodaya |

Some ecovillagers spoke about being guided to their lifestyle by God, some spoke of communicating with plants and nature spirits, and some described themselves as staunch atheists. Amid these philosophical and religious differences, I was struck by their even deeper commonalities. From more than 140 in-depth interviews, I gleaned the following convictions that infuse ecovillage culture:

- The mounting ecological crisis is also a crisis of human meaning.
- The web of life is sacred, and we are integral members of that web.
- We can harmonize our lives with the web of life if we learn to co-create with nature.
- Community is an adventure in conscious relational living – ecologically, socially, and psychologically.

At the heart of these convictions lies one simple premise: that we are inseparable from nature – and the sooner we wake up to this fact, the better for everybody.

Every culture enacts a story, whether tacit or explicit, about the nature of reality and humanity's place in the cosmos. At the dawn of industrialization, the story of humanity's separation from nature may have served a useful purpose, but that perspective is increasingly maladaptive. Our world hungers for new stories of belonging, stories that could spark a cultural renewal. Besides their material and social experiments, ecovillages are also storytelling laboratories. Within the diversity of their stories, I discerned one simple but profound core story that describes both humanity's plight and the solution. In a nutshell, the story is that, having come directly out of nature and thus being inseparable from nature, we can harmonize our ecological, economic, and social relationships by tapping into the evolutionary intelligence that brought us to our current juncture. The story is not unique; indeed, it is cropping up all over the world. Ecovillages just happen to be enacting it in a highly focused and integrated way.

In this chapter, the lessons we glean from ecovillages are not about what we can *do* but how we can *be*. If we want to integrate the ecological, economic, and social dimensions of sustainability, then we must allow ourselves to be transformed in the process. In other words, we have to integrate ourselves. Consciousness is the vitally important subjective dimension of E2C2. Whatever our metaphysical beliefs, sustainability turns out to be an inside job.

## Box 6.1 Sarvodaya's Peace Meditation

One morning, as I was eating breakfast in the Sarvodaya dining hall on the gritty edge of Colombo, I struck up a conversation with a venerable gentleman who happened to be Sarvodaya's senior meditation instructor. Meditation, Mr Mahanama Seneviratne explained, is more than a private matter. It is a dynamic force for progress. At the core of Sarvodaya's vision is the belief that all social problems – war, poverty, environmental destruction, the oppression of women – are rooted not in legislation, institutions, or even behavior but in human consciousness.

"Therefore," he said, "if we want to establish peace among ourselves and with nature, we must first establish peace in our own minds." Mr Mahanama offered to teach me the peace meditation, and that afternoon I took him up on his offer.

I recalled reading about Sarvodaya's mass meditations in the 1990s during Sri Lanka's bloody civil war. These events drew up to a million people – impressive in a country of 20 million – and they were Buddhists, Hindus, Muslims, and Christians. Rather than protesting *against* political policies, these demonstrations both *for* and *of* interethnic harmony were a resounding expression of the politics of yes.

Vishwa Niketan, Sarvodaya's meditation center where I met Mr Mahanama in the heat of the day, has grand wooden columns, a lotus pond and cascading orchids. I felt worlds away from the noisy city and

151

grateful for this respite that doubled as a research opportunity. Here are the instructions I received. You will also find them as an audio download on this book's companion website: www.ecovillagebook.com. I invite you to experience Sarvodaya's peace meditation for yourself.

> Sitting in a comfortable position, silently honor your own religion or belief system. Recognize that every religion is a reflection of the truth.
>
> Now become present in the body, and notice the mind relax. Gradually become conscious of the in and out breath as it moves through your nostrils. Do not change the breath; only observe it. Notice that there is nothing you can call *I* or *mine* in this process. See that this air was and will be breathed by millions of sentient beings. So too are the warmth (the fire element), the fluids (water) and the hardness of the body (earth) all part of the universe. Feeling this connection to all life, realize that you cannot harm another without harming yourself.
>
> Watching the mind, notice how sensations, perceptions, volitions, and thoughts arise faster than lightning. Observe the stream of consciousness as it flows. By returning to the breath, notice the mind becoming still.
>
> Understanding that there is neither *me* nor *mine* in the body or in the thoughts, allow the entire world to grow closer to your heart. As loving kindness and compassion fill your mind, extend these qualities to everyone: people you know and don't know; people you like and don't like; and finally to everyone and all beings. Allow these compassionate thoughts to extend in all directions, and also to the past, present, and future. Feel yourself connected to all things through these waves of compassion. Then quietly return the awareness to your body and your surroundings.

During the meditation, even as I felt acutely alive to every sensation – from the sultry air and the sweat dripping down my belly to the sounds of traffic and sublime birdsong – I seemed to enter a vast stillness. Rather than retreating into an otherworldly bliss, I felt myself embedded in a web of air, water, sunlight, and relationships, both human and nonhuman. At Vishwa Niketan, I found within in my own consciousness one small seed of a culture of belonging, as it surely is for each of us. Ultimately, deep interdependence is more than a story; it is the very warp and woof of our existence.

## The Great Unfoldment

Liz Walker opens her book, *Eco Village at Ithaca*, with a haunting story about her 8-year-old son. An avid "nature boy," he came home from school one day in tears after learning that species are going extinct faster than at any time since the dinosaurs. "I wish humans would just die off and let the rest of the world survive," he sobbed to his mother.[2] While we might debate the merits of teaching young children such overwhelming facts, I've learned from twenty years of lecturing on these issues that, when faced with the facts, many of us are vulnerable to what I call "the misanthropic temptation." Few of us give ourselves over to such raw grief as this 8-year-old, yet still we are vexed by the question: Is there something irremediably wrong that makes humanity behave like a planetary plague?

We might even find some dark humor in the situation. I like to start my lectures with a relevant cartoon. One of my favorites is as an "eco-depth gauge" that asks, "How deep is your ecology?" Near the top are "shallow" responses like "The planet Earth is a good tool, and, like every good tool, should be used wisely." At the bottom is the "abysmally deep" response: "Humanity is a blight upon the planet. A quick and painful extinction is the only just punishment." This cartoon, which comes from a deep ecology magazine, gives me hope: surely a species capable of such self-ridicule can find its way out of this mess! Yet the eco-depth gauge also highlights the same painful reality that brought Liz's son to tears: our species has somehow developed a way of life that is out of sync with the rest of creation. As one environmental philosopher puts it, we are "the natural alien."[3] When we find ourselves seriously doubting whether we belong here, then the environmental crisis is no longer just something "out there." Now it lives "in here" as an existential crisis, a crisis of meaning that demands a personal response.

In times of crisis, enduring cultural myths lose their credibility, and the doors of the human mind open to new stories and new ways of making meaning. We are living in such a time, and we have some pivotal choices before us. As a scientist, I want my stories to accord with the facts. Yet, as a scientist, I also know that many stories can be consistent with the same facts. I therefore find myself drawn to stories that align simultaneously with reliable scientific knowledge and inspire us toward our highest potential. Can we tell a plausible story about our current predicament without becoming a Pollyanna, a Cassandra, or a cynic?

As it turns out, the core premise of ecovillage culture – that we

[2] Liz Walker, EcoVillage at Ithaca: Pioneering a Sustainable Culture, New Society Publishers, 2005, p. 1.
[3] Neil Evernden, *The Natural Alien*, University of Toronto Press, 1993.

are not separate from nature – contains within itself the germ of a better story. The basic premise of the ecovillage story is this: as an integral part of nature, we can tap into the same evolutionary intelligence that brought us here. In so doing, we can forge a viable human future. Ecovillagers differ in how they describe and access this intelligence, but they all adhere to the same basic story line. Some tell it in spiritual terms and others use secular language; some observe nature meticulously while others meditate and pray. However we may do it, the crucial point is that we must access a larger intelligence to guide us through these times. Thomas Berry calls this "the Great Work" of our time; Joanna Macy calls it "the Great Turning."[4] Not surprisingly, I found books by these and other tellers of the new story on ecovillage bookshelves around the world. "Work" and "turning" describe what we must do, and the story itself I think of as "the Great Unfoldment."

At first glance, trusting a greater intelligence sounds like faith-based religion, but the new story I encountered among ecovillagers is consistent with science. The new story is essentially the narrative of cosmological and biological evolution retold lyrically and, most importantly, with a sense of urgency. The story unifies a range of apparent dichotomies: humanity and nature; biology and geology; and, for some, nature and spirit. Mathematical cosmologist Brian Swimme, perhaps the best-known new storyteller in this vein, is a household name in ecovillage circles. He infuses "the Universe Story," as he calls it, with magic and meaning. Consider his synopsis: "This is the greatest discovery of the scientific enterprise: You take hydrogen gas, and you leave it alone, and it turns into rosebushes, giraffes, and humans. . . . If humans are spiritual, then hydrogen is spiritual."[5]

Here is a slightly more elaborated version of the same story. All the matter and energy in the universe have their origins in the Big Bang – what Swimme calls "the primordial flaring forth." With time, stars formed and clustered into galaxies. When some of these stars exploded into supernovae, they gave birth to every element save hydrogen and helium. On our own home planet these elements mingled and, roughly 3.4 billion years ago, rudimentary life forms emerged. Over time, the biosphere "learned" to modify the circulation of matter and energy in ways that were conducive to life. James

[4] Thomas Berry, *The Great Work: Our Way into the Future*, Broadway Books, 2000; Joanna Macy, www.joannamacy.net/thegreatturning.html.
[5] Quoted in Carter Phipps, *Evolutionaries: Unlocking the Spiritual and Cultural Potential of Science's Greatest Idea*, Harper, 2012, p. 305.

Lovelock, the atmospheric chemist who discovered this self-regulating capacity of the Earth system, gave it a name: Gaia. For eons, Gaian innovation followed each cataclysm, leading in due course to a flowering of life in the aftermath of the dinosaurs. This age, the Cenozoic, saw the most magnificent diversification of life in Earth's story: birds, flowers, deciduous trees, mammals, and eventually *homo sapiens*, with all of our cultural diversity.

Now, in just a blink of time (geologically speaking), industrialized societies, enacting a story of separation, have altered Earth's face and are bringing the Cenozoic age to an abrupt close. Climate change and the mass extinction of species are the primary signs that we have entered a new geological age. Scientists call it the Anthropocene, the era dominated by the human presence. In other words, the upshot of the story of separation is that we are now the protagonists in the Great Unfoldment. This is our current evolutionary predicament. The question now is whether we can embrace a cosmology of wholeness and harmonize our lives with Earth's community. With their lives, ecovillagers are voting on the side of "yes." If they and other sustainability pioneers succeed, perhaps the Anthropocene will take a cue from Thomas Berry and bear a more humble name: the Ecozoic – the ecological era.

I never heard the science-based saga of the Great Unfoldment in Africa or Sri Lanka, where immediate survival is the focus, but I encountered variations of this theme in every other community I visited. Ecovillagers speak of humanity as "the eyes of the universe," "the mind of Gaia," and "Gaia's soul." Gaia is front and center in the Global Ecovillage Network curriculum: Gaia Education, where science and spirituality are woven together into a holistic worldview.

While the narrative of the Great Unfoldment has taken root in ecovillage culture, I see there is a gap between this epic perspective and my own subjective experience. Conceptually, I can accept that the energy that impels me originated in the Big Bang and that the elements that constitute my body were unleashed in a supernova explosion. Yet I experience myself as a fairly self-obsessed middle-aged woman harboring a dark fear that I'm just a writhing lump of matter, subject to the laws of entropy. So how do I translate my intrinsic connection with nature into lived experience? How do I make the leap between feeling separate from nature and feeling one with nature? My hunch is that this transformation comes only through spiritual practice. As it turns out, five of the communities I visited – Findhorn, Damanhur, Auroville, Sarvodaya, and Konohana – are rooted in this premise. Except for Konohana, they also happen to be the largest places on my itinerary, suggesting that spiritual responses to our contemporary quandary can be inspiring.

Because of its size and it age, Findhorn has been called "the mama ecovillage," but the three mystics who founded this spiritual community in 1962 did not have ecology on their minds. Rather, Peter and Eileen Caddy and Dorothy MacLean were, in their words, "attuning" to divine guidance through prayer and meditation, and following this guidance wherever it led. None of them had ever gardened, so they were surprised to receive detailed instructions on soil building, planting, and harvesting from what they understood to be nature spirits. They grew a 42-lb. cabbage, thriving roses in an inhospitable spot, and a host of other extra-large crops on the sandy soils of windswept north Scotland. By the early 1970s, their astonishing harvests brought scientists, the media, and thousands of young people to their doorstep.

The founders eventually left, but decades later I still was able to participate in some of the rhythms they established. I particularly enjoyed the morning meditations in the Nature Sanctuary. The seating – several concentric circles radiating outward from a centerpiece of a candle lit among flowers – added to the sense of communal focus before each work day. I would then walk to Cullerne Gardens, where I marveled at how "attunement" transformed our collective work into spiritual practice. Whether meditating or working in the fields, people at Findhorn seemed intent upon following the founders' basic instruction: "Attune to Spirit, attune to Earth."

Still, I had the sense that Findhorn's melding of spirituality and ecology was not seamless. Several residents mentioned that Dorothy MacLean, now in her eighties, would soon be moving back to Findhorn from her home near Seattle. They reported that she was concerned that the community's strong ecological focus was detracting from its core spiritual mission. Later, I was able to confirm this in an interview with Dorothy in which she said that this, indeed, is her perception. I found that some residents concurred and others did not.

I put the question to Angus Marland, a permaculturalist who, as focalizer for the Sanctuary, also led the community's dawn meditations. Angus joined Findhorn in 1972, left in 1979 to start a renewable energy business, and returned twenty years later when he sensed that Findhorn was entering a new phase. As a green businessman and self-proclaimed mystic, Angus seemed like a perfect person to address Findhorn's apparent tension between spirituality and ecology.

"As I see it, they are harmonics of the same quality," he said. "For some people, Gaia is a living system; for others she's a spiritual being. In the sixties, some communities went spiritual, some went ecological. These streams diverged for twenty years, and now they are coming together. That's what the ecovillage movement is about. Findhorn's role is central because spirituality has always been the glue here. It's invisible but it's the essence of the place."

He said that the daily meditations in the Sanctuary are what maintains and builds the energy field around the community. "This clear and strong energy field is Findhorn's signature," he said, "and it is what draws so many people here for a remarkable process of soul integration." Each year, tens of thousands of people converge on Findhorn to see world-renowned teachers like Carolyn Myss and Eckhart Tolle. To my mind, there is a certain irony in an ecovillage depending so heavily on jet travel – even if the purpose is spiritual growth. I put the question to Angus.

"About the business of travel, I don't get too hung up on it. The way people move around the planet these days is by jet. When you feel it's time to integrate your life as a soul, *nothing* gets in your way! We're at a critical moment because humanity is very special."

And how is humanity, the author of a planetary state of emergency, "special"?

Angus lit up. "Humanity is at a turning point. After billions of years, life can consciously return to its source. We're a galactic phenomenon, and our galaxy has a big sign: 'Know thyself!' Consciousness is the source, and it always produces forms through which it can know itself. Silence is the front door to this source, but the door is often hidden by a tangle of brambles and the key is very often rusty."

Through my own meditation practice, I am familiar with the transformative power of silence. If an evolutionary intelligence is within me, I know I am far more likely to find it in silence than in my noisy mind. And yet if my mind is telling itself stories, why not choose the one where I am consciousness over the one where I'm a lump of matter?

While the Great Unfoldment showed up in every ecovillage I visited, it was most evident at Damanhur. The complexity of Damanhur's culture, which includes its own language, dances, and rituals, is far beyond the scope of these pages, but the core beliefs are fairly straightforward. I received some help in understanding these beliefs from Condor Girasole, a dignified Italian man in his late fifties known by the playful Damanhurian name Condor Sunflower. Dissatisfied with political activism, Condor joined Damanhur's founder in 1977 and, along with ten others, helped to build the Temples of Humankind. Now he was one of Damanhur's senior meditation teachers.

"We start from a big myth of a prime Divinity that chose to enter into completely new territory by breaking itself into many forms,

157

like a mirror, and entering matter. Each piece could only perceive reality through its own differentiation. So begins this big adventure, of becoming aware of this world and remembering our divine origin. Eventually, human beings become a kind of bridge. We can become aware of our divine essence not only in ourselves but beyond ourselves. The goal is to divinize this world of forms, to reassemble the pieces of the mirror – but with added value through differentiation. This is Damanhur's dream and we can only fulfill it through action."

So far, this story of the universe as an unfolding field of consciousness is familiar, but how is it relevant to ecology?

"For us," Condor said, "the subtle forces are just as important as physical forces, and there is a constant interaction between these levels. The divine ecosystem overlaps the physical ecosystem. When we develop the inner senses, meditation, dreams, or channeling, we can get to know these forces. These are the things that I teach."

Condor might be right about the "divine ecosystem," but I have no way of knowing. Several Damanhurians told me about "spiritual physics" and I attended a talk by Falco, Damanhur's founder, about time travel. However fascinating these ideas might be, I was in no position to validate them in two weeks. So I steered the conversation back to the physical plane and asked Condor about the Temples.

"Our planet is a living, sensing being, and it communicates energetically across 'synchronic lines.' These lines are like Earth's nervous system, and they only intersect in a few places. We built the Temples exactly where four synchronic lines meet so that our meditations and all that we do here can influence the rest of the world."

Again, I had no way of investigating the veracity of "synchronic lines," but neither Condor's words nor anything I read could have prepared me for the Temples. Seven underground halls, some reaching sixty feet in height, overflowed with gorgeous frescoes, murals, sculptures, mosaics, and stained glass cupolas. Macaco, my guide, explained that an invisible network of wiring and pipes between the Temples provides light and protection from water. Each hall is dedicated to a particular aspect of terrestrial existence, including water, earth, light, and the history of human civilization. As Macaco expounded, every square inch seemed to be imbued with esoteric meaning.

Of all the Temples, the Hall of Metals has the lowest ceilings and is therefore the most human-scale. A circle of sculpted metal pillars depict men and women in dramatic poses. Mosaics on the floor represent greed, vanity, dishonesty, and other unpleasant states, while benevolent beings on the fresco stretch downward protectively. One of Damanhur's core beliefs, Macaco explained, is that each of us must contend with an anti-life principle that is within creation. It is not evil so much as forgetful of divinity. We can overcome this anti-life principle, she said, through love, joy, and playfulness.

Having wrestled with depression for much of my life, I could resonate with the possibility of an anti-life principle – which might, in fact, be the source of my depression, my fears of being just a morsel of matter that's prey to entropy. In retrospect, I find this possibility somehow comforting.

Our last stop, the Hall of Mirrors, is one of the most awe-inspiring structures I have ever visited. The theme here is light: sunlight, spiritual light, air, and flight. My eye was drawn to an enormous colorful cupola overhead, which, despite being far underground, gave the impression of being infused by sunlight. It is, Macaco told me, the world's largest Tiffany-style glass dome. The hall was suffused with golden light and appeared to be filled with icons. Only gradually did I discern that I was surrounded by innumerable reflections of myself that seemed to recede into infinity. Macaco gave me a moment to have my own experience before explaining that the hall was designed to give each person who enters the feeling of being both a distinct individual and in relationship with the entire universe. The effect was so powerful for me that, despite a wave of vertigo and feeling of exhaustion, I was drawn to meditate in this room. I had intended to take notes but instead entered a deep silence, and, when I returned to normal consciousness with a blank notebook on my lap, I had the sense I'd slept for hours. I found that I'd been sitting for only twenty minutes. I felt totally rejuvenated.

While Damanhur may have contained the most dramatic and detailed articulation of the Great Unfoldment, I found expressions of this new story throughout my travels. Part of its magic is that it can be told in secular, religious, or spiritual language. In this sense, it is not just a story about the universe; it is a universally human story. I met atheists, Muslims, Jews, Hindus, Christians, Buddhists, and pagans who were integrating this new story into their worldviews – and, most importantly, aligning their lives with it. In a time when fear and despair threaten our capacity for positive action, the chronicle of the Great Unfoldment can serve as a source of humility and inspiration, reminding us that we are an integral part of a vast cosmological and biological coherence.

Until now, evolution appears to have been an unconscious affair. While humanity shares a common origin with stardust and a bacterial ancestry with all other species, we also have the capacity for

Figure 6.1 Damanhur's Hall of Mirrors in the underground Temples of Humankind

*conscious* evolution. In the new story, the contemporary predicament becomes a developmental opportunity rather than an unmitigated tragedy or a drama of good vs. evil. If we are the universe being born into self-awareness, then current conditions may very well be the labor pains of that birth.

## Box 6.2 A Green Sorcerer's Apprentice

In chapter 3, I described Earthaven's tightly integrated Gateway Farm as "the Mighty Mouse" of agricultural experiments. I asked one of the farm's founders, Chris Farmer, to tell me how the farm reflects his worldview. This is what he told me.

"We all live by stories. Here's mine: I believe that we're all apprentices to the Source – "sorcerer's apprentices" – we exist for a reason: to give thanks. Our gratitude is like food. It nourishes the cosmos and unfolds its hidden potentials.

"For example, I believe our gratitude for the magical spell of agriculture actually stabilized the climate. If you look at the charts, carbon dioxide and temperature rise and fall together. When they're down, which was true for most of the last 600,000 years, there's a mile of ice covering Chicago. But, about 10,000 years ago, they went up and stabilized. Plows didn't exist so people slashed and charred before they cultivated. The agricultural revolution created the most life-conducive climate this planet has seen for over 600,000 years.

"When the sorcerer takes on apprentices, there's a danger that they'll fall into a common trap. Remember the Disney movie *Fantasia*? The apprentice had to carry water. Chop wood, carry water: these are sacred responsibilities! But the apprentice preferred leisure so he cast a spell and had the broom do it. For a while, it worked great, but he hadn't cast the spell appropriately. He wanted to escape his responsibilities. And since his spell wasn't grounded in gratitude – it wasn't returning the power back to the source – it took on a mind of its own. So he started casting more spells to fix the mess, but those weren't cast appropriately either, and things really got out of hand.

"Disney is a multinational corporation, which means there's got to be a lie in the Mickey Mouse story. Here's two. One: Disney, and most of modern culture, insinuates that magic is supernatural and pretend. Well, it's neither. Fire is magic, agriculture is magic, electricity is magic, money is magic. Two: in the Disney story, when everything's going to hell in a handbasket, the sorcerer comes back to fix it all. But the sorcerer is not coming back to clean up our mess, because the sorcerer never left! The sorcerer is the Source, and the Source is everywhere. There's nothing that is not the Source of our lives, and we are apprentices to that mystery.

"The Source needed us to stabilize carbon dioxide. And what's going to bring down the whole show? Climate change. We've been taking the gifts without grounding our spells, without using them to benefit the whole. But the planet *needs* us to stabilize the climate. We've got to quit fossil fuels and sequester that carbon into the soils of our farms.

I tell myself this story. It's just a story, but it fits the data. Gateway Farm is only one solution. It's small scale, but that's how we're going to do it: watershed by watershed. Exxon, Shell, BP – they're not going to do it. We have billions of years of evolution embedded in the neural pathways between our neocortex and our opposable thumbs. Will that fix all the problems? I don't know, but it's worth a shot!"

Whether or not there's a Source that needs us to stabilize atmospheric carbon dioxide, I cannot say, but Farmer's story is consistent with the rise of civilization during a rare interglacial period. By burning 100-million-year-old carboniferous deposits, modern societies have unwittingly cast a planetary spell. Like the apprentice, we've opted for leisure and now find ourselves casting other spells to fix (or worse, deny) the mess. Because our transition to a life-sustaining society will be rooted in a new story of our place in the cosmos, Farmer's tale may contribute as much to the Great Unfoldment as Gateway Farm.

## Many ways to oneness

As I internalized the evolutionary story I found circulating in ecovillage culture, I had some big questions. Since most people in the world identify as members of one religion or another, how does the Great Unfoldment fit with those religions? Christianity in particular, the dominant faith in my own country, has a long-standing quarrel with evolutionary science. Likewise, "tapping nature's intelligence" might sound like New Age baloney to a scientific ear. What happens to the scientific method in the new story? Finally, integrating nature and spirit sounds like a great ideal but what does it mean in practice? As with all of my questions, I found illuminating answers across the metaphysical spectrum.

Los Angeles Eco-Village is a fairly secular ecovillage – so much so that a proposal to hold hands in silence before community meals was defeated by a handful of atheists who saw it as a religious ritual. Yet LAEV was also the most religiously diverse community I visited, with far more Christians, Jews, Buddhists, and Muslims than atheists. Several members expressed a longing for a stronger sense of collective spirituality, but secularism prevailed – perhaps because it served as a lowest common denominator.

I met Lara Morrison, an ecologist, a Christian and a self-described "mystic by nature," in the LAEV permaculture courtyard. Lara graduated in the mid-seventies from the University of Washington, where I teach. Back then, UW had no environmental studies major so she designed her own by combining forestry, biology, geology, and urban planning. Definitely a woman ahead of her time. Today, environmental studies is UW's fastest growing major. I asked Lara if there is a connection between her scientific training and her mysticism.

She said yes. "For me, the universe is self-revealing. It's a matter of listening to reality and attending to both our internal and external experience. Throughout history, people have done things like communicating with plants. That's partly how cultures adapted to particular places. Science moved us away from this, but now we're called to use *both* ways – intuition *and* science – to consciously create culture. This is a tall order!"

Lara added that in order to live consciously, we need science. "We would want to calculate the carrying capacity for each watershed, for instance, and then plan our resource flows. People could share their surplus across watersheds, which would mimic the way ecosystems are structured. That's basically what species do when they migrate seasonally. We need this kind of science if we're going to live sustainably. If the universe is self-revealing, then we need every kind of knowledge to understand it. There's a Sufi saying: Nature is the only manuscript that will enlighten its reader."

She then demonstrated that the New Testament says something quite similar, reading a passage from Matthew 7:7, beginning "Ask and it shall be given." The gist of this passage is that when we follow our deepest longings with sincerity, we essentially open ourselves to the evolutionary intelligence of the cosmos.

"This is about having an intimate connection between yourself and the world," Lara said, "by treating desire as a self-revelation of the universe. Underneath, that's the approach that most people in ecovillages are taking, though virtually none of them has ever read this!"

And Lara's probably right about that; in my observation the Bible is not a universal text in ecovillages.

I resisted the temptation to title this chapter "Spirituality" for the simple reason that a fair number of ecovillagers – especially in Europe – balk at the term. Not surprisingly, I encountered this aversion most strongly at Svanholm, the Danish commune that takes pride in its pragmatism – even while expressing a profound reverence for the cosmos.

René Van Dam, one of Svanholm's chief builders, met me at his studio. His email said I would find him painting and, given the construction I'd seen at so many ecovillages, I expected to find him working on a building. To my surprise, he was making a large, colorful abstract oil painting. René fixed me a cup of tea and told me about his life at Svanholm: raising three children, teaching art, and building creative structures. He defined the essence of ecovillage life as "playing and being open to being infected by new ideas."

When I broached the question of spirituality, René was blunt. "*Phhh!* I'm a very skeptical person and I don't want bullshit. Yes, we have love and beauty here, but don't call it spiritual! That makes it sound magical, not real."

Yet when I asked René how he responded to Gaia, the idea that Earth behaves like a self-regulating living system, his face lit up. "Oh, *yes*! We're like a collection of micro-organisms on this super-organism! But that's biological, not spiritual." After a long pause, he added, "I don't want to say I'm not interested in spiritual things. They might be out there. Places like Damanhur are fine. It's just not what we're doing here."

Likewise, Bø Lassoe, Svanholm's first organic farmer, spoke of feeling "a little allergic to people who become too holy." When I asked him whether he had a spiritual practice, he replied, "No . . .

well, yes." After a pause, he continued in a lower voice. "I have a big respect for nature. Sometimes I ask myself whether this is a religious feeling. I'm most connected to it when I'm outside, but I don't discuss it. It's a private thing."

While those at Svanholm shy away from spiritual language, I suspect that some of its experiments in communal living are more effective in softening the boundaries of ego than lofty meditation practices. The community's ability to stay the course over three decades is largely due to the social trust that comes from sharing income and property. Because the prevailing economic system in the world is about looking out for "me and mine," this arena of trust and sharing serves as a powerful laboratory for harmonizing human life with the Great Unfoldment. However much they shunned God-talk, Svanholm members were clearly dedicated to something far larger than themselves.

There is another reason for not drawing too sharp a line between the spiritual and the secular: in ecovillages, that split seems to be dissolving. Dieter Halbach, a former leader of the German peace movement and the man often credited with starting Sieben Linden, helped me to understand this transition. Dieter recalled that the divide between spiritual and political communities ran deep during the 1970s and 1980s. Intent upon transforming society only after attaining enlightenment, spiritual communities were generally hierarchical and lacking in economic transparency. Political communities, on the other hand, were more egalitarian but frequently dissipated their energies on lengthy meetings.

"Because of my bitter experiences in politics and communities, I saw from the outset that we needed someone to help us to cultivate our inner culture. So I brought in a friend, a Buddhist psychotherapist and an organic farmer. Now we've come to a point where we can accept some hierarchy. We've learned that when we find the right person for the job and trust them, things flow better. This frees up time and energy to give back to the larger society. Sieben Linden started out as political, but now we're bridging the old divide. It's very exciting. We're now in a position to help spiritual communities, and they're calling on us."

My sense is that the transition among intentional communities described by Dieter reflects a larger cultural shift. The old polarities – religion and science, the secular and the spiritual – seem to be giving way to a more unified worldview. The emerging integrative vision is rooted in our new story, the one that understands the web of life as sacred and human beings as vital members of that web. We can see evidence of this shift in the plethora of popular books at the inter-section of spirituality and science, ecology and religion. Ultimately, however, the Great Unfoldment cannot be told in words; it must be enacted through relational living. Because ecovillages excel in this department, we can look to them as cultural forerunners.

## The light inside the dark

Having watched my students struggle with fear, anger, grief, guilt, and despair – and having personally grappled with these dark emo-tions for decades – I have learned to value them as potentially pow-erful catalysts. Without turning the classroom into a group therapy session, I like to end my lectures with a few minutes of personal reflection and sharing. The overwhelmingly positive student response confirms what most of us already know from experience: in the absence of emotional engagement, cognition alone can be a dry and disempowering exercise. According to public opinion polls, most of us *know* that the climate is changing. Yet if we allowed ourselves to truly *feel* the magnitude of this fact, would we go on with business as usual? And what does our psychic numbing desecrate within our-selves? I've come to believe that our greatest danger is apathy – the failure to feel. When we repress our anguish, which has its roots in our caring for the world, we simultaneously deaden our hearts and undermine our capacity for effective action. When we openly express our distress in an atmosphere of care and compassion, we can liber-ate that energy and channel it into life-affirming responses to current needs. While I have seen this alchemical transformation writ small among my students, it was on my ecovillage journey that I saw it writ large. Ecovillagers have developed many practices for diving deep into their concern for the world and allowing their lives to be trans-formed accordingly.

Some of the most powerful deep-diving practices I encountered were developed by Joanna Macy, a spiritual teacher and activ-ist who helped to popularize socially engaged Buddhism in the West.[6] I attended Joanna's workshop "From Despair to Personal Empowerment" in 1982 and will never forget weeping for the first time with a large group of people – most of them priests, ministers, and

[6] Joanna Macy's first encounter with socially engaged Buddhism came in the 1960s through her development work in India and Sri Lanka. Her first book, *Dharma and Development*, introduced Sarvodaya's peace meditation and its ground-breaking village programs to the West.

nuns twice my age. That workshop was tremendously empowering and no doubt colored my pedagogical style as a professor years later. So I was intrigued to find Joanna's workshops, now under the banner of "Deep Ecology" and "The Work that Reconnects," cropping up in so many ecovillages.

Gabi Bott, a Sieben Linden member who was trained by Joanna Macy, helped me to understand this connection. Gabi said the German ecovillage and the "Deep Ecology" workshops integrated her twin passions for spirituality and political activism. Two decades ago, when she worked for the Green Party and as a yoga teacher, she "had two sets of friends: political activists and spiritual practitioners. I needed them both," she added, "and I could never understand why they refused to bring politics and spirituality together."

Eventually, Gabi quit both jobs and traveled to California for intensive training with Joanna Macy. "The training changed my life," she said, "and Joanna encouraged me to bring this work to Germany. She said my country needed healing from its divided past." So that's what Gabi did.

One example of the work she has done is the Aufbrechen Initiative, a movement in Austria and Germany where small groups gather to, as Gabi put it, "share inner and outer ecology." The word *aufbrechen* means both "breakdown" and "breakthrough," suggesting that creative forces are unleashed when people come together and allow their hearts to break open in the face of darkness.

Gabi visited Sieben Linden in 2000 and knew immediately that she would stay. "It was what I'd always wanted: a young community with a huge potential to be holistic. People here are into peace on both the inside and the outside – ecology, political change, communication, and spirituality. I offer the 'Deep Ecology' workshops all over Germany but Sieben Linden is really the perfect place for them."

That may be true, but when I later read Macy's *The Work That Reconnects*, I saw that this work extends far beyond the relatively small world of ecovillages. The basic principles are universal in their scope, yet intimate to our personal intuition.[7] Here is a glimpse:

- The intelligence that guides our own evolution and interconnects us with all other beings is sufficient to the task of building a sustainable world, if we but align ourselves with it.

---

[7] Paraphrased from Joanna Macy, *Coming Back to Life: Practices to Reconnect Our Lives, Our World*, Canada: New Society Publishers, 1998.

- Our capacity to respond to our own and others' suffering is a vital aspect of that intelligence. In following the thread of our own experience, we weave ourselves back into the fabric of life.
- When we reconnect with life by willingly enduring our pain for it, the mind regains its natural clarity and generates new possibilities for relational living.
- These self-healing powers can be fully effective only if we trust and act upon them.

While we can do some of this work in solitude, the experience of diving deep is far more potent in a group – particularly with a skilled facilitator. Whether we come together in our workplace or classroom, our neighborhoods or places of worship, each of us can engage in this reconnective work. Finding our way through the global sustainability predicament requires more than the mind's light; it compels us to open our hearts to the ecological morass that is happening on our watch. The only way out is through.

The most heartbreaking experiences of my journey were in Senegal and the Gambia, and the fortitude of some of the change agents I met there was far beyond anything I've been called upon to muster in my own life. Even on a map, the shadow of global injustice that hangs over West Africa is apparent. Like most of Africa, this part of the world reflects centuries of land-grabbing by European colonizers. The Gambia, a former British colony named for the mighty river flowing to the port city of Banjul, looks like a long narrow bite taken out of the former French colony, Senegal. Upon arriving in Banjul, the closest city to Colufifa's headquarters in southern Senegal, I watched the passengers on my flight – every one of them Caucasian – board several large tourist buses. A lone baggage attendant asked me if I was planning to visit Slave Island. I shook my head, guessing that he meant James Island, the World Heritage Site mentioned in all the tour books. Despite being one the world's smallest countries, the Gambia was once a geopolitical linchpin for Britain in its domination of world trade in gold, ivory, and slaves. For untold thousands of slaves, the final stop on their home continent was James Island at the mouth of the Gambia. Now the island is a major tourist attraction for Europeans who flock to Africa's beaches in wintertime, but it is being swallowed by the sea. In a cruel twist, this historic hub of the global slave trade, a source of precious income for local Gambians today, is literally crumbling as a consequence of greenhouse gases emitted primarily in the global North. Today's cheap slaves come in the form of fossil fuels but, once again, Africa finds itself on the losing end.

167

The most religious people I encountered on my journey were in Colufifa's villages. Most were Muslim and a sizeable minority was Christian or animist, making interreligious sensitivity a primary concern for Colufifa. All the people I interviewed described themselves as deeply religious. It would be easy to chalk this up to cultural mores: secularism is hardly an option where tradition runs strong and illiteracy is the norm. But these West African villagers were also the most economically destitute people I met. Desperation, I learned, can serve as a powerful fuel for both religious faith and transformational change.

On my third day at Colufifa, I traveled through the bumpy outback linking Senegal to the Gambia in a jeep full of village organizers, most of them men in their thirties. The French term for their position is *agent polyvalent*, which I mentally translated as "multi-tasking experts." As an *agent polyvalent*, you might find yourself teaching organic farming and poultry management, running a microfinance program or teaching literacy. Or you might find yourself tending sick chickens in the middle of the night. As one of them joked, "We do anything, anywhere, anytime."

In the evening, the men sat around a campfire and shared stories about their lives; as usual, the women stayed away. Whether because of my age, my race, or my status as a guest, I was welcomed into the circle. The story of Balla Biaye, a 33-year-old young man, was typical. "Before working for Colufifa, I had left school to support my family but could not find work. Many young men have *never* been employed! I have ten younger brothers and sisters, and I'm the only one employed. I also support my mother, two wives and my five children."

I did the math. "That makes eighteen people you are supporting!"

"Yes, that's right. And I pay school fees for all of my children. It's very hard to get money here. One of my brothers died on his way to Spain. Another man I know started out for Spain a few weeks ago, but it was so cold his boat turned back."

At this point, all the men around the fire started telling stories about men who had died on their way to Europe. The atmosphere grew animated as each one told of family and friends who had gone or tried to go. Then, as the fire died down and the gravity of the situation sank in, a dark silence engulfed us. At last, I asked Balla if he had any beliefs that helped him in his work.

"Oh, yes," he replied. "I am a Muslim. Whatever I am doing, I focus my mind on God, and this gives me energy. God is the All Knower and the All Decider."

Another man added, "If we didn't believe in God, we would all kill ourselves." The others nodded and murmured their agreement until, once again, everyone fell silent. This time the silence of desperation was suffused with a prayerful mood. I felt a sense of deep solidarity with these hardworking men. My life of privilege was worlds away from their lives, but in that moment we were united in our common humanity.

Balla continued. "Only religion makes people stay with their families. Otherwise, we would all leave. I want people to hear from my heart so that the rich countries can see our work and support us." I heard him well but did not know how to support Colufifa beyond offering a small bit of money and writing this book.

As I lay in bed on my last night in Senegal, the usual humidity gave way to a blustery, dry wind that blew from the east. Though this was far more ferocious, it reminded me of the desert winds that sometimes blow from the east over Southern California. The combination of my bodily experience and my mind's knowledge about desertification overwhelmed my capacity for sleep. I struggled to grasp the implications even as my throat grew parched. From my years of co-teaching with atmospheric scientists, I knew that global warming is expected to exacerbate the encroachment of the Sahara. But this theoretical knowledge was flimsy in comparison to the visceral experience: the Sahara, hundreds of miles away, was literally breathing down my back. Could it be that global warming will inflict untold misery on the world's most vulnerable and simple-living people? Yes, of course it will. I had read the scientific assessments, but my body was internalizing the data on an entirely different level.

As I lay sleepless in Senegal, my admiration for David in the face of Goliath gave way to a sense of foreboding. A sprinkling of tiny ecovillages around the world hardly seemed a match for the specter of climate change in an unequal world. My flights to India the next day would emit far more greenhouse gases than a typical African villager generates in a year. Once again, my heart broke open with the pathos and the wonder of it all: this tangled web of injustice is precisely how humanity has come to be linked together as a global species. After witnessing so much faith and courage in Africa, paralysis could never be an option for me. In the darkness of the night, I felt my life tied inexorably to the lives of Balla and his friends, and I redoubled my commitment to a viable human future.

## Box 6.3 Abiding by the Cosmic Laws

At the southernmost tip of Sri Lanka, white sand beaches stretch out toward a crystal-clear aquamarine ocean, framed against a tropical backdrop. I was on a village tour with Sarvodaya's 77-year-old founder, A. T. Ariyaratne – Dr Ari as he is affectionately known. As we entered the village of Galle, our view of this jewel-by-the-sea was blocked by a barricade of ugly buildings.

"This is the village where I was born," Dr Ari mused. Gazing at the long rows of hotels, the cheap and expensive restaurants catering to the full range of tourists, and the ayurvedic massage parlors with signs saying 'Foreigners Only,' I felt a pang of sadness. It may have been an idyllic place to grow up, but the encroachment of commerce was jarring.

"I worked hard to bring Sarvodaya's work to this area," Dr Ari said, "but the force of globalization was too strong."

I reflected the many similar scenes I had seen in my travels. I said, "I've visited so many wonderful ecovillages, but they're just drops in an ocean of mostly destructive development."

"You're right," Dr Ari replied. "So much of what is happening in the world seems destructive. But on a deeper level, these drops are more important than the whole ocean because they are in harmony with the cosmic laws. Only what abides by the cosmic laws can survive. This tremendous wave of globalization feels like a tsunami, but it cannot last."

For a moment, "the cosmic laws" sounded mysterious, but then I realized that Dr Ari was referring to ecological principles. Of course, he was right: only what is sustainable can be sustained. In the long run, sustainability is not a luxury; it is inevitable. Allowing my mind to widen into this larger perspective, I relaxed into a soft expectancy. As a mother, I know that birth can be a painful and bloody process. No doubt, something is being born through this planetary upheaval.

Still there is here and now, and I grieve for the devastation.

## 'Tis a gift to be simple

Wendell Berry suggests that spirituality and practical life should be inseparable. "Alone, practicality becomes dangerous; spirituality, alone, becomes feeble and pointless," he writes. "Alone, either becomes dull. Each is the other's discipline, in a sense, and in good work, the two are joined."[8] Intuitively, I agree with him, and ecovillages seemed like a good place to see what this might mean in

[8] Wendell Berry, *Home Economics: Fourteen Essays*, San Francisco: North Point Press, 1987, p. 145.

practice. For every ecovillager I interviewed, spirituality is about this world and not some afterlife. Yet if this world is our primary concern, won't our attention be so riveted on external reality that we neglect the inner life? When I set out on my journey, I imagined that most ecovillages would be so busy shrinking their ecological footprints that they would have little time for introspection. Instead, I found that they tend to place a high value on integrating inner and outer reality. I expected, for instance, members of Club 99, Sieben Linden's simple-living neighborhood, to be obsessed with their vegan agriculture and fossil-fuel abstinence. Yet I had some of the most numinous conversations of my journey in their ultra-low footprint straw-bale common house. Maybe I shouldn't have been surprised. After all, for thousands of years, monasteries and ashrams have given witness to the connection between material simplicity and inner growth. Perhaps today's ecovillages are rediscovering this connection and giving it a contemporary twist.

I even encountered a few postmodern monks on my journey: those who had taken on the practices associated with Damanhur's Way of Monks. Goura, a soft-spoken adherent in her mid-thirties, explained that the role of the monks is to access higher forces and bring them into Damanhur's work. Like religious monastics, the Damanhur monks practice celibacy and engage in fasting and silence in order to better contain the spiritual forces. Before coming to Damanhur seven years earlier, Goura had lived in London and practiced Buddhist meditation, but she wanted something more practical. She also worked for awhile as an organic farmer, but was dissatisfied with farming. Eventually, she stumbled upon Damanhur's course on astral travel and, to her amazement, found that she could travel outside her body. The moment she entered the Temples, she knew she had found her home.

"I never thought I would be able to do something like this. My contact with the universal forces grows with experience. It's hard to explain: I just feel it and refine it through discipline and practice."

I was curious about how she experienced the intersection of spirituality and ecology.

"My contact with the forces becomes stronger when I am more coherent in my everyday life," Goura said. "For example, I couldn't contact any forces if my behavior did not reflect the path I have chosen. The more I live my values, the more I can contact the universal forces. It's a material and spiritual refinement at the same time. Before, I was 'eco,' but I didn't have much understanding. Now that I'm more sensitive, I can really care about things."

Throughout my journey, ecovillagers spoke to me about this synergistic relationship between material simplicity and inner growth – and nowhere more so than at Konohana in Japan. Named for the legendary goddess of compassion said to inhabit Mount Fuji, Konohana is first and foremost a spiritual community. Its primary field of practice, however, is literally in the expansive vegetable and rice fields at the base of the mountain. In each action, word, and thought, members are expected to seek divine guidance. Their motto, "Before cultivating the field, cultivate the mind," informs everything from Konohana *kin* (the fermented brew they drink each day) to the nightly harmony meetings the entire group attends. Behind it all, and sometimes in front, is Isadon, Konohana's founder, a man who seemed to be always working – and always smiling.

It's not easy to categorize Isadon's philosophy. His worldview is compatible with many religions, but he adheres to no religion. Asked about his teachers, he said that, when consulting others, he often finds new ideas coming up. This he experiences as "a remembering process." He added that he meditated for years but "stopped when it was no longer necessary."

Isadon summed up his teachings in these words: "Forget about yourself and give. This is how all other living things live. Because we have such a high capability, we have been able to disconnect ourselves from the natural way. This is why people suffer."

Though he had never heard of "the universe story," Isadon's teachings seem to be a blueprint for the Great Unfoldment. I asked him how he sees humanity's disconnection from nature.

"It was just part of a long and natural process. Nature's intention is the same as the Divine intention. We were generated by nature; we did not create nature. It seems like we will destroy nature, but nature is more powerful because nature is the source of our lives. Even a millionaire cannot survive without food, air, and water.

"Nature is giving us so many messages now," Isadon added.

My mind traveled to my course syllabi: deforestation, climate change, toxic waste, the extinction crisis ... "How do you see the future unfolding?" I asked.

"I can't really see it like American science fiction movies. My vision is that human beings will learn how to live in harmony with nature. The time since the industrial revolution helped to draw out the human potential by building the ego. Nature's message is not to go back to the past, but to use technology to live in harmony with nature. Rather than living separately, people will live in a more sharing way. Because they are needed, communities will sprout up without plans being made for them. We didn't plan Konohana. The direction was in front of us, but no plan. Plans generate attachment, which reduces flexibility."

Isadon made it all sound so easy but I noticed that he never seems to stop working.

"I work," he said, smiling, "but it is not hard! For us, prayer and work are the most important things, so I am always doing both. If we enjoy our work and talking to God, we never get tired. We only get tired when we are stressed."

"I get tired!" I said. I was tired at that very moment!

"I think you are tired because you have an irregular life. You travel and teach, but someday you might want to try farming. Agriculture is the best way to have a regular life – especially if you keep animals. You can't take a day off!"

Later that day, I strolled through Konohana's lush fields and reflected upon the simplicity of Isadon's demeanor. A biblical injunction came to mind that seemed to encapsulate the intersection of spirituality and ecology: "to live like a lily of the field." Whatever Jesus might have meant 2,000 years ago, the phrase took on a sense

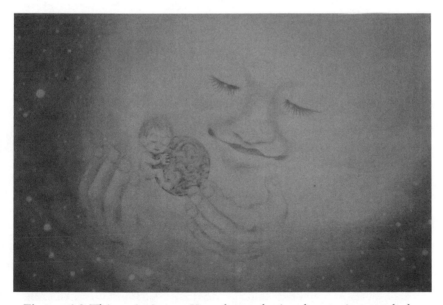

**Figure 6.2** This painting at Konohana depicts humanity as a baby holding Earth's fate in its hands while also being held by the Divine

*Source*: Painting by Shunsuke Shimura, photograph taken by Isao Yoshikoshi

of immediacy under the gaze of Mount Fuji. What would it feel like to know myself as belonging to the cosmos? With all my worries and plans, all my personal and scholarly complexity, how could I possibly live with the simplicity of a flower? Surely there must be a state of simplicity on the other side of all this complexity! As I watched the glacial waters tumbling down the granite aqueduct, hand-carved centuries ago by farmers, two terms came to mind: to be grateful and *to trust*. With those bridges, I felt myself more as a verb than a noun, one tiny tributary in the Great Unfoldment.

## Box 6.4 Music of the Plants

When I learned about Arboricoli, the tree-house "nucleo" where Damanhurians say they communicate with plants, I was skeptical, to say the least. The concept of a universal intelligence is one thing; the idea of chatting with a petunia quite another. Still, as a researcher, I wanted to test the veracity of these claims. So when Lucertola Pepe (Lizard Pepper), who had specialized in this work for twenty years, offered to demonstrate plant communication, I accepted.

Arboricoli is a cluster of tiny tree-homes, all built by hand – some without nails – and linked by a network of swinging aerial bridges. We climbed up to the community dining room, where we sat by a sun-splashed window. Lucertola connected electrodes from an electronic instrument to the roots and leaf of a white cyclamen in full bloom. After some time, a pleasant but somewhat monotonous tune came through the speakers.

Lucertola explained that this sound was coming from the cyclamen and was its "music" for that time. "Plants produce different kinds of music," she said, "depending upon who is around them at the time and that person's mood." She added that plants learn to become better musicians, especially after listening to classical music, and that the plants teach each other. "When we put an experienced plant next to one that has not learned, the new one learns immediately," she said. "They seem to pass information instantaneously."

The cyclamen's simple arpeggio carried on as Lucertola described various concerts involving as many as four plants and four musicians. "Music is a universal language," she concluded.

As a music lover, I silently concurred and felt a ripple of joy at the thought. At precisely that moment, the music shifted to a tinkling series of high notes in a complex and beautiful pattern. Within moments, the simple arpeggio resumed. Not noticing any other change in the room beyond my mood, I found myself entertaining the possibility that the cyclamen had responded to me.

"The plants react to people's intentions," Lucertola said. "When someone plans to cut a plant's leaf, it stops making music. When you are sad, a plant can really help you. And when skeptical people come, the music changes." Just then, the music stopped.

"It's listening," she said. "Would you like to make a communication?"

I stepped forward awkwardly, thinking I hadn't the slightest idea of how to talk to a cyclamen. I touched one of its leaves softly, I admired the translucent beauty of the white petals of its flower in the sunlight, I thanked the plant for its beauty – all to no avail. The monotonous music continued unabated. I felt a flash of irritation with myself. I saw that I was being sentimental and insipid. Through my genial babble, I was squandering an opportunity to communicate with another life form! If a universal intelligence united me with this cyclamen, I *wanted* to access it! Once my resolve was clear, I fixed my gaze on a particularly luminous flower, stilled my mind, and entered into an intense concentration. At that moment, the music transformed into one exceptionally high, sustained note, an utterly distinct and ethereal sound. I had no doubt that the plant had "heard" me and responded. Speechless and satisfied, I relaxed my gaze. As I resumed my seat, the music returned to its familiar refrain.

"So this is it," I said at last.

Lucertola smiled. "This is only the beginning."

## A new we

It is quite normal to hear ecovillagers saying things like "I live in a cauldron" and "We're surrounded by mirrors here." Unlike other personal growth workshops, you don't get to leave community life behind at the end of the weekend. You've made your home in an evolutionary laboratory, and the main point of your relational experiment is to foster new modes of human beingness. In this sense, the engaged spirituality of ecovillages is not just about tapping into nature's intelligence. It is a collective endeavor, deepened by the power of seeing others and being seen by them – *truly* seeing and being seen. I think this is why ecovillagers everywhere told me that human relationships were both the most challenging and the most rewarding aspect of community life.

Paul Caron, a 60-year-old builder at Earthaven, described this collective work as much more demanding and meaningful than building ultra-green homes. "It's far easier to change how you build your houses than to change yourself," Paul said. "Being here is like being in a fire. Your lack of trust, your anger, your family neuroses – everything that separates you from the rest of the world is going to come out here!"

"Do you ever question working so much on yourself when there are so many big problems in the world?" I asked.

Paul had obviously given this some thought. "You have to think about long-term effectiveness. When things break down, people will just need a little sign for which way to go. If people don't see other options, they'll keep their noses to the ground. But when the crisis comes, if people see even a small hint of another possibility, they'll respond. People need to see, and most of all *feel*, that something else is possible. The real hallmark is getting over our individualistic culture. That means remaking ourselves. To me, that's what Earthaven is about."

"Sounds daunting," I said.

"It's a huge adventure! To me, what's at stake is everything, and I'm willing to give it everything." Paul paused, his eyes misting. "When people ask, 'What's it take to live at Earthaven?' I say, 'What've you got?'

"The whole ecological problem is about us," he added. "Humans are a different order of reality. We're part of nature, but we're the part that becomes conscious of itself and takes responsibility. We have something to live up to that the rest of nature doesn't have. We're an unfinished species. I think we have maybe a hundred years to prove that we deserve to be here. From what I can see, I think we're doing all right!"

Feeling myself as very much a work in progress, I like the thought that we're an unfinished species. If we're the species that takes responsibility, then we have to do so internally as much as externally. After all, consumerism is fueled as much by fear and desire as it is by petroleum. If we want to go beyond individualism, then we need to be in communities of practice that encourage us to face whatever it is that separates us from other species. For most of us, reading books and doing solo spiritual practice are not enough. There is a transformative power in truly being seen by others, particularly when these others are also committed to living a new cultural story.

Ironically, as I've mentioned, ecological beliefs themselves can be prominent sources of division in ecovillages. Michiyo Furuhashi, my translator at Konohana, offered a personal example. "When I came here, I was an 'ego-village' person," she recalled. "I wanted to change Konohana's systems for water, energy, and waste. I was so critical! I wanted to play God and tell them how to live. From our harmony meetings, I saw that I was causing conflict. It was very hard to see this, but

I found that when I stopped resisting, I could enter a flow. As a consequence, I am more relaxed and my relationships are more harmonious."

Across the metaphysical spectrum, ecovillagers share a core belief in the power of the group mind. I heard it countless times: the whole is greater than the sum of its parts. Consensus decision-making and other experiments in participatory democracy, of course, are rooted in this assumption, but some communities take this premise a step further and apply it to spiritual awakening. Findhorn and Konohana, for instance, try to communicate with the Divine in order to work together as one body. Reflecting their belief that community life is the very basis for spiritual growth, Damanhurians greet one another with *Con te.* In essence, they are saying, "My soul is with your soul." Likewise, Auroville sees itself as a field of collective yoga. Like traditional mystics, these people are seeking an intimate relationship with the Divine, but to do it, they aren't retreating alone to a cave or a cell. They are seeking "together" while remaining "engaged in the world." In the words of one ecovillager, "It's easy to be enlightened on the meditation cushion. Try being a Buddha in a community meeting!" Although this was not my personal experience on the cushion, I could see her point. Human relationships are where the spiritual rubber meets the road.

Surprisingly, I first encountered the term "collective intelligence" in two German ecovillages, neither of which had a strong spiritual identity. Compared to the United States, Germany is a fairly secular culture, so I didn't expect to find a spiritual teacher there working specifically with communities. Yet nearly half of the people I interviewed at ZEGG and Sieben Linden spoke about being transformed through their work with Thomas Hübl. These were some of the most mentally clear and emotionally accessible people I met on my journey. Several had just finished his one-year training with eighty people from fifteen German communities. From what I could gather, the gist of the training was to learn how to go beyond one's own conditioning and inhabit the collective field that unites us all. In other words, it was intensive schooling in how to participate consciously in the Great Unfoldment.

Thomas was away at the time, so I did the next best thing: I "googled" him. At first glance, he seemed too young and stereotypically good-looking to be a legitimate spiritual teacher. Reading on, however, I could also see that he's onto something. And I could see from my visits to these communities the positive influence he's had on ZEGG and Sieben Linden.

The following summer, two events drew me back to Germany: a community conference on collective wisdom in the heart of Berlin and, at Sieben Linden, the General Assembly of the Global Ecovillage Network for Europe and Africa. The conference, in simultaneous English and German translation, included Thomas Hübl's first public presentation for the non-German community movement. Over a dozen ecovillages were represented, including a sizeable contingent from Findhorn. The underlying theme of Thomas's talks was the Great Unfoldment. He suggested that, in the modern era, people have crystallized a physical, emotional, and mental sense of self, but that we are actually more like rivers than fixed objects. According to Thomas, we each reside at a specific "cosmic address" from which we transmit our entire past and future. He described the shift from individualism to universalism as being like "moving from particle consciousness to field consciousness."

"In this next level of evolution," Thomas said, "we are learning that we are not a collection of 'I's,' like a six-pack of beer where the bottles clash together when we move. The contraction of the 'I' limits our energy. When we see through our habits and become aware of the space between us, this space that is holy, we free up our collective intelligence. Then we can talk *from* life, not *about* it."

While Thomas's worldview was not much different from the evolutionary story I found percolating through ecovillages, his ability to convey that worldview experientially through small-group practices was something new for me.[9] In one exercise, we were instructed to pair up, sit in silence, "read each other like a book," and then check our perceptions with each other. Not only did my partner glean that I was a teacher and a mother, he also discerned my emotional and physical state quite accurately. I sensed that he worked with his hands and had an unhappy childhood. He turned out to be a carpenter with a happy childhood; the sadness I detected was a consequence of his recent divorce. Never having thought of myself as energetically sensitive, I was surprised by the accuracy of my perceptions. I was also surprised, and somewhat disarmed, by how much a complete stranger could know about me without my saying a word. Indeed, silence seemed to be an essential ingredient in entering the field of collective intelligence – what Thomas called "this space that is holy."

When Thomas asked how many of us felt seen by our partners, everybody's hand went up. I found myself wondering, how much we

---

[9] Some of Thomas Hübl's practices are outlined in his small book, *Transparence*. Available in print or as a free download at www.media.innerscience.info/index.php?main_page=product_info&cPath=90&products_id=270, accessed June 18, 2013.

normally censor our perceptions of one another and how much we unconsciously broadcast to others. I left the conference feeling alive to new possibilities of socio-spiritual synergy.

To experience collective intelligence in action, all we needed was an ecovillage, which is where I went next – to Sieben Linden for the General Assembly of GEN-Europe/Africa. Sieben Linden, in many ways a model ecovillage, was the ideal setting for the gathering. Never was a toilet flushed, every drop of unused water was recycled into the landscape, and most of our food was grown on-site. For five days, I lived with nearly a hundred ecovillagers from twenty-five different countries as they shared their best practices, celebrated their achievements, planned educational programs, and elected new leaders – luckily for me, all in English. Meetings were both heartfelt and focused, with only a couple of bogged-down episodes around GEN's meager finances. Songs were aplenty. Each evening, several ecovillage initiatives gave pithy, jam-packed presentations. I learned about the Anastasia ecovillage movement in Russia; Kibbutz Lotan, an ecotourism ecovillage in Israel; Guneskoy Village in Turkey; Eco-Yoff in Senegal; and the Estonia Ecovillage Network, convened by some of the leaders of that country's famous Singing Revolution. I found my mind stretching to grasp the breadth and depth of the global ecovillage movement. The five-day gathering was a phenomenal experiential download, to say nothing of the ten gigabytes of photographs and PowerPoint presentations I downloaded. So many stunning images!

I was not the only researcher at the GEN assembly. An Austrian filmmaker, Stefan Wolf, was making a movie about the European ecovillage movement. We compared notes on our travels and found ourselves agreeing that the most important work of ecovillages is the inner work. The title of his movie, now available online, makes the point nicely: *A New We*. In ecovillage culture, the pathway to social change is through personal transformation in the crucible of community.

Most of us do not live in ecovillages, but we each can rewrite the story of separation through our own lives by exploring the uncharted territories of collective intelligence. The key is to come together with others in a field of practice with agreements that help us to move beyond our habitual self-contraction. As we bring awareness and deep listening to our relationships, we are essentially reconstructing reality at the level of collective consciousness.

## All life is yoga

I wrestled with the question of whether to travel to Auroville, which calls itself not an ecovillage but a "universal township." Auroville is a member of the Global Ecovillage Network, but only because some of its members wanted to see their community represented. With more than two thousand members from forty-three countries and spanning a large geographical area, this "township" is in a class of its own. First and foremost, Auroville is a spiritual laboratory, founded in 1968 as "a site of material and spiritual research for a living embodiment of an actual human unity." Auroville's sustainability experiments are well known in ecovillage circles, but, rather than stemming from ecological tenets, they emerge from the teachings of Sri Aurobindo. In contrast to the traditional yogic disdain for worldly phenomena, Sri Aurobindo opens his magnum opus, *The Synthesis of Yoga*, with the epithet "All life is yoga."[10] In other words, the universe – including every aspect of human experience – is an evolutionary unfoldment of divine consciousness. This is a familiar idea in Findhorn, Damanhur, and Konohana, but it goes well beyond the ecovillage consensus. Not only is life sacred for Aurovilians, matter itself is considered an embryonic form of consciousness. In scientific circles, this is a hot topic, but it's far beyond the scope of this book. Still, if sustainability is ultimately an inside job, then Auroville had to be on my itinerary.

It was this intersection between spirituality and ecology that drew Bhavana Dee, an American woman of sixty, to Auroville thirty years earlier. "I was uncomfortable with my middle-class existence," she recalled. "I just couldn't believe that the point of life was to make money and get things. So I came to India searching and immediately sensed what I wanted. But I didn't buy the whole equation that spirituality equals renunciation. Even before finding Auroville, I wanted to *work for* the world, not *escape from* it."

Noting the simplicity of Bhavana's home, a small thatch hut, I asked about her environmental beliefs.

"When I first read about ecology, I felt, *this* is a spirituality of matter. In the early days of Auroville, our main work was tree planting. For me, this was Vedic sacrifice in the truest sense – giving ourselves to the future. We carried water in clay pots to each tree as if they were our children. People talk about the environment, but it's

---

[10] Sri Aurobindo, *The Synthesis of Yoga*, Vol. 23 of *The Complete Works of Sri Aurobindo*, Pondicherry: Sri Aurobindo Ashram Trust, 1999.

really about our relationship with matter. It's about the right use of things."

For Bhavana, "the right use of things" also translated into starting the Auroville Village Action Group, an umbrella organization for many of Auroville's development projects. These include microfinance loans, literacy programs, cottage industries, and cultural education. "We are surrounded by forty thousand villagers, and I was pained by their poverty," Bhavana said. "The only way for me to relate to them with integrity was to help them get out of poverty. Otherwise, what could 'human unity' really mean?"

For Bhavana, this human unity is Auroville's most important work.

"I don't see how humanity can make it without a change of consciousness. Instead of having egoism as our default setting, *the whole* needs to become our default setting. This is what I've learned from thirty years in Auroville: that it is possible to live for the whole."

During the year of my journey, I met many people living for the whole, or at least very much aspiring to – probably more than I ever had before. I kept wondering how their small efforts could be scaled up. Each time I left an ecovillage and was jolted into the harsh reality of highways and airports, I found myself grappling with the limited impact ecovillages seemed to have on the whole. Whether the ultimate problem is about consciousness, action, or material reality, we're facing some big problems. As the largest and most dynamic community on my itinerary, Auroville seemed a good place to look for clues – and Joss Brooks, an Australian who moved to Auroville in 1969, seemed an ideal person to address my questions. For Joss, Auroville's real work is to share its successes with the bioregion.

I met Joss one Sunday afternoon on his veranda overlooking the thriving forest he'd planted decades before. Joss told me about how, over the years, the radius of his work had expanded from tree planting in Auroville to conservation projects throughout the South Indian state of Tamil Nadu. Joss was particularly excited about his most recent undertaking, which he described as "the possibility of not just creating heaven on earth, but creating heaven in hell." As he divulged the project's complexity and scope, I found myself surprisingly eager to leave the comfort of Auroville in order to see it firsthand.

Two hours north of Auroville is Chennai (formerly known as Madras), India's fourth-largest city and home to nearly ten million people. Conditions in much of Chennai are dreadful, with frequent outbreaks of malaria, tuberculosis, and cholera, and still the population is growing. Thronged along its waterways, where the city meets the Bay of Bengal, is one of the Chennai's worst slums. This is the spot where the city's chief minister put the challenge to Joss: "Are you willing to bring the best of Auroville right here into the worst of Chennai?" One of the primary results of that conversation is a 60-acre ecological and social restoration project known as Adyar Poonga.

At Adyar Poonga's entry gate, I recognized the distinctive images of wildlife painted on rock tablets – clearly an Auroville export. Joss explained that, while he was the primary Aurovilian working on Adyar Poonga, fifty to sixty others were also involved.

As we set out, Joss laid out the mission. "Our goal is to transform a sewer into a living ecosystem." For two sultry hours, we meandered through the maze of sandy trails and shantytown homes, all surrounded by towering air-conditioned office buildings. In some places, we stepped gingerly over human excrement. Still, I saw abundant evidence of Auroville's forty years of experimentation in education, cottage industries, afforestation, reed-based water filtration systems, effective micro-organisms, natural building, and more. It wasn't heaven by any stretch, but it was on its way. Even though the project was not yet open to the public, city officials from around the world were already asking to visit.

As we circled back to the gate, Joss described himself as a poet at heart. Why would a poet want to leave the green tranquility of Auroville to spend his days in the scorching cesspools of Chennai?

He smiled. "I am a bit out of my element. Sometimes it's scary to function in the world of reports with hundreds of people working under me, when we have to come up with master plans for the chief minister and these corporate guys. Everything depends upon how tightly I'm holding the Divine's hand. I get the CEOs and ministers to hold the other hand, and they get the energy. Then we walk through the shitting fields of Chennai together. Their reality is reports and plans; my reality is holding the hand of the Divine will. If you get that will strongly by the hand, then you get things done."

"How do you know when you've got the Divine's hand?" I asked.

"Sri Aurobindo calls it 'the vast noise of the creative urge.' I tune into that," Joss said. "And I like to remember the Quaker saying that there is that of God in every man. It's when you doubt or try to do it yourself that things get messy."

Joss helped me to see that a change of consciousness is not just an internal matter; nor is it simply an individual matter. Given the right conditions, it can be a profoundly creative force and it can even be contagious. Auroville's spirituality of matter was showing tangible results in the swampy ghetto of Adyar Poonga. Yet each time I thought of Joss metaphorically holding the hands of government ministers and corporate executives, I had to wonder whether this invisible transmission wasn't actually his most significant work. In the end, I dropped my either/or thinking and concluded that the transformation of consciousness and socio-material transformation are inextricably interwoven, the warp and the woof of human development.

---

## Box 6.5 The Ecological Footprint of Enlightenment

For Aurovilians, the Matrimandir, an enormous golden globe at the community's center, is "the soul of Auroville." Every element of this edifice, from its "sacred geometry" to its ultra-thin layer of gold "skin," is laden with deep symbolism and complex engineering. Each morning of my visit, I cycled through the forest, climbed the stairway to the Matrimandir, donned a pair of mandatory white socks to protect the white carpet, and scaled the circular ramp to the expansive inner chamber. Twelve enormous white columns support the white domed ceiling. Each day, my attention was captivated by the crystal sphere – the world's largest – at the chamber's center. The luminous globe is penetrated by a shaft of sunlight traveling from the ceiling overhead clear down to a marble lotus pond far beneath the Matrimandir. The complex solar tracking system that captures and directs the sunlight is an engineering wonder, to say nothing of the structure itself. As much as I enjoyed gazing at the crystal orb and contemplating the Matrimandir's alchemical meaning, I always closed my eyes and basked in the silence. Because each shuffle reverberated throughout the chamber and a sneeze could sound like an explosion, I remained utterly still and entered into a concentrated state that left an impression throughout each day of my stay in Auroville. In the late afternoon, I would sometimes sit in one of the twelve "petal" chambers, each a different color signifying spiritual qualities like faith, gratitude, and courage. Again, the silence was palpable and the atmosphere intensely focused. On a purely sensory level, I was glad for the respite from South India's sweltering climate, for the Matrimandir was Auroville's only air-conditioned building.

Like Damanhur, with its elaborate Temples of Humankind, Auroville believes that the Matrimandir is a sacred vessel for the transformation of human consciousness. Given my own experiences in both places, I am open to this possibility. Yet these structures are tremendously resource intensive. In terms of energy and material use, no other building in either community comes close to the resource requirements of these sacred structures. My inner artist and mystic were delighted, but my inner ecologist was dubious. Three years later, I've still not resolved my own internal debate.

Throughout the ages, people have poured their most sophisticated technologies and their more glorious artistry into their places of worship. Why should today be any different? We may even need these spaces now more than ever; perhaps they are quintessentially the right use of things. Yet I feel uneasy in the same way as I did with Angus's remark about jet travel: "When you feel it's time to integrate your life as a soul, *nothing* gets in your way!" Really? Nothing?

I did not become enlightened on my journey, but I did grow tremendously. I also emitted more greenhouse gases than twenty typical Africans do in a year. If everybody on Earth followed my example, we would essentially fry the planet. So I wonder: do we really need to consume copiously in order to wake up to our interdependence and live accordingly?

I returned from my journey with a firm resolve to pursue my own path of inner growth with a substantially lower footprint.

Figure 6.3 The enormous banyan tree adjacent to Auroville's Matrimandir also serves as a sacred space for the community

## Connectivity – ever deeper, ever wider

The universe becoming conscious of itself, a new we, collective intelligence – these are lofty concepts. But this need not deter us from pursuing them. So was democracy lofty in 1776, and, even at that, it excluded women and slaves. Our big ideas run the risk of becoming empty slogans, however, if we do not allow them to *inhabit* us. If we sincerely want to participate in the Great Unfoldment, then we cannot simply deploy feel-good concepts. In *living* the story and not merely telling it, we allow ourselves to be transformed in unexpected and radical ways. We need to direct ourselves toward our North Star and be patient along the way with our inevitable stumblings and detours. In our movement beyond hyper-individualism, as much as we might hunger for the sense of belonging that comes from living as cells in a larger organism, the transition from separation to coherence will be awkward at times. Ecovillages are dancing on this edge.

As I see it, standing in the fire of community – especially a well-functioning community – is quite possibly the single best way to rewrite the story of separation with our own lives. Whether we find ourselves playing music, baking bread, running a microfinance program, building a temple, communicating with plants, or caring for a dying friend, in community every dimension of life becomes an opportunity to move beyond individualism. We each encounter such opportunities every day. My sense, however, is that we can expedite this cultural transformation by intentionally coming together with others to breathe life into a story of belonging. In this way, ecovillages are laboratories for conscious participation in the Great Unfoldment.

We need not live in an ecovillage to learn from their experiments. Whenever we come together with others for the purpose of planting a seed for a viable human future, we are essentially creating a crucible for the transformation of consciousness. And while consciousness is beyond words, beyond story, the stories we tell ourselves about our place in the cosmos do matter. Whether they call themselves secular, spiritual, or religious, ecovillagers are telling – and, most importantly, living – new stories of belonging. When we approach life as an integrated whole, revering "the space between," we are consciously reweaving the scattered strands of the prevailing culture. Ecology, society, economics, politics, and spirituality then assume their rightful places as intertwined aspects of a unified life.

As I spoke with ecovillagers around the world, I found my mind's dichotomies softening into a bigger picture. Science vs. mysticism, Christianity vs. evolution, simple living vs. big-picture thinking,

185

selfishness vs. altruism – these old antinomies were making peace in my mind. As my either/or categories dissolved into a more embracive, both/and perspective, my internal experience of myself and the world felt larger and more generous. I began to see my own foibles and those of others as transitory deficiencies of consciousness, rather than irredeemable character flaws. I came to view the story of separation as a means of creating individuals capable of consciously giving themselves to the whole. In framing our contemporary predicament as a developmental process, rather than the catastrophic consequence of human stupidity or God's punishment for our sins, I could see larger possibilities for action and compassion – possibilities that grow exponentially in the context of community. I could see that each of us has the potential to become, quite literally, a force of nature.

The message of every religion is that at root we are one, linked inextricably in that oneness through love. Now, science tells us that we come from a common origin and are connected through a vast network of material and energetic exchanges. Today, *oneness* is becoming more than a concept; economically and ecologically, we are increasingly entwined into a global oneness. No doubt, most of us do not live in an internal state of oneness, but the world itself seems to be conspiring to push us there. At a minimum, planetary exigencies are calling us to internalize the reality of interdependence and come home to our place within the larger community of life that sustains us. Our species is operating as a geophysical system – albeit unconsciously – and our inner lives seem to be playing catch-up with our technological creations. It is not so much a question of whether we will make it as a species. As members of an exceptionally weedy and brainy species, some of us will most likely adapt to whatever conditions we catalyze. The real question is what *kind* of species we will be, and this is a question of consciousness.

Globalization has given us the material infrastructure for planetary connectivity. Can we develop the inner connectivity to live as one species, in all its splendid diversity, on our one Earth? We can look to ecovillages as living laboratories for answers to this question. And we can ask ourselves, "What stories will future generations tell about what we did to further the Great Unfoldment?"

# — 7 —

# SCALING IT UP

Since returning to my home in the Pacific Northwest, I've shared my journey with dozens of audiences. A common response is, "That's all fine for those lucky ecovillagers, but what about the rest of us?" This reaction always brightens my day because it means that people are taking the message to heart. As I've reiterated, we don't need to join ecovillages or create new ones – though I support anybody who makes that choice. The point, rather, is to glean lessons from ecovillages and apply these to our lives, right here and now. That means taking action in our homes and neighborhoods and towns, which is a primary theme of this chapter. Yet the problems facing our species – and the most comprehensive solutions – require more than local action. This point was driven home for me by a colleague, an international political economist who responded to my talk with the simple query: "How do we scale it up?" At the time, I felt unsettled because I had no clear answers, but I knew he had asked the right question.

My journey was a paradoxical one. I was an international relations scholar acutely aware of the global nature of our problems, yet I was touring micro-communities in search of seeds for a viable future. Even including Sarvodaya's 15,000-member villages, most of which are only slightly more sustainable than the norm, the total number of ecovillagers on Earth is probably two million, at most 0.03% of the world's population. Yet I am convinced that these seedlings have something to teach us at every scale of human existence. Time is far too short to construct ecovillages for seven billion people, but not too short to apply their lessons everywhere, from our individual homes to our imperiled planetary household. Given that some of Earth's life-support systems may have already passed the tipping point, success is far from guaranteed. What *is* guaranteed, though, is a sense of shared adventure and worthy purpose – qualities I found in abundance in ecovillages.

Social purpose, I believe, is for humans much like water is for fish: absolutely vital to existence, yet largely unexamined. Ecovillagers have managed to move out of the mainstream and orient their lives around the core purpose of sustainability. They are rethinking the values of convenience and comfort, profit and growth, and building a culture that reflects and amplifies their sense of purpose. Considering all that we've accomplished in the pursuit of technological mastery – from the miracle of the micro-chip to wonders of the Hubble telescope – what might we accomplish if our core purpose were to harmonize our lives with our home planet?

Ecological sustainability means living in the circle of life, which is my shorthand for subsisting within nature's capacity for self-replenishment. The message of climate change and biospheric depletion is that our game of technological mastery is over. We seem to have checkmated ourselves into partnership with nature – and a junior one at that. The first step is to embrace this core purpose at every scale, starting with the power of one: ourselves. So long as we consider sustainability an afterthought, like recycling a Coca-Cola can, we will persist in our utterly unsustainable lifestyles. When, however, we have yoked ecology to our economies, communities, and consciousness – the other three windows into sustainability – to this sense of purpose, then our thinking becomes systemic and E2C2 takes on the kind of dynamic, self-reinforcing character we find in ecovillages. With sustainability as a core purpose, one that is consistent with other objectives like happiness and democracy, we can then tease out the basic principles of ecovillage living and begin to scale them up.

The most obvious starting point is permaculture's twelve design principles (outlined in chapter 3). Ecovillages have already taken the initiative here, scaling them up from the single property owner to the community level, but we can go further. Imagine neighborhoods catching and storing energy, cities producing no waste, businesses using small and slow solutions, countries responding creatively rather than pursuing myopic policies. Yet as thrilled as I might be to see every level of governance jumping on the permaculture bandwagon, I would hope for more. As an ecological design strategy, permaculture offers little insight into the other three windows into sustainability. To my mind, the truly exciting synergistic possibilities emerge with the full E2C2 – when ecology, economics, community, and consciousness join forces. Permaculture's ecological principles are a good start but are also more complex than we need.

188

In order to export the ecovillage experience, we need a few simple principles that reflect the integrative character of that experience while attending to larger social and economic realities. Taking sustainability as a core purpose, I suggest the following five principles:

1. *Systemic thinking* is a key ingredient in ecovillage success stories. Architecture, transportation, and food production, for instance, are structured in ways that promote and amplify the core values of social trust and ecological sustainability. What if we joined together to grow food in our parks and backyards? What if parents, rather than driving their children to school, organized "bike trains?"[1] This integrative approach to E2C2 differs sharply from prevailing piecemeal approaches to city planning, national policy making, and international institutions – but change is afoot.

2. *Subsidiarity*, the idea that social and political decisions should be made at the lowest level practicable, has its roots in democratic theory, Catholic social teaching, and EU international law. An ecological reading of subsidiarity would meet human needs with the lowest possible resource consumption and waste disposal. That means relocalization – a corollary to energy descent. Yet if we wish to sustain a global civilization, then our reading of subsidiarity might be something like, "Export your photons but leave your molecules at home."[2] On this measure, ecovillagers tend to be model planetary citizens, localizing their material consumption while remaining engaged in world events.

3. *Sharing* is the essence of both ecology and community. Ecovillages offer models for sharing everything from land and cars to self-governance, skills, and life stories. As we scale up, the sharing expands to include schools, parks, roads, waterways, the atmosphere, the biosphere, the internet – anything that sustains us in common and, we might add, anything for which we pay taxes. Full-cost accounting and other policies that protect "the space between" simultaneously foster ecological, social, and economic sustainability. Sharing does not spell the death of the individual but rather her or his coming of age as she or he develops from what Thomas Hübl calls "particle consciousness" into "field consciousness."

---

[1] Maya Jacobs, "How to Build a Bike Train," www.yesmagazine.org/planet/how-to-build-a-bike-train, accessed June 20, 2013.
[2] This slogan has been attributed to Denis Hayes, founder of Earth Day.

4. *Design* with an eye to the future is a vital element of ecovillages and their scalability. Even with planning, communities at every scale – especially those least responsible for the problems – will face enormous stress from climate change and energy descent; without careful forethought, there is a real possibility of systemic collapse. If we take our cues from ecovillages and downshift today, we greatly enhance our prospects for tomorrow. The key is energy, the master resource. As Ozzie Zeher demonstrates in *Green Illusions*, even with an all-out effort, renewables cannot come close to fueling today's energy consumption, much less a world of ten billion people hoping to live like the global North. Yet Zeher admits that renewables will eventually supply most of humanity's energy needs. The catch is that we need to *create* the kind of society that *can* be powered by renewables.[3] That means mirroring an ecovillage design strategy, one that prioritizes quality of relationships over quantity of stuff, at every level.

5. *The power of yes* is greater than the power of no. Focusing on the most practical issues of life, ecovillages embody a kind of hands-on, do-it-yourself politics. They are creating parallel structures for self-governance within the prevailing social order while demonstrating how to live well with less. Ecovillages themselves are scaling up this *power of yes* through Gaia Education and other training programs, but there are countless constructive initiatives sprouting every day. Whether it is one person stringing a backyard clothesline or the hundreds of cities in the International Consortium of Local Environmental Initiatives (ICLEI), a positive example is compelling – and likely to become more so in the future.

With these five principles and our compass pointed toward sustainability, we are equipped to apply ecovillage lessons on every human scale, from the neighborhood to global governance – the primary task of this chapter. And, as we shall see, ecovillages are having a ripple effect at every scale. First, however, a note about government. Ecovillages are self-governed micro-societies yet, like the rest of us, they are also embedded in local, state, and national governments. Politically speaking, ecovillagers are not easily categorized: some subscribe to a kind of green libertarianism while most see a vital role for government. From my own perspective, the mounting global

---

[3] Ozzie Zeher, *Green Illusions: The Dirty Secrets of Clean Energy and the Future of Environmentalism*, Omaha: University of Nebraska Press, 2012, p. 342.

mega-crisis needs all hands on deck: nonprofits and businesses, governments and intergovernmental structures at every level.

## Neighborhoods

As human-scale experiments, ecovillages are most easily emulated at the neighborhood level, where proximity facilitates face-to-face relationships and the sharing of everything from meals and appliances to child care and cars. Given the anonymity of contemporary life, the first step may be to meet our neighbors and begin to build trust. Eventually, whether or not we all share the core purpose of sustainability, we can begin by asking what our community needs. Whatever the answer – a covered bus stop, a clothing swap, cooperative child care, a group purchase of solar panels, or simply a monthly potluck – the conversation itself will launch a process of democratic deliberation and enhance the possibilities for future sharing. In some Seattle neighborhoods, these conversations have led neighbors to take down fences and create community gardens. One of my favorite models is the partnership between private homeowners and aspiring young farmers, whereby the former make their yards available to the latter in exchange for a weekly allotment of vegetables. Another emerging "neighborhood commons," ubiquitous in ecovillages, is the tool library.

As people recognize the need for a revivified neighborhood commons, resources are arising to help meet that need. City Repair, for instance, is a grassroots organization in Portland, Oregon, that (like ecovillages) doesn't wait for government to implement needed projects – they just do it themselves. City Repair's guerilla approach to urban revitalization was so successful that Portland officials invited the group to assist with city planning. The model has since spread to other US cities. Likewise, internet-based sharing tools emerged in the wake of the economic downturn of 2008. NeighborGoods.net matches people with goods, and two attorneys published *The Sharing Solution* and a companion website to help people with the social, logistical, and legal aspects of sharing property. Localharvest.org began connecting individuals with nearby farmers' markets, community gardens, and family farms. And traffic skyrocketed on freecycle. org, another online venue for matching people with goods. Freecycle's mission statement reads like the kind of integrated approach to E2C2 that we find in ecovillages: "Our mission is to build a worldwide gifting movement that reduces waste, saves precious resources, and eases the burden of landfills while enabling our members to benefit from the strength of a larger community."

In order to create a neighborhood-based economy of solidarity, we need to get serious about sharing – and developing – our skills. For this, a neighborhood skills-map is essential. Services we need might be close to home, but, without engaging our neighbors, we will never know. Moreover, a sustainable local economy isn't just about hiring our neighbors for conventional services: haircuts, plumbing, web design, or an automotive tune-up. It is also about learning and sharing new skills: gardening, poultry care, food canning and fermentation, rainwater catchment, bicycle repair, midwifery, and so on. The Transition Towns movement calls this "The Great Reskilling." During the fossil-fuel interval, many of these functions were mechanized, and our lives were so highly individualized that we didn't seem to need others – at least not people we would ever meet. Because reskilling means rethinking the values of speed and profit, it is closely allied with the new "slow" movements: Slow Food, Slow Money, Slow Cities. Slowing down and learning new skills is more than a lifestyle choice; it is an act of resistance to fossil-fuel-driven culture, highlighting the value of what cannot be bought and sold.

If we seek to make our neighborhoods more like ecovillages, we will probably find, as many ecovillagers have, that people are both the most challenging and most rewarding aspects of our work. Making the epic transition from hyper-individualism to relational living requires trust, which can only be built incrementally through sharing our lives, both outer and inner. As useful as the social media might be, it cannot replace face-to-face relationships in reweaving the web of life. According to Peter Block, a prominent leader in community building, "communities are formed by conversations that build relatedness."[4] Fortunately, we have access to a wealth of resources to facilitate those conversations, including what I encountered in ecovillages: Nonviolent Communication, World Café, Compassionate Listening, Appreciative Inquiry, and Forum. Ecovillage life supports Block's claim that "the small group is the unit of transformation and the container for experience of belonging." As we incorporate the kinds of relational practices I encountered in ecovillages into our neighborhoods, we create a culture of belonging – the kind of culture that can weather the coming storms.

---

[4] Peter Block, *Community: The Structure of Belonging*. San Francisco: Berrett-Koehler, 2009.

## Cities and towns

Most people live in cities – the proportion grows daily – yet ecovillages are primarily rural. If the human future is urban, which seems likely, then what do ecovillages have to teach? The answer, I believe, is twofold: the specific practices of urban and suburban ecovillages and the scaling up of the basic principles of ecovillage life. As incubation chambers for a whole-systems approach to E2C2, ecovillages hold lessons for anybody who wants to think systemically about sustainability, wherever they might live. As currently constituted, cities are ecological parasites, commandeering vast resources from the countryside and distant realms. If the human future is to be urban, then we need to get serious about the subsidiarity principle and think systemically about how to consume less, share more, and do most of it closer to home. In other words, our cities and towns must be revamped. Fortunately, in some quarters that process is already underway.

David Owen opens his book, *Green Metropolis*, with a story about moving in his youth to an ecological community where per capita greenhouse gas emissions were less than a third of the average American. The secret of that green utopia, which turns out to be New York City, is a combination of density, public transit, and walkability. Owen then presents a powerful case for naming the car, arguably the most prominent symbol of hyper-individualism, "Global Environmental Enemy No. 1."[5] Whether our cars are fueled by petroleum or solar-powered batteries, it is difficult to see how dragging around tons of matter with our bodies can ever be sustainable. The ecovillage solution entails sharing and relocalizing, which is the essence of public transportation. Some cities, like Portland (USA), Hanover (Germany), and Dongtan (China) are taking this a step further with linked "eco-districts" at transit stops.

For those times when we need to go solo, it turns out that the most energy-efficient mode of travel is the bicycle. At LAEV, located in the heart of American car culture, bicycling is a badge of honor. I had a memorable experience cycling through Hollywood at what Jimmy Lizama calls "the most democratic speed." I saw that Los Angeles, with its wide, flat streets and dry climate, has the potential to become a cyclist's paradise. A year later, the city's mayor came to the same conclusion. After attending an international climate conference in

---

[5] David Owen, *Green Metropolis: Why Living Smaller, Living Closer, and Driving Less Are the Keys to Sustainability*, Riverhead Trade, 2009, p. 2.

Copenhagen, where he experienced a bicycle-friendly infrastructure firsthand, the mayor resolved to build a citywide network of 1,663 miles of bikeways. Diplomatically, the conference was an abject failure, but the ripple effects of thousands of city officials sharing strategies for addressing climate change are more difficult to calculate. At a minimum, we know that the "power of yes" flew from Copenhagen to Los Angeles.

We might ask whether networks like Cities for Climate Protection, the Aalborg Charter of European Cities, and Towns Towards Sustainability are sufficient to counterbalance the laggardly pace of international law. Nonetheless, they represent bottom-up efforts to harmonize human and natural systems at scales beyond the ecovillage. Findhorn's Living Machine, for instance, which recycles 10,000 gallons of water every day, is impressive but small potatoes compared to urban wastewater treatment plants using many of the same technologies. The Calera Creek Water Recycling Plant in California recycles four million gallons of water daily – and boasts a fully restored wetland. Likewise, when cities adopt new mixed-use zoning codes that enable people to live near their workplaces, new ways of schooling for sustainability, and new policies that expand urban food production, they are, in effect, scaling up the ecovillage model – even if they've never heard of ecovillages. The same can be said for congestion pricing on public transportation or charging households by the volume of their garbage or adopting land-use planning strategies that incorporate wildlife corridors. And some urban initiatives, like the Living Building Challenge (which promotes buildings that heat and cool themselves, collect and store sunlight, produce food, and recycle nearly all of their water and waste) go beyond any technologies I encountered in ecovillages.

The ecovillages, in turn, are broadcasting their strategies. From the beginning, EVI hoped to serve as a model for Middle America, and in 2011 that aspiration got a big boost through a partnership with Tompkins County. Together, they won an EPA Climate Showcase grant to create models for climate-friendly zoning and building codes. "Twenty-one years in, and we're finally helping mainstream development!" Liz Walker observed. EVI's third neighborhood, TREE, which was being planned when I visited, will model best practices like passive house and high-density construction, car-free common spaces, multi-use structures, community gardens, and mixed-income housing. Incorporating two other projects, an urban "pocket neighborhood" and a 26-acre suburban development, the EVI–county partnership is forging a new pedestrian neighborhood zoning ordinance. "If it

194

works," Liz said, "we'll disseminate it to other cities, states, and national levels."

I noticed that the EPA's notion of a climate showcase was all about material structures, so I asked Liz about the social fabric of these pedestrian neighborhoods. "That's the question of the day," she said. "We hope it will develop organically. The 26-acre project includes a clubhouse with a kitchen, so there could be shared meals and social events." It's a step forward, but an integrated approach to E2C2 requires more.

A big piece of that "more" is found in the Transition Towns movement, which encompasses hundreds of cities planning for climate change and energy descent. Rob Hopkins, author of *The Transition Handbook* (the movement's inspiration), had been an ecovillager and a permaculture designer himself. "My basic realization," Rob said, "was that permaculture, ecovillages, and their tools, principles, and insights are vital to the wider societal transition. Ecovillages have spent many years testing and refining the technologies, both social and physical, that a sustainable world will need. Yet it struck me that they are sometimes reluctant to engage deeply with the mainstream. So transition is a way of rapidly scaling up those insights." A transition town, then, is essentially an expanded ecovillage.

Rob was only partly right about ecovillagers; many are eagerly engaging with the mainstream. By 2012, Gaia Education was offering its Ecovillage Design Education (EDE) in thirty-two countries and nine languages, with support from city and national governments, as well as the EU. May Fast, a Findhorn resident who helped write EDE curriculum, grew up in São Paolo and was keen to bring the EDE to Brazil's largest cities. Her courses in Brasilia, Rio de Janeiro, and São Paolo have attracted funding from these cities. "We ran the EDE in São Paolo's largest slum and had a hundred students, mostly on scholarships," May said. "All told, we've trained 15,000 designers, and these change agents are sparking every kind of social and ecological enterprise you can imagine."

May's primary work is running a United Nations CIFAL, the French acronym for International Training Center for Local Authorities. Her Findhorn-based training center operates on a village scale, but the other eight are located in large cities. Agreeing that the human future is urban, May recently opened another CIFAL office in Edinburgh. "Cities make up 12 percent of the Earth's land and consume 83 percent of its resources. If we spend our time on what can't be replicated in cities," she said, "we're losing time."

I share May's concern but my travels in Africa and Asia convinced me that traditional villages remain an essential piece of the sustainability puzzle. China's growing New Rural Reconstruction Movement has reached the same conclusion. While this vibrant movement does not speak about "ecovillages," its vision closely mirrors that of Colufifa and Sarvodaya. The movement promotes small-scale organic farming and revitalizes villages by coupling traditional knowledge with new green technologies. Every developing country is facing a similar set of problems. The mega-slums of Sao Paolo, Shanghai, Lagos, and other cities of the global South are swelling with people who can no longer eke out a living in their villages. The factors driving this mass exodus are complex, ranging from depleted soils to WTO trade rules, but policies that promote rural sustainability – including the ecovillage model – will also be helping cities. While mega-cities are new to the human scene, the village model has, at least until recently, withstood the test of time. This is why Sarvodaya, Colufifa, and other grassroots rural initiatives are so important.

## The nation

My year of ecovillage living sensitized me to the vital role of human purpose. Every time I left an ecovillage for "the real world," I underwent culture shock. As I read billboards and observed crowds, I asked myself: what is the core purpose of this global fast-paced, hard-edged culture that has permeated the planet? The best answer I could find was economic growth. Surely there are other human purposes, but the overarching one, the one with the most visible effects is growth. It spans the political spectrum, from right to left, with the only variation being the question of how we will grow. By and large, growth is the touchstone of national elections – and in places where people are hungry and malnourished, it probably should be. The question is how it is achieved.

If governments' mandate is to send goods and capital scurrying around the globe, they've done an admirable job. There's only one catch: infinite growth on a finite planet is impossible – a fact that ecovillages have internalized. No wonder, then, that venturing out into "the real world" felt so jarring – the two cultures are living at cross-purposes! Ultimately, sustainability is not optional; it is the sine qua non for earthly habitation. "Degrowth," as ecological economists call it, is inevitable, which means that we can look to ecovillagers as our forerunners. And, I might add, those of us in affluent societies can also learn from those who are living closer to the earth.

196

Heretical though it might sound, a new breed of economists is thinking about how societies can flourish while downsizing. Many of their ideas – like valuing human relationships over material wealth and internalizing environmental costs – are standard fare in ecovillages. With an awareness that affluence is neither sustainable nor the fast track to happiness, ecological economists are devising alternatives to GDP/capita to measure progress.[6] In 2012, the Happy Planet Index, which measures sustainable wellbeing, ranked Costa Rica as No. 1 and the United States as No. 114.[7] National governments, including the United Kingdom's Office of National Statistics, are taking this work seriously and developing means other than GDP/capita to measure national wellbeing.[8]

Like governments, ecovillages subsidize what they value. Ecovillages create a viable future by supporting common spaces and amenities, healthy food, access to clean water, and strong relationships. For reasons ranging from entrenched ideologies to corporate lobbying, governments often end up bankrolling a highly *undesirable* future. Think, for instance, of the trillions of dollars spent on militarizing the Middle East. A major step toward creating a positive future would be to end subsidies for programs that foster fossil-fuel dependency, a move that is particularly urgent in the United States and Canada. The rush to excavate unconventional hydrocarbons threatens to destabilize the climate and undermine any possibility of creating a society that could be powered by renewables. Rather, our tax dollars need to leverage our fossil-fuel-based wealth toward a low-carbon economy. In the short run, the resulting "green jobs" could extend the life of the growth economy, even as they move us to a steady-state economy. Germany and Denmark, with their enormous investments in renewable energy, are betting on this strategy. There is also a moral question at stake. As one ecovillager put it, "If we don't pay the real cost for our energy, then we're essentially thieves, aren't we?"

While full-cost accounting is essential to sustainable living at every level, governments have a distinct advantage: they enjoy the twin powers of taxation and regulation. This is why national governments are the primary arbiters of today's commons. Sweden, for instance, finances most of its environmental programs by taxing polluters. Likewise, product stewardship laws, which make manufacturers responsible for end-of-life disposal, are popular in Canada, Europe,

[6] Carol Graham, *Happiness around the World: The Paradox of Happy Peasants and Miserable Millionaires*, Oxford University Press, 2012.
[7] www.happyplanetindex.org, accessed June 20, 2013.
[8] www.ons.gov.uk/well-being, accessed June 20, 2013.

and some US states. Yet such laws – or any full-cost accounting measures, for that matter – are unlikely to receive US congressional approval so long as corporate money dominates the electoral process. Thinking systemically, then, we see that campaign finance reform may be a prerequisite to a strong sustainability commitment in the United States.

Applying the subsidiarity principle, national governments could play a catalyzing and coordinating role in developing state and municipal design strategies for local self-reliance. As a major source of funding for local roads, education, agriculture, health care, and social services, national governments are already engaged in this multilevel governance. The new and crucial element would be introducing *sustainability* as the organizing purpose. Imagine civilian service programs modeled on the Peace Corps or Teach for America; we could call them Re-energize America or Farm the UK. It's being done – I met several young Germans doing "alternative civilian service" in ecovillages – but why not expand it! Dozens of my former students would jump at the opportunity to build a sustainable future in exchange for having part of their student loans forgiven.

Beyond being a source of lessons, ecovillages are beginning to be taken seriously as models by national governments. A case in point is the US EPA's decision to make EcoVillage at Ithaca a Climate Showcase Community. The US Department of Agriculture also funds Groundswell, a farmer-training center started by EVI's two farms and a consortium of other local farms. These kinds of training centers are playing a role in the "Great Reskilling" that is already underway. Likewise, the EU and the German government now offer scholarships to low-income students who attend Gaia Education's EDE courses.

Nowhere, however, are ecovillages being taken more seriously at the national level than in Senegal's National Agency for Ecovillages. With support from fourteen national and international partners, the newly appointed Minister of Ecovillages, Babacar Ndao, intends to transform 14,000 existing villages into ecovillages by 2020. Starting with Mbackombel, a model village of a thousand residents, the agency is integrating green technologies – solar panels, organic farming, aquaculture, and sound water and forest management practices – into traditional rural life.[9] The pioneering work of

---

[9] Koffigan E. Adigbil, "Ecovillages Breathe New Life into Rural Senegal," InterPress Service News, July 3, 2012, http://odewire.com/263175/eco-villages-breathe-new-life-into-rural-senegal.html, accessed June 20, 2013.

Colufifa and existing Senegalese ecovillages like EcoYoff will facilitate this program, which could provide a model for other developing countries.

The "power of yes" is already operating at every scale of human life, from Colufifa's microfinance programs to Michelle Obama's White House garden; in a globally connected world, it has the potential to go viral at any moment – witness the Arab Spring. The point is to learn from one another, and for this we have the internet. As incubation chambers for a whole-systems approach to E2C2, ecovillages offer powerful lessons. At the national level, the key lessons are to value the commons, subsidize a viable future, promote local self-reliance, and foster positive examples.

## Business

Commerce operates at and across every social scale yet, as the place where full-circle living seems most at odds with the growth imperative, it deserves special attention. Scaling up ecovillage economics means incorporating the principles of full-cost accounting, right livelihood, and cooperative ownership into our business models. With respect to production, this means cradle-to-cradle manufacturing, the end of excessive packaging, and a rigorous adherence to the triple bottom line (economic, ecological, and social). Companies like Patagonia offer an environmentally conscious manufacturing model. With respect to consumption, the future is in sharing, or collaborative consumption, through businesses like ZipCar and second-use stores. With respect to ownership and decision-making, the wave of the future lies in cooperatives and decentralized leadership through team-based organization.

Much has been written elsewhere about the ecology of commerce; there are many models.[10] Among light-green practices, we find businesses like Bayer Corporation that are far from sustainable and yet adopt policies that surpass legal requirements. On the dark-green end, we find the BALLE network (Business Alliance for Local Living Economies), which more closely mirrors the ecovillage model. Beyond this, there are a few businesses that manage to operate in the gift economy.

---

[10] For two models of sustainable business, see www.naturalstep.org and www.ceres.org. For a critique of much so-called sustainable business, see Peter Dauvergne and Jane Lister, *Eco-Business: A Big-Brand Takeover of Sustainability*, MIT Press, 2013.

These fledgling dark-green initiatives, however, are likely to remain weak so long as the growth model enjoys substantial governmental and social support. They will be vulnerable, as Crystal Waters' farmers were, to the prevailing bottom line: profit. Just as successful ecovillage economies are contained within a larger social context of solidarity and participatory governance, so too must viable economies at every scale be sustained by supportive social structures. Social trust is not only the glue of community, it is also the glue of a viable economy.

## Globalization from below

Can globalization be consistent with sustainability? Thus far, international law has been wholly inadequate to the task. The 2012 declaration from the Rio+20 Earth Summit was called "the longest suicide note in history."[11] We cannot expect better so long as national governments see their primary purpose as promoting fossil-fuel-driven growth. The most powerful global actor today is the multinational corporation, which drives nation-states and the international institutions operating at its behest. As a counterbalance, "globalization from below" holds out the possibility of a humane and sustainable global civilization. Ecovillages are part of this "blessed unrest," as Paul Hawken calls this movement of movements, comprising perhaps a million initiatives, which he likens to a planetary immune system.[12]

Ecovillages, in particular through GEN, have a global presence through UN initiatives, North–South partnerships, and international gatherings. In 2012, a landmark year for GEN, 500 people from twenty-eight countries gathered in Colombia to establish CASA (a Spanish acronym for the Council of Sustainable Settlements of the Americas). Besides the growing Latin American ecovillage movement, the network brings together eco-barrios, Transition Town initiatives, eco-caravans (nomadic sustainable communities), and permaculture centers to develop and disseminate models of sustainable living. An ocean away, representatives from sixteen African countries met at Sekem, a farming ecovillage in Egypt, to launch GEN-Africa. Because most people in the global South are only one generation away from

---

[11] Kumi Naidoo, Director of Greenpeace International, quoted in Bryan Walsh, "What the Failure of Rio+20 Means for the Climate," *Time*, June 26, 2012.
[12] Paul Hawken, *Blessed Unrest: How the Largest Movement in the World Came into Being and Why No One Saw It Coming*, Viking, 2007.

their ancestral village, networks like GEN-Africa and CASA can serve as critical knowledge banks.

Faceless, placeless globalization is a historical anomaly; human cultures developed in place-based communities. Part of the ecovillages' appeal is that they're rooted in real relationships with people and resources. Can relationships of integrity exist on a global scale? The jury is out but, if they can, it will require scaling up the ecovillage experience. A sustainable global civilization would mean harmonizing human life with Earth's great biogeochemical cycles – "thinking like a planet."[13] At a minimum, such a civilization would require sufficient clean energy and communication technologies to share knowledge (particularly about the biosphere) and some form of governance. Applying whole-systems thinking and the subsidiarity principle, the key question would be: what functions are most appropriate to the global scale? The measure would be their social and ecological impact. A global internet might pass the test, but most world trade and travel would not. And then there is the perennial human question: who gets to decide and how? Natural and social scientists are coming together to study these questions under the rubric of Earth-system governance.[14]

A whole-systems approach to global sustainability would scale up the core ecovillage principle: sharing – in this case, equitably sharing planetary resources. Global justice turns out be as much a matter of pragmatism as ethics. If, after wrecking the climate, we retreat to our fortresses, we have no ethical leg to stand on, but the problem is also material. The global South, representing 80 percent of the human population, is catching up to the North in affluence just as planetary resources are reaching the tipping point. The South is unlikely to alter its trajectory without the sort of exemplar that ecovillages provide, nor without financial and technological assistance from the wealthier and more culpable North. Climate change will only aggravate these tensions. As the Bangladeshi delegate told an international climate summit, "We will march with our wet feet into your living rooms!" In an era of climate refugees, geo-engineering, and species triage, an insular strategy is inadequate. Local sustainability initiatives like Transition Towns and eco-neighborhoods will be far more compelling when pursued under a global umbrella. Just as trust is the social glue

[13] Karen Litfin, "Thinking like a Planet: Gaian Politics and the Transformation of the World Food System," in Peter Dauvergne (ed.), *Handbook of Global Environmental Politics*, 2nd edn, Cheltenham, UK: Edward Elgar, 2012.
[14] Frank Biermann et al., "Earth System Governance: Navigating the Anthropocene" *Science*, March 16, 2012: 1306–7.

in an ecovillage, so too must it be in a sustainable global civilization. At every scale, the relational turn underpins sustainability.

## At home in the global ecovillage

I have told many stories in this book – stories of ecovillages and their pioneering members, as well as the story of a professor getting educated. But the overarching story is that of our species, groping its way toward sustainability. The ecological and social debt of fossil-fueled affluence is coming due, no doubt, and the circle is closing. The question is not so much whether the circle will close without us, but rather who we will be within it. As arguably the weediest species on Earth, human survival is probably not at stake: the local is our modus operandi. What is at stake is the tremendous achievement of a global civilization. In the face of energy descent and a changing climate, then, what kind of world do we want and how do we use our collective power to go about creating it? The future depends upon how wide our circles of wisdom and compassion are today. If we want to live as a global species within the circle of life, then we need to scale up the lessons from ecovillages commensurately.

Humanity is operating as a geophysical force, yet most of our members are utterly unaware of our perilous entry into the Anthropocene.[15] At the same time, globalization has given us the material infrastructure for planetary connectivity. As we cross the threshold into this new era, the question is whether we can develop the technological, social, and spiritual connectivity to live as one species on our one Earth. To my mind, rising above endless consumption and aiming for connectivity is a worthy purpose. It is a purpose that supplants the old story of separation for it brings us home to ourselves as integral members of the Earth community. On a microscale, ecovillages are at the leading edge of this homecoming and can therefore help to illuminate the path. It is, however, a pathless path; we make it by walking forward together.

The Anthropocene calls us to a larger sense of identity and responsibility. In this emergent identity, we can experience a global citizenship that simultaneously transcends and includes our bounded self and our existing social identities. In stretching our loyalties, we

---

[15] This new geological era is characterized by human-induced destabilization of Earth's life-support systems. See Johan Rockstrom et al., 2009, "A Safe Operating Space for Humanity," *Nature* 461: 472–5.

are each enlarged – particularly when we join with others who are embarking upon this pathless path. As much as anything else, it is this sense of shared adventure that I find so compelling in ecovillage culture. Yet in this shift beyond hyper-individualism, the individual is also the key, for she or he is constantly asking herself: What is my unique contribution to the whole? In a world of separate individuals, we might be tempted to give up. What can one person do? Yet in a world where everything is hitched to everything else, one person's gesture can have monumental impact! My global ecovillage journey convinced me that humans everywhere have access to an innate evolutionary intelligence. Tapping into this, our thinking becomes expansive and E2C2 takes on the dynamic, self-reinforcing character that we see in ecovillages.

As we consider what it means to be living at a hinge time, we might consider the evolutionary roots of our intelligence. We think of mammals as latecomers to the terrestrial scene, but animals of our class apparently coexisted with dinosaurs for 135 million years, many no larger than mice, hiding in burrows and eating insects by night. In the shadows of the predatory dinosaurs, our tiny predecessors developed fur, keen eyesight, milk-producing glands, more complex social habits, and, most of all, an enlarged brain. When dinosaurs and most other species were driven to extinction in the aftermath of a catastrophic asteroid impact, the number and diversity of mammals exploded.[16] We cannot know for sure what enabled our mammalian ancestors to survive the last extinction crisis, but we can be fairly certain that brainpower and social connectivity played a part. No doubt, brainpower and social connectivity will also play a vital part as we navigate the uncharted waters of the Anthropocene.

Ecovillages are seeds of hope, but they are sparsely sown across the global landscape and time is short. Fortunately, ecovillages are but one facet of a vast decentralized sustainability movement, and in today's tightly networked world, change can happen very quickly. In 1997, "Google" was just a silly word and smartphones were the stuff of science fiction. Like the potential ripple effect of one individual, rapid nonlinear change is a feature of highly interconnected systems – for better or for worse. If prevailing human systems are unsustainable, then they will cease. The only questions are "when" and "how." In that light, ecovillagers may be running some critically important

---

[16] T. S. Kemp, *The Origin and Evolution of Mammals*, Oxford University Press, 2005, pp. 3–4.

experiments – as are the rest of us who embark upon the pathless path of harmonizing human life with our home planet.

After all, when dinosaurs ruled the Earth, who could have imagined that a handful of tiny mammals would be the evolutionary success story of their day?

# EPILOGUE

I returned home to Seattle more inspired than I had felt in years, yet also concerned that ordinary life would dampen my enthusiasm. One morning, I was walking through my neighborhood and came upon a sign: Edible Garden Tour. Following the arrows, I met a middle-aged couple living in a permaculture paradise, complete with rainwater catchment, solar panels, and an edible landscape. They sent me off with a map. Up the hill was a young woman raising ducks in her family's backyard. Just around the corner, I met an elderly woman with a veritable orchard. "I grow far more than I can eat," she said, "so I mostly donate it to the food bank." Having lived in the same home for fifteen years, I thought I knew my neighbors – but apparently not. These urban farmers, I learned, were part of a citywide sustainability network. Most were also involved in transportation planning, renewable energy, and creative conflict resolution. Everything I had encountered on my journey was happening in my own neighborhood. So ecovillages are not *the* answer to our problems. They are *one* answer – or, more accurately, they are micro-laboratories running loads of experiments. We need all the well-designed experiments we can get.

While ecovillages aren't the right solution for everyone, some people yearn for the intimacy, focus, and integrated solutions of ecovillage life. My journey demonstrated to me that that I am such a person. I returned with a clear sense of my dream: a small group of people dedicated to deep solidarity, personal transformation, and living lightly on Earth. "Some day," I told myself.

That day came sooner than expected. On Valentine's Day of 2009, I fell in love – with a beautiful farm on Whidbey Island. I cannot explain it, but I knew: "This is it." I could almost feel my dream incubating there. The land – mostly rolling pasture, with a view of the

205

Olympics – abounds with wildlife, yet I could commute to the university by mass transit. I took a flying leap and a second mortgage on my Seattle home, and was soon the proud owner of land I didn't know how to tend and the sole member of a new community. "SkyRoot," I christened it, evoking the integration of earth and the heights to which we aspire. I was alone and unskilled, but I had one thing going for me: a timely vision deepened by a year of inspiration from around the world. Surely the detour would enhance the book by grounding it more deeply in real life, I thought, and surely the right people would come. I believe I was right on both counts; I just seriously underestimated the time involved.

Three years after starting SkyRoot, I fully concur with Diana Leafe-Christian: community is definitely the longest, most expensive personal growth workshop I've ever taken! In hitching my life to a dream, I've soared high and also fallen into tremendous self-doubt. Of one thing, however, there is no doubt: I've learned more about myself at SkyRoot than in any other three-year period of my life. I've been humbled by my tendency to take on too much, I've learned from others who are more innately generous than I, and I am continually grateful for my own staying power.

Figure 8.1 This tapered-wall wooden yurt, where I wrote this book, was the first new home built at SkyRoot

Since 2009, SkyRoot's six-bedroom farmhouse has been home to eleven people, six of whom live here at the moment. I fervently hope they will stay, and I know they could leave. The comings and goings of companions has been a source of joy and sorrow.

At one point in the fall of 2011, when only one woman remained, I threw up my hands. "I don't know what to do!" I said.

"You don't need to do anything, Karen. Just be a lighthouse," she replied. Her words helped me through those dark months. And the long writing process, which sparked memories of the ecovillage pioneers I had met, brightened my light.

Perhaps my greatest learning has been grasping the foundational importance of core purpose. As people have come and gone at SkyRoot, I've learned that people are attracted to community for numberless reasons, many of them unconscious. Each of us, including myself, is a mixed bag. In giving myself to the core purpose of integrating E2C2 – ecology, economics, community, and consciousness – I have entered a crucible of clarification and refinement. The key to an intentional community is *intention*; without it, a group is merely a collection of individuals. Shared intention is the loamy soil where seeds of trust and sharing can take root and flourish, and the key to this intention is *attention*: moment-by-moment focus.

Additionally, I've learned some very practical skills: how to build a first-rate fire; how to operate a composting toilet; how to build a tapered-wall wooden yurt; how to care for goats, turkeys, and chickens; and how to kill a chicken.

In the spring of 2012, SkyRoot got a tremendous boost when a young farmer and her partner moved into the farmhouse with their toddler. Soon afterward, another farmer came on board, and SkyRoot Farm was born. In the summer, a second couple, who had recently retired, bought a house nearby in order to join us. So now there are eight of us with a shared vision for a multigenerational co-housing community with an integrated approach to E2C2. With a spirit of deep solidarity and a spirit of adventure, we are planting one more seed for a viable human future. Truly, it's a whole new life!

# RESOURCES

ECOLOGY

Coleman, Eliot. *The New Organic Grower*. Chelsea Green, 1995.

Crawford, Martin. *Creating a Forest Garden: Working with Nature to Grow Edible Crops*. Totnes: Green, 2010.

Holmgren, David. *Permaculture Principles and Pathways beyond Sustainability*. Petersfield: Permanent Publications, 2010.

International Living Future Institute, http://living-future.org/, accessed June 3, 2013.

International Passive House Association, www.passivehouse-international.org, accessed June 3, 2013.

Jeavons, J. *How to Grow More Vegetables*. Berkeley, CA: Ten Speed, 2002.

Jenkins, Joseph. *The Humanure Handbook*, available as a free download at http://humanurehandbook.com/, accessed June 3, 2013.

McNall, Scott. *Rapid Climate Change: Causes, Consequences, and Solutions*. London: Routledge, 2011.

Solar Energy International, www.solarenergy.org, accessed June 3, 2013.

Tertzakian, P. *A Thousand Barrels a Second: The Coming Oil Break Point and the Challenges Facing an Energy Dependent World*. New York: McGraw-Hill, 2006.

Zehner, Ozzie. *Green Illusions: The Dirty Secrets of Clean Energy and the Future of Environmentalism*. Lincoln: University of Nebraska, 2012.

## ECONOMICS

Eisenstein, Charles. *Sacred Economics: Money, Gift, & Society in the Age of Transition*. Berkeley, CA: Evolver Editions, 2011.

Hall, Charles A. S. *Energy and the Wealth of Nations: Understanding the Biophysical Economy*. Springer: 2012.

Jackson, Tim. *Prosperity without Growth: Economics for a Finite Planet*. London: Earthscan, 2009.

Korten, D. *The Great Turning: From Empire to Earth Community*. San Francisco, CA: Berrett-Koehler, 2006.

Leonard, Annie, www.storyofstuff.org, accessed June 3, 2013.

New Economics Foundation, www.neweconomics.org, accessed June 3, 2013.

Pickett, K. and Wilkinson, R., *The Spirit Level: Why Greater Equality Makes Societies Stronger*. Bloomsbury, 2011.

PostCarbon Institute, www.postcarbon.org, accessed June 3, 2013.

Robin, Vicki, et al. *Your Money or Your Life*. New York: Penguin, 2008.

Schumacher, E. F. *Small Is Beautiful: Economics as if People Mattered*. London: Blond & Briggs, 1973. www.smallisbeautiful.org, accessed June 3, 2013.

## COMMUNITY

Buck, J., and Villines, S. *We the People: Consenting to a Deeper Democracy: A Guide to Sociocratic Principles and Methods*. Washington, DC: Sociocracy, 2007.

Christakis, N., and Fowler, J. *Connected: The Surprising Power of Our Social Networks*. New York: Little, Brown and Company, 2009. http://connectedthebook.com, accessed June 3, 2013.

Christian, Diana Leafe. *Creating a Life Together*. Gabriola Island, BC: New Society, 2003.

Cohousing Association of the US, www.cohousing.org, accessed June 3, 2013 (includes international co-housing communities).

Eurotopia, community directory and magazine: www.eurotopia.de/english.html, accessed June 3, 2013.

Fellowship for Intentional Communities: Community Directory and *Communities* magazine, www.ic.org, accessed June 3, 2013.

International Consortium for Local Environmental Initiative, www.iclei.org, accessed June 3, 2013.

Rosenberg, M. *Nonviolent Communication: A Language of Life.* Encinitas, CA: PuddleDancer, 2003.

Seeds for Change: Resources for consensus decision-making. http://seedsforchange.org.uk, accessed June 3, 2013.

Sociocracy, www.sociocracy.info, accessed June 3, 2013.

World Cafe Community, www.theworldcafe.com, accessed June 3, 2013.

## CONSCIOUSNESS

Berry, Thomas. *The Great Work: Our Way into the Future.* New York: Bell Tower, 1999.

Dowd, Michael. *Thank God for Evolution: How the Marriage of Science and Religion Will Transform Your Life and Our World.* New York: Viking, 2008.

Elgin, Duane. *Awakening Earth: Exploring the Evolution of Human Culture and Consciousness.* New York: Morrow, 1993.

Harding, Stephan. *Animate Earth: Science, Intuition and Gaia.* White River Junction, VT: Chelsea Green, 2006.

Litfin, Karen. "The Sacred and the Profane in the Ecological Politics of Sacrifice," in Michael Maniates and John Meyer (eds), *The Environmental Politics of Sacrifice.* Boston: MIT Press, 2010.

Macy, Joanna, "The Work That Reconnects," www.joannamacy.net, accessed June 3, 2013.

Natural Genesis, an annotated bibliography on the Universe Story, www.naturalgenesis.net, accessed June 3, 2013.

Phipps, Carter. *Evolutionaries: Unlocking the Spiritual and Cultural Potential of Science's Greatest Idea.* New York: Harper Perennial, 2012.

Uhl, Chris. *Developing Ecological Consciousness.* Lanham, MD: Rowman & Littlefield, 2003.

## INTEGRATED SOLUTIONS

Astyk, S. *Depletion and Abundance: Life on the New Home Front.* Philadelphia, PA: New Society, 2008.

Community Solutions, www.communitysolutions.org, accessed June 3, 2013.

Global Ecovillage Network resources:
  GEN Oceana and Asia, genoa.ecovillage.org, accessed June 3, 2013.
  Ecovillage Network of the Americas, ena.ecovillage.org, accessed June 3, 2013.
  GEN Europe, www.gen-europe.org, accessed June 3, 2013.
  Gaia Education, www.gaiaeducation.net, accessed June 3, 2013.
Hamilton, M. *Integral City: Evolutionary Intelligences for the Human Hive*. Gabriola, BC: New Society, 2008. www.integralcity.com, accessed June 3, 2013.
Higgins, P. *Earth Is Our Business: Changing the Rules of the Game*. London: Shepheard-Walwyn, 2012.
Hopkins, R. *The Transition Handbook: From Oil Dependency to Local Resilience*. Totnes, England: Green, 2008.
Meadows, D., and Wright, D. *Thinking in Systems: A Primer*. White River Junction, VT: Chelsea Green, 2008.
Natural Step, The, "Accelerating Change Toward Sustainability for Businesses and Communities," www.naturalstep.org, accessed June 3, 2013.
Resilience, www.resilience.org, accessed June 3, 2013.
Resurgence Magazine, www.resurgence.org, accessed June 3, 2013.
Schumacher College, "Transformative Learning for Sustainable Living," www.schumachercollege.org.uk, accessed June 3, 2013.
Solutions for a Sustainable and Desirable Future, www.thesolutions-journal.com, accessed June 3, 2013.

# INDEX

213